"As Dawn took the steps
substance abuse, she did
and the bad, would not b
her story to this day. Nov
shelter of anonymity and
only one person but with everyone. No doubt many will be helped by her
courage and desire to help others."
Rev. Elden Landvik,
Retired Lutheran Pastor,
Former Missionary to Brazil

MW01284359

d

"So many physicians, including myself, start training with big dreams,
of missionary health in Africa, curing disease and making a big impact
on the world. Dawn describes how, as physicians, we get caught up in
'life,' losing hold of our dreams. Dawn discovered how to reconnect with
her dreams, by giving of herself. Her openness, honesty, willingness and
faith have brought her the fulfillment she dreamed of as a medical student. In traveling the world and giving openly of herself, she has received more than she has given. This is what life is all about. The old
cliché, 'the more you give, the more you receive' stands true in this book.
She is living proof anything is possible."
Rosanne Iversen, M.D.
Owner of Steamboat Family Medicine

"A bright new voice is heard in this engaging story – a tale of life with
which all too many of us can relate. A doctor, wife, mom, missionary,
writer, and addict, Doc Dawn takes the reader on a journey that is at
once inspiring, enlightening, and educational."
J. L. Hardesty
Author of The Lost Legend Trilogy

"With candor and introspection, Dawn shares how service to others and
to God can truly change lives."
David K. McFarland, M.D.

"Having traveled the world sharing her medical skills with those in desperate need, Obrecht gives us a glimpse into the transforming world of
short-term missions. When we pursue a lifestyle of sharing our gifts and
talents with a hurting world, God uses our efforts not only to help 'the
least of these,' but to stretch and grow us as well. *Mission Possible* will
entertain and motivate you to step up and seek out new opportunities to
share God's transforming love outside the safety of your personal comfort zone."
Jane Dratz, Editor, Dare 2 Share Ministries;
Columnist, Christian Post

"Dawn and I have been friends since we were nine, but until our 20th high school reunion I had no idea of the things she was struggling with as we grew up. It is like a miracle to have her own account of her growth as a person, a doctor, and a missionary. Dawn has ministered to me in many ways, as a teacher about addiction, a source of inspiration as I have followed her many adventures, and as a friend and sister in the Lord. Her book will encourage many to use their talents, whatever they may be, to help needy people around the world."
Elizabeth (Buff) White
Smith College '70
Northwestern Univ. MSJ '73
Text Editor, AMA Family Medical Guide (Random House, 1982)
Missionary with South America Mission, serving in Brazil

"Dr. Dawn's book invites us to share her journey from depression, addiction, medical school, and recovery to a higher 'Positive Addiction' which is more habit-forming than alcohol or drugs, more expensive than either, but where the 'high' is far greater than any attainable from any possible substance, that of orthopraxis of her Christian belief: serving the poor in the name of the Lord!"
Jack L Wasinger DDS, MA, PhD, ThD candidate
Dental Missionary, Veteran of multiple missions to Papua, New Guinea

"As pastor of a local church, I consider Dr. Dawn's commitment to offer her encouragement and expertise to the hurting in our community truly a blessing. Thanks for all you do for our people! ... I find her willingness to share her time and genuine care to the hurting in the outermost parts of the world truly an inspiration! Keep up the 'good' work, Doc!"
Troy Lewis
Pastor, Steamboat Christian Center

"Very easy and entertaining read. Doctor Obrecht's passion for medicine first inspired me as a college student as I was beginning my own journey into medicine. Her compassion and caring for all patients, but especially those that she helps with her unique perspective and life experience, continue to inspire me today."
Mario J. Carmosino, M.D.

"A remarkable and compelling story of one person's journey to find healing while helping to heal others. Dr. Dawn takes us with her as she finds a far greater purpose for her life than she would have ever imagined. A story of her healing... A story of a life given away so that she might keep it... A story of finding Hope... and a story that will give every reader Hope. A book to read and a book to give as a gift."
Chuck Stecker, D.Min.
President, Founder
A Chosen Generation

MISSION POSSIBLE

A Missionary Doctor's Journey
of Healing

By

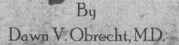

Dawn V. Obrecht, M.D.

Mission Possible
A Medical Missionary's Journey of Healing
By Dawn V. Obrecht, M.D.

Library of Congress Cataloging in Publication Data
Obrecht, Dawn V.
Mission Possible: A Medical Missionary's Journey of Healing / By Dawn V. Obrecht, M.D.
1. Medical missions
2. Addiction and recover, alcoholism, drug addiction
3. Spiritual healing
4. Travel, Honduras, Ecuador, Bolivia, Viet Nam, Brazil, Indonesia, Louisiana, Hurricane Katrina

ISBN 144047138X
EAN-13 9781440471384

Cover design by Sofia Rossi

Table of Contents

Foreword i

Universal Law of Service ii

Prologue iii

Part 1 Introduction: To be, or not 1

Part 2 Honduras 11

Part 3 Ecuador 51

Part 4 Bolivia 69

Part 5 Viet Nam 93

Part 6 Brazil 113

Part 7 Indonesia 133

Part 8 Louisiana 207

Generalities 242

Epilogue 246

December 4, 2008

I had no idea turning my scribbles into a book was such a process. I only knew that I did not know how to do it. I thank God for giving me the wonderful people who have made it possible.

First, my editor Stacey Kramer, without whom I would still have only scribbles. Your expertise in writing, editing, layout, teaching and more is unparalleled. You helped me *see* the possibility of creating a book, and then stayed with me until it became a reality. You have coached me through writing, organizing, revising, whining, procrastinating, excitement, complaining, near melt-downs and persistence. Your support has helped me believe in myself and my writing. Thank you for the precious gifts of kindness and friendship. You are the best Jewish Mom a girl could have! I look forward to our next project...after a short break.

Troy Reichert, my agent, is much more than just "an agent". Thank you for the coaching and guidance and helping me to define the direction of my writing. And Chuck Stecker, thank you for Troy!

Thank you to Keith Kramer for his copy edit and Sofia Rossi for her cover design, to my readers and endorsers for the kind words and encouragement, and to Jo Hardesty for reminding me to use my own voice. Thank you to my wonderful patients for keeping me grounded in the here and now and allowing me to share your struggles, and to my brothers and sisters who journey through personal growth of all kinds. Your process encourages me.

Most of all, thank you to my husband, Erik Landvik, for being my partner in everything. Your support in yet another of my endeavors, your constancy, your ability to live on a spiritual basis and remind me that God is in charge, all help me to be the best person I can be.

– D. V.O.

*This book is dedicated to everyone, everywhere,
who helps to make the world a better place*

Foreword

Once in a great while, we have the privilege of sharing deeply in another's journey of self to wholeness. Dawn Obrecht makes this journey through the work of medical service to others.

Mission Possible takes the reader to many exotic locations throughout the Third World where medical care is the exception, not the rule. Here infant mortality, childhood epilepsy, unchecked infectious disease and trauma are the norm. The stories are fascinating, the human suffering unspeakable. Through the author's eyes we are present as the gamut of maladies is treated: an eighty-year-old man who travels hours by horseback seeking help for pain; a child treated for meningitis without modern diagnostic equipment; and countless others who are comforted and cared for following a tsunami.

We are also taken on the author's deeply personal journey of spiritual growth beginning with the pain of alcoholic parents, through her own addiction and finally to a place of healing and peace in recovery. As Dr. Obrecht so aptly teaches, recovery is a process – a lifelong work in progress, not an arrival. In transitioning from the mind-numbing shutdown place of childhood fear and anguish to the acceptance of pain and forgiveness of self, we begin a process of opening. It is in this opening of self that we are able to experience compassion for others and are drawn to a life centered on service. Our gifts and talents are given to us to help us serve. In serving others we grow spiritually.

Dawn Obrecht has written an exceptional book with many valuable lessons for all of us. She is an accomplished physician and an extraordinary individual. I should know – she's my sister.

W. Fred Obrecht, M.D., anesthesiologist; veteran of multiple missions to the Dominican Republic and North Carolina State Medical Team physician responder to Hurricane Katrina victims

This is the Universal Law of Service
We Always Get More Than We Give

Spiritual growth, service, overcoming fears to do what we think God wants us to do; these are all addressed in *Mission Possible*, a book about one woman's surviving and thriving while being of service and getting closer to her God.

Each chapter ends with a summary of lessons from that mission. By bringing these lessons to consciousness and articulating them, they can be internalized and used.

For those who are held back from serving by their fears, *Mission Possible* can encourage them to move forward, helping them see how they can overcome what is holding them back, do what they want to do, and consider alternative ways to serve. Not everyone is meant to go to Asia or South America to build churches or care for the sick, but many can help by collecting supplies, providing publicity, fundraising with a bake sale or garage sale, or just encouraging those who will go. There is always a way to help and work to do by *anyone* willing.

Enormous emotional and spiritual growth comes from service, whether one is on the front line or behind the scenes. By doing what we think God wants us to do, not letting our fears paralyze us, we grow in ourselves and in our relationship with Him.

Prologue

My name is Dawn and I am a recovering addict. I am also a physician, wife, mother, grandmother, athlete, Christian, American, and fit into a few other categories as well. Mostly I am a child of God down here on earth doing the best I can.

I have found that if I am open and available, I get to be help-ful, often by doing bits of medical care in a variety of different set-tings. Those with other gifts – sewing, singing, babysitting, art and so on – are able to give in ways I cannot; medicine is my way.

My spiritual support group includes people from all socioeco-nomic standings, all educational backgrounds, and all walks of life. I am often asked medical questions, or to look at an injured body part. Recently I spent a few minutes prior to a recovery meeting with a somewhat older man, newly sober, uninsured, unemployed and with no resources. He had been having foot problems and explained that he had suffered pain on the sole of his right foot on and off for years. It was bothering him more and more and he found that there was a hard lump that was the specific source of his pain. He had repeatedly soaked his foot and removed some of the callous, finding a dark spot he also removed; he was concerned that it might be something seri-ous he should be doing something about. He had clean feet, clean socks, and was generally very much like any other patient I might have seen in any routine medical practice. A few minutes before the meeting began we found a bench where he could remove his shoe and sock. The culprit on the bottom of his foot was obvious from his de-scription, a plantar wart, now without its seed. It should heal well without him spending money he cannot afford to go to a clinic. He was very grateful for my time and expertise, and I got to feel good about having the ability to help someone.

Last year, a long-time acquaintance at a camping retreat we were both attending asked me to look at her eye. For several days she'd had the sensation there was something in it, but was reluctant to go to a doctor. The biggest "feel good" for me was that she stopped worrying about her eye when she found out I would be at the retreat. She said just knowing that Doc Dawn would be there was reassur-ing. Janelle is perfectly able to see any doctor she wants, including an ophthalmologist. She lives in a city where they are plentiful and has the means to pay for anything she needs. I am flattered that she chose to have me look at her eye. She did, in fact, have a sliver of something imbedded in the cornea. The only location with good lighting in this campground was the shower facility, so we set up a chair; her boyfriend held a flashlight for additional direct light and I instructed her to sit very still. I was able to remove the sliver with a tiny needle I had in the medical kit I take everywhere with me, even to campouts, and her eye felt better immediately. I asked her to see an ophthalmologist in Denver the next week and he confirmed that the sliver was gone and her cornea was healing from the tiny nick I had made to do the procedure.

Another friend and member of the same group called me recently to ask about getting an antibiotic for her urinary tract infection. It was a weekend, her doctor not available, and the time and money to go to an emergency room in Denver exorbitant. What a joy to be able to help this single working mother by phoning in a prescription. Again, I asked her to see her regular doc to confirm adequate treatment when she finished the medication.

The more anxiety-provoking "opportunities" are those that involve emergencies. I have responded to cardiac arrests in airports more than once, having doctors in other specialties move over and defer to me when I tell them I am trained in emergency medicine and am glad to try to intubate the person on the floor who is in cardiac arrest. Several times I have sat with passengers who developed chest pain while on a flight and consulted with pilots to decide if they should turn the plane around and land as soon as possible. The flight attendants and emergency crews that meet the planes are uniformly grateful for the little I do. In one case, the flight attendants moved a sick passenger to first-class seating putting me beside him for the duration of the flight from Washington, D.C. to Denver. He remained stable and paramedics in Denver took him immediately to a local hospital. I heard from him a few days later – he had improved. He was very appreciative of my help, and relayed a message from his cardiologist that he, too, was glad I was on board and had thought to give him an aspirin, for its cardioprotective not its pain-relieving properties, and to monitor his pulse.

On a long international flight from Miami to South America, a Brazilian doctor who was also a passenger and I were asked to consult about a flight attendant having abdominal pain. She was in a significant amount of discomfort with dizziness and fatigue. The option to land immediately was not there, as we were flying over jungle. We gave her some medication and found a place for her to lie down until the end of the overnight flight.

Long ago, as a resident in emergency medicine at Denver

General Hospital, now Denver Health and Hospitals, when I was considered a "baby doctor" (not a pediatrician, but a new and very inexperienced doctor), I had several opportunities to help skiers. There was an arrangement with the local "front range" ski areas, all within sixty miles of Denver, where doctors could get day passes by signing in with the ski patrol and carrying a radio. We would ski all day while being available to ski patrol to help with anyone ill or injured. This was a terrific deal, as we were paid below minimum wage as interns and residents, if you count all the hours we spent overnight in the hospital. None of us had any extra money for recreation and we actually did not have the time either. Many of my ski days were the days when I was on a night shift in the emergency room. I was always up all night, unlike night shifts elsewhere in the hospital when I could count on a few hours of sleep. At the end of the shift, some of the E.R. nurses and I would often drive directly to the closest ski area and ski all day, hoping to grab a few hours sleep in the early evening before returning to the hospital to work the next night. No time, no money, no problem; we still found a way to ski!

As the ski patrol doc, I reduced dislocated shoulders, splinted fractured limbs for transport, put in hundreds of stitches, and consoled parents and partners of injured skiers. The medical work added a dimension to my days of skiing that simply enhanced the joy. Sunshine, exercise and being able to take a few minutes out to use my relatively newly acquired skills to help someone, all made for many great days.

One day at one of the ski areas less than an hour from Denver, I had stopped for lunch. Just as I was taking off my coat and gloves, I got a call on the radio to come to the base area outside of the cafeteria. Only thirty seconds away, I immediately ran outside to find a middle-aged man lying on the snow, a worried look on his face to match the one on the faces of the two ski patrol EMTs beside him. I rapidly took the briefest of histories while feeling his pulse and scanning his overall appearance. He had simply developed dizziness and weakness, to the point of needing to sit and then lie down, at the end of his last run. The ski patrol had, appropriately, kept him horizontal, not moving him until I checked him out. He denied having chest pain, although he acknowledged a strange feeling in his chest. While he was telling me this, I was, simultaneously, detecting a very irregular pulse. My now ex-husband, a psychiatrist, was with me and offered to go to our car and get the black medical bag I always carry. In it I had a very few and very important medications, one of which was used to treat cardiac arrhythmias (irregular heartbeats). I was able to get an intravenous line started and a quick bolus of lidocaine into this man while telling the ski patrol to call the Flight for Life helicopter. He could have gone into cardiac arrest at any moment – the sooner I got him some help, the better. He needed immediate transport to a cardiac care unit where he could be monitored. The significance of the cardiac arrhythmia was probably that he'd had, or was having, an acute myocardial infarction (heart attack). A large percentage of heart attack victims die from the subsequent arrhythmia. The heart stops beating effectively and skips beats, beats with too shallow a force, or just flutters around, not pumping blood to the organs, especially to the heart itself, causing death within minutes. Kneeling in the snow next to this man was nerve-wracking! Finally we heard the whip-whip of the helicopter. The pilot landed on the snow (the parking lot was full and no chance of getting everyone off of the slopes to move their cars). I breathed deeply as I watched it take off with my patient on board.

About three weeks later, after I had long forgotten this day, stuffing my brain with tens of thousands of pieces of information and pushing out anything not absolutely necessary for continued residency education and performance, I got a phone call. The man called me and simply said: "I just want to thank you for saving my life!" I was stunned. He had tracked me down, probably from my name on the report I gave to the nurse on the helicopter. Clearly his cardiologist had clued him in that the anti-arrhythmic medication I had given him intravenously had probably kept him from going into cardiac arrest. How thoughtful of him to take the time to call me, and how thoughtful of his doctor to inform him that we did a good job out on the snow with minimal equipment. This experience reminds me of how much I like the practice of medicine!

I also stop at traffic accidents if help is not already there. The summer after Erik and I had moved into our rural home in northwest Colorado, I was stopped in a line of vehicles, engines off, occupants standing outside their cars, trucks and campers. Since I was in one of the first vehicles in the line, I got out to see what was halting my progress home after a day working in town. An unmoving body was on the ground in the middle of the narrow county road, several people kneeling beside.

I ran to the scene and found her alive, conscious, in pain and confused, not moving, but able to answer my questions. Her mother was there with others who had found a blanket to cover her and had called local emergency services. Her cycling helmet was beside her and a semi truck was parked a few feet away.

The girl was a fifteen-year-old competitive cyclist, riding on this narrow road with no shoulders. Her mother was cycling behind her when her daughter went under the wheels of a passing truck. When I introduced myself to the mother saying that I was a physician with emergency medical training, her relief was visible and audible. During the nearly thirty minutes it took for an ambulance to reach us, I was able to examine her daughter, determine she did not appear to have brain damage and clearly had either femur or pelvic fractures or both, probably not major abdominal injuries, and most likely had a good chance of recovering.

Finishing this and finding nothing more I could do for the teenager, I turned to the distraught man pacing beside his truck who had just given his report to a police officer. Approaching him, seeing the fear, pain and questions on his face, I impulsively asked if he needed a hug. Affirmative. I was then able to tell him the girl was going to be okay and the mother, riding behind her daughter, specifically said the accident was *not* the trucker's fault; her daughter had either swerved, skidded, or been pulled under the wheel. The accident was just that, an accident, with no one at fault, no one needing or wanting to blame. Air currents under trucks, gravel on road edges, simply the danger of riding on a narrow road all contribute to accidents.

A few weeks later, again after I had moved on and all but forgotten the day, flowers from the trucker arrived for me with the message, "Thank you for your help and compassion. It was appreciated more than you know." Again, my greatest service was in comforting the mother and the driver of the truck. When we later met the teenager and her family, she had no recall of the day and was on her way to full recovery from a fractured pelvis and other injuries.

I answer questions, look at rashes, into ears and eyes, and at extremities. I get to do this at any time and place. I think many doctors do this, as it is one of our ways of relating. I feel especially blessed for having had the broad emergency and general medical training. My psychiatrist friends don't really like being asked to look in a toddler's ear. In fact, my psychiatrist, radiologist, and pathologist friends are some of those who ask me to look in their children's ears!

I have been in the men's locker room at a masters swim meet, called in when an adult male swimmer was having chest pain. The coach and teammates of the swimmer escorted me in, shouting, "woman in the locker room." We sent the patient off in an ambulance, but not until I had spent twenty minutes or more with him, my male teammates staring at me, then going about their business of showering and changing. After all, I am a doctor.

I have run out onto the field or playing court at more than one high school game. My daughters are athletic and my husband and I attended most of their games. Once at a volleyball game, a young girl collapsed. I was only a few feet away in the stands and immediately went onto the court to care for her. The man sitting next to us was stunned and said to my husband, "Isn't she afraid of a lawsuit?" This possibility had *never* occurred to me or to my husband, who responded with, "I think she is just concerned about the girl." The man questioning my actions was, of course, an attorney. I am grateful I get to function with faith, not fear.

Much of the time, I have no real medical care to offer, usually do not have appropriate equipment or supplies with me, especially when I am a spectator at a game, or out on a run or bike ride. What I provide most is reassurance for the patient and his friends and family.

My day is always enhanced by these little opportunities to help. I have been blessed with a legacy of support and encouragement that taught me to do what I believe I am supposed to do, to pursue my dreams. I don't let the negative stuff get in the way. When the mother of a friend said, "You don't want to be a doctor, you want to marry one," my jaw dropped. I had never thought about marrying a doctor; I just wanted to *be* a doctor. When I was starting college in 1966, the roommate of a boyfriend said, "You'll never do it." He could not imagine having women in his class. I promised to contact him when I finished. I don't recall that I ever did... maybe I'll send him this book.

Part One

To be, or not...

Adventure, joy, frustration – these three words epitomize the essence of my short-term medical missions to Asia, South and Central America, and the Southern United States. The physical journey connected me with ordinary people, some medically trained, most not, who provide valuable services, and to people who do not have regular access to medical care and are thankful for us just showing up. My personal journey attests that no one leaves a mission unchanged.

△◆
Chapter One
△◆

Age twelve was a pivotal year for me. I decided on my life's profession and I also decided I wanted to end my life. I don't remember ever having just one thought at a time, one feeling, or one plan. I was planning to be a doctor – no clue what that meant, but I was going to do it – and simultaneously I was planning to die.

Having grown up in a family with a preacher grandfather, I was raised going to church and Sunday school, so my idea of being a doctor was to be a missionary doctor in Africa. I had heard missionaries talk about their lives in other countries and found that adventurous and exciting. Undoubtedly there was also an element of wanting to get away, really far away from my family, as well as just wanting adventure. As the years progressed, the dream of being a missionary doctor in Africa faded. I got sidetracked with marriage, children, and something even more challenging – addiction.

My grandmother, who was born in the 1880s, told me that being a doctor was the second most important calling, after being pastor of a church. Unlike most women of her time, Mammy was college-educated and very supportive of me and my desire to go into medicine. She even knew a woman doctor from her mother's generation, the late 1800s! My grandfather was a Southern Baptist preacher in the Carolinas in the early 1900s. He preached in the days when preachers were the last to be paid, the days when they were given chickens and vegetables, but no money. He had to take other jobs to support the family; as a ticket taker on a train, then a night watchman. Mammy took in boarders from the college, did laundry and cooking, taught piano, and did anything else she could to support the family. My mother and her sisters grew up with little material wealth but lots of love and adventure. She followed her dream and became a writer, working as a journalist for several major newspapers.

When I decided at twelve to become a doctor, it was 1960 and girls rarely became doctors. I was an asthmatic child, sick a great deal with respiratory infections including episodes of pneumonia. I was very active between asthmatic periods and often suffered minor injuries, and sometimes more-than-minor injuries that required more medical care than available from the bathroom cabinet. Once I tried to climb out of my second-story bedroom and into the nearby tree. I planned to meet some friends and stay out much later than I would have been allowed to at age fourteen. I started my escape attempt by holding onto the gutter on the side of the porch off of my bedroom. Misjudging my jumping capacity, or perhaps just the distance between house and tree, I fell through the enormous branches of the pink magnolia that was designated as "my tree." The one beside it, with luscious white flowers blooming all summer, was my brother's tree. Both trees had tree houses, courtesy of Dad's expert carpentry skills and his support of our tree-climbing ability. Upon landing, only one ankle hurt and I was still able to hobble inside. The next day I finally told my mother and we went to the doctor, who diagnosed a fractured ankle. I am fortunate that was all I broke, although many who know me have wondered, judging by my behavior over the years, if I also might have hit my head.

As a result of my illnesses and injuries, I got to know my doctor quite well. This wonderful pediatrician made house calls, something I also did on occasion many years later. I remember so clearly when he would come to our house to see me in the early morning before his office hours and again late in the evening. Children in the 1950s and '60s were often hospitalized and those with asthma and allergies often had tonsillectomies. I think my doctor must have been ahead of his time because he never put me in the hospital and I still have my tonsils.

Further demonstrating his progressive mindset, Dr. Stiffler took me seriously when I announced during one of his house calls that I had decided to be a doctor. After diagnosing yet another respiratory infection and calling in a prescription to our corner drugstore, he took time to talk with me about being a doctor. He made a point of telling me I needed to study hard, get good grades in school, go to college, study even harder, continue to get good grades and apply to medical school. His wife was also a doctor at this time when so few women were, and his son was also planning on a career in medicine. I did as he suggested and went to medical school at the University of Maryland, just one year behind his son, Bobby.

△♦

Chapter Two

△♦

It was important to be taken seriously by my doctor, but more important to be taken seriously by my own parents. In many ways they too were ahead of their times and, despite severe family dysfunction, I always felt that there was never a child more wanted and loved by both mother and father. My father, born in 1900, went to work in the family feed company the day after he finished high school in 1918. He remembered one of the customers that day saying to him, "I thought I saw you graduate yesterday. What are you doing working already?" He and his family assumed that he and his two brothers would work at the feed mill starting immediately after high school. They all did. His older brother was a sensitive and sickly man, and wrote poetry while sharing the work of running the feed company. Dad's younger brother, my Uncle Charles, worked at the mill and also was able to attend law school at night. He left the family business to his two older brothers to practice law.

Dad told me that he would like to have been a doctor, but there was really no possibility. Always hungry for more education himself, Dad took classes in farm animal care, perfecting the composition of feed, even learning about veterinary supplies, medications and diagnosing illnesses in animals. It was the closest he could get to a career in medicine.

When I, his oldest child, announced that I wanted to be a doctor, this old man, already sixty (he was forty-eight when I was born and nearly fifty-two when my brother was born), was thrilled. He instantly said he would pay for my tuition. Money to go to medical school was the greatest gift he could give me. Even while suffering with his own problems, consistent support, both emotional and financial, was what he had to give and he did for many years. He was so proud. He told all of his customers and friends that his daughter was going into "medical," always proud and supportive and often with me there to blush and wish he would not talk about me. He frequently reminded me that my education "was one thing they could never take away." I was never sure who "they" were, but my father had lived through the Depression and two world wars and had seen poverty from the inside, resulting in deep fear and negativity, much of which he covered with alcohol. Dad lived to see me graduate from college with honors in chemistry and to finish medical school four years later. He lived to see me have a successful family practice and be self-supporting after all the years he had supported me, making it possible for me to finish many years of school without debt. He also lived to see my two daughters born before he died at age eighty-seven, less than a year after my mother died, and after nearly forty-six years of marriage.

My mother was born in 1910 in the South, the daughter of a Southern Baptist preacher and schoolteacher mother. She was adventurous, secure as the oldest of three daughters and brought up to believe she could do anything she wanted. She raised my brother and me the same way. Ten years younger than my father, she was thirty-eight when she gave birth to me, her first child; three prior babies had not lived. Mom had been a reporter at the *Baltimore Sun* and *Washington Post* newspapers in the 1930s and '40s. Big adventure and excitement drew this southern girl north to Baltimore, alone and looking for a journalism career. There were very few women in journalism back then and she had a sports column even though women were not allowed in the press boxes. She covered some of the most spectacular events of the time, including the horse race between Seabiscuit and War Admiral, never once going into the press box.

No wonder that she was completely supportive of my medical career; she assumed I could do whatever I wanted. She taught me there were no barriers and not being able to do something was never discussed. I remember being fascinated by the tales she told of her career and thinking that journalism would also be an exciting profession. Medicine had my heart, though, and has held it for almost fifty years now. I am grateful for what it has given me.

△◆

Chapter Three

△◆

My parents, besides being supportive and doing the best job they could with what they had to work with, were both sick. I caught the disease from them, although it did not manifest until a few years later at about age fourteen. The disease is alcoholism.

I now know that the rage I felt toward my father for his drunkenness and the verbal abuse he displayed toward my mother, my brother and me, was the source of my desire to leave life as I knew it. Perhaps seemingly bizarre to those unfamiliar with alcoholism, this kind, supportive man, my father, could suddenly become a vicious abuser terrorizing us only hours after sitting in church or spending time with us in the garden. Mom began drinking as a way to escape her own pain.

I saw no way out. As a child, I was a victim; children are. Adults may feel like victims, but children truly are victims of the adults in their lives. I remember so many times from preschool to the year I finally left home at age seventeen, when evenings were spent hiding from Dad. I alternated between begging him to stop screaming at Mom and begging her to leave – for the evening, forever. He never stopped; she never left.

The next day, and there was always the next day, everyone would act as if nothing was wrong; we were just a normal family. Verbal violence, the occasional physical violence, and always the fear of what he was going to do next, were a way of life. I got the message and went about my "next days" the best I could; confusion, hatred, rage all had nowhere to go. I was warned not to tell anyone about my father's drinking, not that I would have known how to anyway, but that message further cut me off from other people. As is usually the case, I turned my anger and pain in on myself and became depressed. Seeing no way out, I made the decision at only twelve years old to end my pain. I overdosed on all the medications in our bathroom cabinet, drinking the children's cough syrup, the "sleeping medicine" our doctor had prescribed when my mother told him I was anxious and having difficulty sleeping, and swallowing all the pills I could find. I was quite disappointed and angry when I awoke the next day and realized I was going to live.

A little more than a year after trying to take my own life, I did find the solution for my pain: Alcohol. And cigarettes. Alcohol and cigarettes covered my pain! I could be raving drunk, slurring my speech, losing my balance, and eventually throwing up, or just have a "little buzz." Either way, everything was better. I found a way to cover the anger, sadness, fear and pain. Cigarettes did the same for me, just to a lesser degree. They allowed me to push down the feelings. Think about it: the simple action of bringing a cigarette to your mouth and inhaling can be seen as bringing a puff of smoke into your body to push down the pain. Don't feel. Take another drag off of that chemical cloak. Cover up and deny the existence of the anger and sadness, the loss and loneliness.

Eventually I progressed to using other drugs because alcohol and cigarettes were not working so well by the time I was eighteen. The anger and pain were breaking through. My parents continued to be supportive of me and their own disease continued to progress. I hated them more every day, yet I was dependent on them for support during the eight years of college and medical school. I controlled my alcoholism and drug addiction while in school, getting extremely drunk and high when I could, studying extremely hard when necessary. I am typical of most addicts (an alcoholic is just an alcohol ad dict), in that I was very functional. Only a small percentage, some say three percent of alcoholics, are street drunks – the rest look like you and me. I know that those years of using drugs helped me survive the pain of childhood. The pain was too much for me to feel and to live with unless I covered it up with something external, a mind-altering chemical of some kind. The addiction saved my life.

The end of the story of my addiction is that it nearly killed me before I began to get help and recover. My daughters were three and six and the drugs had again stopped working. I was in pain, anger, despair and rage on a daily basis. The memories of my childhood abuse, emotional and verbal, and of watching my mother abused, surfaced with the birth of my own daughters; my childhood was in my face as I watched my little girls. Unconsciously I was reliving my own little girlhood.

Through a series of events that I now believe were all "God things" or coincidences (one of God's aliases), I landed in a recovery group and began to heal. Angels appeared in my life at every turn; I saw addicts recovering every day. People of all shapes and sizes, all ages, colors, educations, socio-economic standings, including other doctors, were healing, not using drugs *and* not wanting to die. For the first time in my life, I felt as if someone understood! The others in my support group had all been there. They knew how I felt without me saying a word. When I did say words, they were able to reply with similar stories and feelings. I was home! I could do what they had done and be free from twenty years of addiction. Maybe I could learn to want to live, not just go through the motions trying to get another day behind me without harming myself.

It worked; and I worked. I worked harder at recovery than I ever had at anything in my life. My life, and the lives of my daughters, depended on my getting well. I have not had a drink or a drug since March 9, 1984. After the first two years, I have been happy most of the time. I am so grateful for my life. I get to be emotionally, spiritually and physically healthy and I get to help others along their pathway to health.

Divorce, recovery and children old enough for me to leave with relatives for a few weeks prompted my return to the childhood dream. The "God thing," in the form of a small ad in a medical journal, was the catalyst and I was able to find a way to begin to live my missionary doctor dream, if only for a few weeks at a time. Marriage, my real one (the first one being the trial run), to an amazing man who had been a missionary kid was, of course, just a coincidence.

△◆
Chapter Four
△◆

Now, after three-and-a-half decades of practicing medicine, I am following in my mother's footsteps, becoming a writer and writing about my medical experiences. Medicine has meant so much more to me than a career. It is a way of life. I am a person, a human being, not just a doctor; but doctor is in every cell of my body and soul. My husband and children see me as wife and mom, and I am as much those as I am doctor, but I was doctor first and feel as if I have always been. I only vaguely recall life before being "Doc Dawn." I never wanted to be or do anything else until now; now I want to write about being a doctor.

Initially I wanted to write this book simply to report on my medical missions. The people and experiences have stretched my brain and given me much more than I gave them. I have been allowed to live some of that childhood dream. I just wanted to report on my trips for anyone who might be interested. As *New York Times* reporter and author Rick Bragg was told by a mother about the death of her son, "People forgets it if it ain't wrote down."

What follows are the stories of my adventures as a missionary doctor. All the events I describe are true and some names have been changed or omitted to protect anonymity. Each of my seven mission trips is unique, each only a few weeks in duration, yet worlds away in every imaginable way from my everyday life as a doctor in this country. It has been possible for me to have these adventures and fulfill my dream of experiencing missionary medicine only because of my recovery from my own illness. In turn, my recovery has allowed me to be a far better human being, and in turn a far better doctor than I would have been. What has happened in the writing and rewriting of this book is the reinforcement of my knowledge that God has had a hand in every part of my life, especially when I did not believe in Him. One of the many recovery sayings is, "I thank God for recovery and I thank recovery for God." I have always known that I had to go through what I went through to get here, but I never fully comprehended that the difficult times would be the pieces that allow me to be of the most service possible to each human being I come in contact with.

In medical school, some of my classmates and I would comment on our hope that certain of our fellow students would go into pathology or radiology, or some specialty where there was minimal contact with real patients, and where they could do the least harm. Having survived my own addiction and recovery, alcoholic parents, two suicide attempts, and getting to a point of almost constant peace, usually joy, in my own life, I am able to help others in a way I could not have learned in school. Some of the parts of medicine that have been the most satisfying to me are the ones I don't get paid for. I love teaching medical students and having them in my office; it is all volunteer. I love giving talks to other doctors, to hospital and medical society groups, most of which are unpaid. And I love doing medicine in developing countries. Not only are these adventures unpaid, but we volunteers have to pay to travel to the countries and support ourselves while we're there. Except for a few specialties, medicine is not a high-paying profession. The doctors who go into medicine for the financial rewards are few and probably very unhappy. My friends are astonished when they find out how little I make. I did not go into medicine to make money. I just love medicine, all aspects of it. There are doctors and then there are doctors. Some have empathy and communication skills; some do not. Some care deeply about their patients; some do not. It has been said, and it is taught in medical schools, that more than eighty percent of the information a doctor gets from his or her patient is from the history. The physical exam and laboratory tests add only a fraction of what a doctor needs to know. Communication, as much intuitive as verbal, is a crucial part of meeting a patient's real need, not just the stated reason for their visit. Hearing, seeing, sensing our patients' needs is much more an art than teachable skill.

As human beings, we travel our own pathways and learn how and what we have to give. My suffering has made me a better physician, perhaps especially to those who have suffered enormous tragedies like the tsunamis and hurricanes, or major trauma like the women in Asia who have had acid thrown in their faces, or those who have lived through poverty and near starvation. These patients have blessed me more than they can know, simply by allowing me to feel their suffering, to identify with them, and to help just a little. I come away, time after time, knowing I am blessed beyond my capacity to understand. I have survived my own tsunami and now my life is calm.

△◆
Lessons
△◆

- Heal, whatever it takes. Do the work of recovering and healing from your life's trauma and pain.
- Serve, help others, in your own unique way, whether it is cooking your family's dinner, sharing a loving and understanding smile, or a mission trip to the other side of the world.
- Develop and nurture your own relationship with God.

Part Two

Honduras
1992

Seizures, meningitis, dengue fever and machete wounds are all part of life and death in rural Honduras, where there are no doctors. Honduras gives me my first taste of providing medical care in a developing country. This is why I had gone to medical school in the 1970s. Now I can live my dream for a few weeks and experience what medicine does and does not have to offer to this community. I will be the only doctor for many miles and many hours, and will know that when I leave there will not be another doctor here for many months.

△◆
Chapter One
△◆

How did this happen?

Here I am, minding my own business, sitting at my desk during a short lunch break between patients in my family medicine office in suburban Denver, Colorado. I rarely have a "real" lunch break and am lucky to get a few minutes to return phone calls and do paperwork while eating some of my brown-bag meal. Today, however, I indulge myself by flipping through a medical journal while munching on leftover elk stir-fry from last night's dinner.

Something different from the usual advertisements catches my eye. A tiny square at the lower left corner of a page near the back of the journal says, *"Physician wanted for short-term Medical Mission to Honduras."* I gasp audibly, glad that nobody else is in my office at the moment. I had gone to medical school thinking I would be a missionary doctor and practice medicine in some Third World country. In my initial dreams, I pictured myself in Africa caring for people with varied illnesses who'd had no access to medical care for much of their lives.

Noticing my sweaty palms, I try to refocus my eyes and re-read the little ad. I don't usually look at this journal; actually I rarely look at any journals anymore, getting most of my continuing medical education from talks at the hospital, or conferences on specific topics. It really does say, *"Physician wanted for short-term Medical Mission to Honduras."* I realize I am holding my breath; I am dizzy, heart pounding, and glad that I am sitting down. Could this be a "God thing?" Of course, everything is, but could I really consider picking up my old dream and going to another country, a developing corner of the world, as a volunteer doctor? Even for a few weeks? Holding my breath again; breathe, I command myself. And keep eating lunch; cannot afford to be dizzy from hypoglycemia, hypoxia, or just stress – incompatible with providing good medical care to the afternoon patients.

Sidetracked from the medical mission dream for the past two decades while going through medical school and residency training, I also got married; moved from Maryland to Colorado; had two children; got divorced; figured out how to do the single working-mom bit; started my own medical practice; got remarried; and on and on – life! As my ex-husband says, "It beats the alternative."

My eyes go from focusing on the ad to glazing over as I begin a recurring daydream, a flashback into my journey to becoming a doctor:

I remember glowing with the encouragement I received from my pediatrician and vowing to follow through and follow my dream. Not many women were in medicine in the U.S. at that time, but many women were doctors elsewhere in the world; today, some estimate that eighty percent of doctors in Russia are female. Medicine is a very maternal profession; women do it well, as evidenced by the fact that nearly fifty percent of medical students are now women, and women doctors are uniformly the first in any group practice to have a full patient load. I continue to be grateful for my pediatrician, a very important man in my childhood, who took me seriously when I risked telling him my dream.

Another huge piece of my support came from my parents. How difficult it must have been for my dad, at age forty-eight, to adjust to the birth of his first child and then almost four years later, to a second child. In spite of his imperfections, there was much good about him and I truly believe that no other children were ever more loved or wanted. This did not, however, keep him from being his sick, alcoholic self. There was verbal abuse, drunkenness and chaos and incongruity throughout my childhood.

My parents promised to provide financially for my education. Money, the getting and saving of it, and finding ways to not spend it, was one of my father's gods. Alcohol was another. He loved my brother and me, and in his own warped way, he also loved our mother. Both my brother and I finished medical school (he is an anesthesiologist) without debt, highly unusual then and now. Dad was very proud of us and of his part in paying for our education; he went to work in the family feed mill business making and selling dog food the day after he finished high school. He never had the opportunity to do anything else. I often say that my dad put me through medical school on dog food.

A knock on the office door startles me back to reality; my first afternoon patient is ready.

A dozen or more patients and four hours later, I am home. I have a chance to make a phone call to the New Hampshire number listed in the journal ad. The small organization, really just a handful of people, loosely supported by a church in New Hampshire, has been arranging for doctors and dentists to go to El Rosario, Honduras for two-week stays about four times a year for the past five years. It sounds like a terrific opportunity to go to a rural community and pro-vide medical care for two weeks, beginning in three months. I imme-diately, although tentatively, volunteer; no one asks for documents or verification that I am a licensed physician. Heidi, the doctor orga-nizing the trip, simply tells me to show up in San Pedro Sula, Hon-duras at a specific hotel, on a specific day, to meet the four others coming from New Hampshire. I will be the only doctor. She also gives me a great deal of information about the community and the mission, telling me what illnesses and injuries are most prevalent so I can spend some time over the next few weeks studying diseases we don't see in the U.S.

A trip like this is an enormous step for me. I will be leaving the comfort zone of my quiet little family medicine and addictions practice, and trying out missionary medicine. I am simultaneously excited and scared; physiologically the same thing, just a matter of the human brain's interpretation of the neurochemical adrenaline. I have never been the only doctor in a community, am unfamiliar with tropical diseases, and am used to high-tech support and everything a hospital has to offer in the way of diagnostic and treatment facilities. Still, I decide to go.

My unsuspecting husband of three years, Erik, arrives home to a very energetic wife who greets him with, "I'm going to Hondu-ras! Want to come?"

Erik, having grown up in a missionary family in Brazil, speaks fluent Portuguese and almost fluent Spanish, and loves to travel. He is not in the medical profession, but has lots of first-aid experience and other practical skills too numerous to name. He agrees to go and to do whatever work needs to be done. There is al-ways something to do for anyone willing to work.

My daughters, Brie and Kara, are fifteen and twelve and happy to stay with relatives for the two-and-a-half weeks we will be gone. I arrange for another doctor to cover my practice and begin making flight plans. Erik and I decide to go into San Pedro Sula on a Friday, two days before the rest of the team arrives. We like to travel and will enjoy the extra time to explore the city before heading out to the small village where we will be working. We also hope to attend a meeting of our worldwide recovery and spiritual support group. We've attended support meetings in Europe and found the same con-nection, despite language differences, that we have had with people recovering in the U.S. It's always reassuring to find people all over the world in recovery supporting each other.

The preparation begins. In further conversations with Heidi, she says to bring whatever medical supplies and pharmaceuticals I can, and leave things I do not use for the next group of workers and for use by community members during the three months between North American missions. Several locals have been trained by previous medical missionaries to dispense basic medications for common illnesses, so there is some minimal care most of the time. I tell my office staff about my plans and ask them to begin collecting extra samples of medications from the pharmaceutical representatives who regularly visit our office. The "drug reps" often have almost outdated medications to give away in quantity when there is a specific need. They also have unusual dosages that have not caught on with doctors in this country but are just as good as more commonly used dosages, and they appreciate being able to donate them to causes like foreign medical missions. We begin to receive donations and our office starts to look like a warehouse. One rep even gives me an extra stethoscope she has among her supplies. My entire staff is excited for my trip and spends lunch breaks repackaging medications.

Pharmaceutical companies package sample medications in absurd ways. They put anywhere from one to four pills in a "blister pack" or plastic bottle, put that in a box, and sometimes put four to six of the boxes in another layer of packing. This makes the whole thing take up lots of space and look like a lot of medication, just to better advertise their brand. The truth is that a one day's dose of a given medicine may be four pills; to even give someone the first three days of medicine, I have to give them at least three whole boxes. It is a tragic waste of trees and plastic. I would boycott these companies, but I need the samples to give to my patients who cannot afford to buy their medications. I have not found a company that does not do this; if I do, I will use that company over and above the others, all else being equal.

The task before my staff is to pack down the samples so that we do not take extra plastic and cardboard to Honduras. We are careful to keep everything properly labeled and try to put about a one-week supply of medicine in each small bottle. Enthusiasm grows as the reps spread the word, and I am offered lots of medications. I accept them all. We soon have four large duffel bags of medications and supplies, all efficiently packed with minimal excess paper and plastic.

The day arrives to send the girls to stay with my aunt and cousins in North Carolina. Erik and I depart the next day with four huge duffel bags of supplies and one carry-on each for all of our personal items. The airport check-in is easy, as is arrival and baggage claim in Honduras. I guess no one cares that we are taking drugs *into* Central America!

△◆

Chapter Two

△◆

On the plane, my mood changes to one of complete relaxation and surrender. Whatever happens happens. I have decided to do this, it is under way, and there is no turning back, so I might as well enjoy the change from my daily routine. Travel always makes me feel like a wide-eyed kid, and while I will miss my girls, I know it's all right to leave them for a short time to have my own adventure. Except for brief trips to Mexico, this is my first time out of the country since doing a rotation in London during medical school. I am more confident about my medical abilities, and more importantly, I have more trust that God is in charge of my life. I let Him deal with it while I relax and enjoy being alive.

On arrival at our hotel, where we will meet the rest of the team in two days, I am grateful that Erik speaks the language. No English spoken here. We take our luggage up two flights of stairs and down a narrow hallway with a warped and slanted floor to our tiny, hot room. It is clean, perfectly adequate with two single beds, a desk and an overhead fan. There is a small bathroom with very old, ragged, but clean towels and a new bar of soap. It feels like what I imagine a hotel in the western United States would have been like about one-hundred years ago. There is no phone, no tourist pamphlet, no television, no bedside table or lamp, just a bulb hanging from the ceiling. We are happy to be here and find this nicer than we expected.

Returning to the front desk, Erik asks in Spanish for a phone book. He finds the number for our support group and uses the reception desk phone, speaking again in Spanish to the person on the other end of the line. I understand nothing. Ah, powerlessness; I relish not having to be in charge right now. In Mexico, almost everyone, especially people who deal with tourists, speaks some English. San Pedro Sula is one of only two cities of any size in Honduras. It is not a tourist town and is so far from any English-speaking country that there is no reason for anyone to learn the language. I have taken a six-week course in "medical Spanish," so I have a few words. Until now, it has not occurred to me that communication would be a problem. Over the years, I have had a variety of non-communicative patients: infants, hearing impaired (although I do know some sign language and there is often an interpreter with hearing-impaired patients), mentally ill, comatose, and non-English speaking. The most common silent patients: angry teenagers. I am sure I will be able to determine what is going on with my patients and find a way to communicate when I get to the clinic in a few days. For now, I have Erik.

While Erik is on the phone, I investigate the lobby. Across the bare tile floor is a set of double doors leading out to a courtyard. A small pool with several lounge chairs is surrounded by blooming trees and bushes; and it is hot. We really are in the tropics. It must be well over ninety degrees Fahrenheit and at least that humid and even warmer in our small upstairs room. My skin is ecstatic. Used to the dry Colorado climate, it is soaking up the moisture in the air and smiling at being uncovered and warm. Even though he grew up in Brazil, farther south where it is even warmer than this, Erik is not so fond of the hot, sticky climate. While not overweight, he does outweigh me by about one-hundred pounds, has a full beard, and looks more like he belongs on a Viking ship than in a jungle; his forehead sweat is visible from across the room.

Erik joins me in a few minutes, having accepted an offer for us to be picked up at the hotel in about an hour by a member of the local support group. Their Friday night meeting starts at eight o'clock, like many do in the States. It's only six-thirty now, so we have time to get something to eat.

Out on the street in the evening heat, the sidewalks alternate between narrow and nonexistent. The humidity is thick, as if it is raining, but the drops are not falling from the sky, merely appearing spontaneously on our faces, necks and other strategic points as evidenced by dark spots on our clothing. Each doorway we pass lends us its own smell — tortillas, corn, meat, vegetables, soups, all tantalizing and increasing our hunger. We are able to change a few American dollars into the local currency, *lempira*, and have a large meal for a fraction of what we would pay at home. By the time we reach the small eatery at the end of the second block, we are ready for the wonderful spicy concoction of pork chili and rice complete with hot tortillas and salsa, hot in temperature and in flavor. It is interesting that even in sweltering heat, hot foods are typical. I have always been adventurous in my eating, buying tacos from the guys with the little carts on the streets in Mexico, seafood from the stands on the beach, and never have had a problem. I do have life-threatening allergies to preservatives, mostly those found in bottled sauces, vinegars or wines (which I don't drink, but is sometimes slipped into a sauce or marinade). One of the joys of eating in other countries is the lack of preservatives; I have to be more careful in upscale restaurants in the U.S. than with low-end food vendors in developing countries. In our restaurant this first night in Honduras, we can see the food being prepared and it's obvious that I have nothing to ask about or to fear; everything is fresh, visible and with no weird additives. I am careful about water, drinking only bottled or canned drinks, and enjoying the types of soft drinks I remember from childhood that are no longer found in the U.S. I haven't seen a six-ounce bottle of Coke or Orange Nehi since I was in grade school.

Few people have paid much attention to us so far; the most we get is a smile and a nod. We must be somewhat conspicuous, blonder and taller than the average Honduran, but they are seemingly used to an occasional tourist passing through the city on the way to Mayan ruins or ocean diving. We walk back to our hotel along the street, sometimes finding a bit of sidewalk, most of the time just on the edge of the road. We are careful to step quickly to the side when cars approach. There are no defined lanes for traffic; motorcycles, cars and trucks all swerve in and out, narrowly missing each other. Pedestrians take their lives in their hands to walk along the edge of the road, but there is no other way to get anywhere on foot. We survive the excursion and are waiting at the hotel when Herman arrives to pick us up.

△◆

Chapter Three

△◆

Herman sees us immediately as he gets out of his car. It is not hard to spot us, we are clearly not locals. He hugs us both, a typical greeting for support group members, even those meeting for the first time, and opens his car doors. I defer to my Spanish-speaking husband and climb into the back seat. Erik says his Spanish is tainted with Portuguese words, so he sometimes gets blank looks when he inadvertently uses a word from his youth in Brazil. With everyone trying, we communicate adequately and immediately feel welcome. Herman is excited and proud to introduce us to his friends at the meeting and get us a cup of coffee. It feels as if these are long-time friends we had never met until now.

The meeting place is a rustic one-room building, quite old with paint chipping from the walls and floors bearing the scars of many years of scuffling feet and moving chairs. Seats for about seventy people are neatly placed in rows and a blue wooden podium, with the recognizable support group symbol painted in white, stands in front on the same level as the chairs; there is no elevated stage for speakers in the simple room. The familiar slogans, steps, traditions and prayers are hanging on the wall, in Spanish, of course. The coffee pot is at the back of the room, and people are lining up to be introduced to Herman's interesting visitors.

I get lots of hugs and welcomes. One lady tries to use some broken English and we smile at each other a lot, neither of us able to say much in the other's language, but both making the effort to express that we are happy to meet. The familiarity is comfortable, even though I do not speak the language. This is the way alcohol and drug recovery meetings all over the world feel – home to those of us who have had our lives saved in this program. Erik and I had planned all along to find a meeting here this weekend, thinking that it would be good spiritual support and a helpful and interesting activity for us, and believing that we could share something of our long-term recovery (eight years for me and four for Erik) with some alcoholics who have little access to the depth and quality of meetings we have in Denver.

Here we are thinking we're going to be these important messengers of long-term recovery and much to our surprise, Herman has been in recovery for twenty-three years. He has not had a drink for twenty-three years and this specific group has existed for twenty-five years! Every Friday night for twenty-five years, alcoholics seeking recovery have met here to help themselves and others achieve and maintain sobriety.

I am often asked why I still attend support meetings (especially now that I have not had a drink for nearly twenty-five years). The short answer is that by attending meetings, I get to remember how I have learned to live life with a different attitude. Recovery is about more than not drinking. It is about changing behavior, dealing with old and new resentments and other feelings, making amends for harm we have done, and growing spiritually. To do this, I need regular reminders and association with people on the same pathway. The more I grow, the more I want to keep growing, and sharing experience, strength and hope is the best way for recovering people to keep growing. Most importantly, my spiritual support groups help me maintain and grow in my relationship to God.

As the meeting starts, Erik translates a little for me. Mostly, I sit and soak up the "vibes," the same sense of peace as in meetings at home. I memorize the serenity prayer in Spanish from the one hanging on the wall. This is a "call up" meeting where the chairperson asks people to come to the podium and speak for a few minutes. After the first two speakers, each of whom talks for about ten minutes, the chairperson calls on Erik. Even though Erik doesn't have a sophisticated adult Spanish vocabulary and sometimes interjects a word or two in Portuguese, he nevertheless goes to the podium and talks for his eight to ten minutes. It's a very special event to have two visitors from the States attend their meeting and Erik receives lots of applause when he finishes. Many people want to talk with him afterward. Recovery is the same in any language.

I am so proud of Erik and so happy to give and get hugs and smiles from all the women in the room while the men shake Erik's hand. Erik says he does not remember exactly what he said, the same thing he says after speaking at a meeting at home in English. Apparently he said something appreciated by the group. Whatever he said, I am now feeling completely peaceful. When the meeting ends, we receive an invitation for lunch the next day at Herman's home.

When our new friend picks us up for lunch, he first gives us a tour of the city, then takes us to his home where we join his wife, Roselita, and their three grade school-aged children for a simple home-cooked meal of tortillas and soup. Five of them live in three rooms. The diminutive gray house is level with the ground. Just a step over the door frame and we are in the living/dining area, barely larger than the table and chairs it holds. A small appendage is just off of this main room, attached but with a life of its own. The wonderful smells coming from it are so strong I think I can actually see them! Herman proudly introduces us to Roselita and then to the plump older lady standing in the doorway of the appendage; she is the cook. I am always amazed at the custom in other countries of having maids, cooks, nannies, even yard workers; we are visiting a poor country and by our standards a very poor home and yet they have a cook. The back two rooms of the house are bedrooms, each only slightly larger than the bed. The children are on the big bed in their parents' room watching television, the only TV in the house, which is an old, small, black-and-white model. It appears as if all three children sleep in one room, or perhaps one of them on the couch, common in many countries I have visited.

There is coffee and pastry for dessert, plus lots of smiles and offers of more food. The language barrier is significant for me, but Erik translates much of the conversation. I am struck by the kindness and generosity of this family. Even though they have very little, they want to give to us, feed us, drive us around and show us their city. We feel so welcome. We are already loving the Honduran people and feeling comfortable in the country and we have only been here twenty-four hours. I internalize this level of kindness and pray to be more like them.

△◆

Chapter Four

△◆

By the time the rest of the team arrives the next day, we already have friends, have been guests in someone's home, have had a tour of the city, and are quite comfortable. They are stunned. They expected us to be bored, feel stranded and isolated, and be anxious for their arrival. We tell them how we made contact and watch the expressions of surprise on their faces. It has never been important to either Erik or me to avoid telling people that we are in recovery from alcoholism and drug addiction. This acknowledgement of our past, and of our current involvement with our support group, has far-reaching consequences during the next two weeks.

The other team members all know each other from their church in New Hampshire. Since it is summer, our team has three students and one other adult who is a nurse; one of the students is her fifteen-year-old daughter. There is a Spanish-speaking, second-year medical student, Christine; an eighteen-year-old high school dropout, Rick; Erik, and me, the only doctor. We also have a local Honduran, Louisa, who will go along as interpreter and knows the route we must drive to get to the town where we will be working, El Rosario.

The first item of business is to rent a vehicle and purchase supplies. We need a truck that will hold all six of us, our baggage, the duffels of medical supplies and all of the food and water we will need for the next two weeks. We split into three groups; one goes to rent the truck, another to buy food and water, the third to change money and make contact with Louisa.

We have limited money, but manage to acquire a truck that actually runs, as well as some supplies. A potential disaster is averted when Erik goes with the teenager, Rick, to change money. We are told we will get a better exchange rate on the streets than at a bank, so they go to the central *plaza*, a square block used as a park, typically in the center of most Latin cities. Lots of local hustlers hang out there, selling their wares, imitation watches, sunglasses, jewelry, other trinkets and services as tour guides or drivers. Thinking they are helping Rick to mature and feel good about himself, the church has entrusted him to hold and exchange all of our money for the entire two weeks. Familiar with similar scenes in South America, Erik goes with him, telling him to be appropriately discreet, not show the money to potential thieves, and to be sure the exchange happens away from the eyes of the many unsavory characters. The safest way to change money on the streets is to show very little of what one has, in this case refraining from advertising the several-thousand dollars, more than the annual wage of some who may be watching. Erik asks some of the vendors to direct them to someone who can change American dollars. Much to Erik's surprise, Rick flashes all of the three-thousand dollars in front of everyone. The money changer makes a deal, giving Erik and Rick the Honduran currency. Knowing that many pairs of eyes are watching this exchange and aware of the extreme danger, Erik is afraid for his life and keeps looking over his shoulder as they half walk, half run back to the hotel. No one follows. I see this as evidence of God's presence on our trip; or perhaps just luck (another one of God's aliases).

A little shaken and glad everyone is safe, we are off with Louisa leading the way in her tiny car loaded down with supplies. Rapidly out of the city and headed into the mountains, the road is blacktop for at least an hour. While not "rush hour," the traffic is bumper to bumper; and although the usual absence of lanes and rules of the road applies, I am amazed at how few accidents there are. I settle into my "I am not in control" mode and pray for safety.

As the oppressive heat of the city lessens and the smog fades, we climb into the hills. The blacktop road comes to an end and a dirt trail, about the width of the truck, appears. We drive for another hour or so, and then the "road" becomes narrower than the wheelbase of the truck. We all get out and assess the situation. The road narrows as it curves around the hillside; the drop-off is several-hundred feet into the jungle and recent rains have washed out this section of road. We had noticed several stream crossings over the past hour; now the consequences of torrential jungle rains may be significant.

Rebuilding the road is the only reasonable choice. There are no other travelers on this road and are not likely to be for days or weeks. The village where we are going has no phone and there have been no phones in the past hour or more of travel away from San Pedro Sula. This is before the days of cell phones, but we are so remote it is unlikely there is cell service even today. Louisa is the only one in our group who knows the way to El Rosario and she is not in shape to walk the rest of the way and ask for help. We are traveling so slowly that we have probably covered less than twenty-five miles in about two hours on the dirt road. The village is likely only another six or eight miles away, but at least a three-hour walk in this terrain. There is no place for us to turn around. Backing up is a possibility, but there are no road crews to call to repair the road for our return. One law I experience over and over on my trips to backwoods locations in Third World countries: we are on our own! Travelers do best if they are prepared to be their own road crew, doctors, plumbers and everything else.

So, we start moving rocks and dirt with our bare hands and are able to make the road wide enough to vote it safe. I am not so sure, so I walk across and only climb back into my seat after the truck is securely on a wider stretch of road. The next hour to the village is, thankfully, uneventful.

On arrival, unsure we are actually in a village as there are only a couple of cement structures and a handful of scattered huts, we are greeted by children, dogs and most of the adults who are not at work in the fields. I am happy, excited to continue in this adventure, and a little intimidated by the finality of being here, our home for the next two weeks. What if no one wants medical care? What if they don't like me? (I remember one of my former nurses in Colorado, Cris, with whom I once had a conversation similar to the one I am now having with myself. Her response was, "What's not to like?"). Soon enough, I quiet the negative voices and enjoy the smiling children already tugging at us with no hesitation, expecting entertainment and fun. We are welcome here.

Our accommodations are in one of only two cement buildings in the town. The structure had been built by previous teams to house up to ten. It is a square cement room with four bunk beds, a corner partitioned off by a three-quarter wall containing a small, technically two-person bed (they must be thinking of two people significantly smaller than Erik and me) and a porch-like affair that serves as the dining area. The outhouse and shower are across the field about twenty-five yards away. The cook house, complete with fire, metal barrel-top to function as burner, and cooks, is a few feet out the back door. Home for the next two weeks.

The almost double bed in its own semi-private corner is clearly for Erik and me, the only couple on the trip. We set up our mosquito netting and put our bags on the floor, then go to the truck to unload supplies. Erik is able to chat easily with the workers, as is the medical student, Christine. I am glad she will be helping me work with the patients.

We spend the evening getting organized and meeting the locals who will be working with us. Two young women, Maria and Angelina, are the "pharmacists," in charge of the medicines brought by North American teams and left here. They do an excellent job of labeling the medicine, its use and the typical course of treatment. They do all this with a sixth-grade education and a lot of on-the-job training by the teams who come for two weeks every three months. It is obvious they are just as smart as anyone on our team, only with less formal education; and they are eager to learn more. We also get to meet the "dentist," Eduardo. He has a third-grade education, more common for this village than the six years of grade school the "pharmacists" have.

As the days unfold, I watch these locals work and am impressed with their knowledge, skill and expertise, having been trained by each medical team to come here over the past five years. The dentists from the U.S. have stopped coming, as Eduardo has been so well trained. The local workers – the "nurses" who take blood pressures, Eduardo, Maria, Angelina, and all the others – ask lots of questions, always wanting to learn more and frequently taking notes. It is easy to see that they are doing an excellent job with what they have, dealing well without so much of what we are used to in the U.S. They have no concept of what they do not have, professionally and personally, so they don't miss it. They eagerly learn as much as possible when teams from the U.S. are here. I learn more from them than they do from me and I aspire to be more like them, happy with what I have, not missing what I don't have. They demonstrate how much can be done with strong desire and minimal formal training. I never hear negative words or even a hint that they can't do something, and I watch with awe as they work so well, conscious of the lack of backup. The nearest help is many miles and many hours down the road.

There is something familiar about the feeling of working with a minimum of equipment and no backup. The sense of being "on my own" is one I have had many times, not only in medical training, but in early recovery as well. So many times I could have returned to drinking. In those first years, before my divorce when my ex-husband was drinking and I was not, when I felt so alone, and after my divorce from him when I was distraught with overwhelming aloneness and single parenting, I wondered if I would make it. When the drinking ceased to be an option, was no longer working to relieve the pain, didn't provide the escape it had in the past, I had to choose. If I was to live, to not return to drinking and all the agonizing it brought, I had to find a way to "have backup." What I did have was help from people who had been there, people who willingly shared their own experiences through recovery. If I could hang on to the hope that I could have what they have, sobriety, peace and even joy, if I could work with the little bit of equipment I had, willingness and drive to survive, then maybe I could make it. This was good as far as it went, but I needed more reliable backup, something constant, available 24/7, even in the middle of the night, someone who is never busy. Eventually, kicking and screaming all the way, I allowed God into my life, and later allowed Him to take charge of my life. I did this only because other recovering alcoholics and addicts told me it worked for them. They did not try to convince me that God exists and cares for me, but just that I need God. The way I was running my life was not working. I had to turn my life over to someone who could do a better job – God.

Here in El Rosario, I have people who will share their experience of working with what they have. I have a minimum of equipment, but it is enough; I have an interpreter, and I have the willingness and drive to do this job. And, I have long since allowed God to be present in my everyday life. I just have to remember He is here and in charge even in El Rosario. All I get to do is the footwork, what I think I am supposed to do, and leave the results up to Him. Tough for me, getting out of the results business and this is a good time to practice.

The cooks are perhaps the most important members of our team. They go through our supplies: fruit and vegetables that have to be used in the next few days as there is no refrigeration, cornmeal, oil, beans and rice. Eggs do not have to be refrigerated. This is one of the many things we learn on this trip. To this day, eggs remind me of that time in Honduras. We also bought chicken that has to be cooked today or tomorrow.

Most people in this village have a one-room hut for a family of four to fourteen. Wealthy people have a pig or a few chickens, and perhaps a home with more than one room. One family has a truck. It is an ancient Ford with more than 300,000 registered miles on it, and probably many additional uncounted ones. Groups of men are seen working on it frequently. Several very wealthy families have horses, and we see a few oxen hooked to plows. When someone in the family works, there is food to eat. If there is no work, if someone is sick or injured, there is no food. The village dogs are very scrawny and fight for the almost nonexistent food scraps. We learn immediately to never feed the dogs. If we have leftovers from the ample meals cooked for us, they go to needy people. So many villagers go a day or two without food when there isn't any. They seem to know that they will eat again in a few days. The main benefit to the cooks who work for us for two weeks is food for their families, in addition to a small salary.

Erik will be working with some locals on a water project to run piping from a holding tank a mile or so uphill to several spigots, one for every six huts, so that people can have clean water without having to haul it for a mile. This project, and public health education, is more important than the minor medical care I will be doing. The real needs of the community are sanitation, a clean water supply, and a storage system for grain and other food so those who are without at a particular time will have a supply to draw from.

△◆

Chapter Five

△◆

That first evening, after a wonderful meal of chicken and fresh vegetables, along with hot tortillas right off of the grill, we head to the bunk house. In spite of all the excitement or maybe because of it, Erik and I decide to have a mini-meeting. We go to the kitchen table, taking some candles with us, and read from our recovery literature. It feels good to focus on thankfulness for all we have, for safety, shelter and the experience of being here. When we first leave the bunk house, some of the others follow. They know we are in recovery from addiction, but that usually has no impact or meaning to most people. How would anyone know what that means unless they have been there? Since they are with us in the kitchen, we invite Rick and Louisa to join us. The immediate "yes" from both of them surprises me, but we just go with it. We read aloud about recovery, living life without drugs and alcohol, acceptance, trusting God, and being the best human beings we can be. Then we talk for a few minutes and ask the others to say anything they want. Louisa is the daughter of an alcoholic father; she tearfully tells us about her painful childhood and subsequent compulsive overeating; she has attended meetings for children of alcoholics in the past and is so happy we are having this meeting tonight. She wants to heal and recover from her childhood pain. Rick stays quiet. We close the meeting with a prayer and thank them for joining us.

Soon after dark we settle down to try to sleep. The buzz of conversation from the other team members, a few feet away in bunk beds, gets gradually softer and the snoring begins. Even though I am not good at tuning out nighttime noises, I decide to get used to it. There is absolutely nothing I can do about the snoring and I need to sleep adequately during the next two weeks.

Success. I know I have slept, because I am startled awake by crowing. It sounds like a rooster is in our room. I sense that Erik is awake. He is much closer to me than we are used to in our king-size bed at home. We hear the crowing again and both start to laugh. I am against the wall, so the window, a square opening in the cement, is beside me. Sitting up, I peer out the window into the pitch dark. I cannot see where the noise is coming from, but I do see a large shape, something four-legged, about six feet from me. As my eyes adapt to the black night, stars come into view between the tree tops. The nearby shape moves slowly, large head bent to the ground – a cow. Again, the crowing. Don't they have a clock? They really should try to not awaken us until at least five or six a.m. I hear someone from the next room get up and go outside, undoubtedly to the outhouse. I decide to wait until they return before I go. I might just as well figure out the routine tonight, especially since I am quite awake.

Crawling over Erik, I find my sandals. We have been warned not to go outside barefoot, as the ground comes alive at night with spiders, snakes and other nocturnal creatures. The spiders live in the holes we noticed that dot the field just outside our housing. They are some primitive species that lie in wait for their prey to step too close. They are shy and do not usually allow themselves to be seen during the daylight, and it is not routine for locals to be out and about at night – no lighting – so spider bites are rare. But, we are told that if anyone is bitten, it is potentially deadly. Great! I don't even consider asking if there is antivenin for spiders or snakes any-where in the country. We certainly don't have any.

The outhouse, a swimming pool length across the field, is be-yond about a thousand spider holes and probably a million snakes! Flashlight in hand, I step out onto the porch. Nothing is attacking me yet. No twenty-foot anacondas or man-eating spiders on the steps. I shine the light on the grass. The holes are still there. I don't see any movement – nothing spider-like looking back at me. Maybe the person who just made the trek across here scared them all back into their holes, at least temporarily. If that is the case, the best tact is for me to go now. I walk fast, afraid to run to the outhouse on the very uneven ground. The outhouse is equipped with a door that closes and latches, a seat and a roll of toilet paper. I have been in outhouses before and this one is nice – clean, as much as an out-house can be, and large enough to be more tolerable than most. The only thing I don't like is that there are lots of critters inside with me. There are the usual spiders, not the hole-in-the-ground ones, as-sorted small insects, and cockroaches in a variety of sizes. If I spend too much time in here, I will get to know them a little too well. I would prefer that they vacate the space on the floor where I place my feet when I sit, but they were here first. They scatter when I shine my flashlight around, all except the spiders in the corners, happily awaiting some of the smaller insects' deaths by entrapment.

As I open the door and shine my light on the ground, I see no sign of dangerous creatures. It would be really ironic and poor form for the doctor to die from a middle-of-the-night spider or snake bite before even seeing patients for one day. I make my way across the yard, tiptoe into my little room and crawl back over Erik. Safely back in my corner, I drift off into early morning sleep.

A few hours later, I hear commotion outside. This time it is from the other side of the building. I think I have slept a little more, but have been aware, on some semiconscious level, of the barnyard under my window. The animals roam freely, showing up randomly under windows and anywhere else they think might either be inter-esting or provide food.

Food is what is causing some commotion outside in the "kitchen." I smell something wonderful. Could it be coffee? I am a coffee connoisseur, love breakfast and have been wondering what will be served. I have never had a cook before this trip, so I go a little tentatively into the dining area portion of our building, just a few feet from the bedroom. I find coffee, tortillas and one other team member. Soon a platter of eggs arrives, then fruit and a bowl of rice, then Erik and all but one of our team, Rick. The cooks are happily chattering away with each other and a stream of visitors to their "kitchen." They seem as if they have won the lottery, laughing and giving food to their family and friends. I marvel at the joy they have in being able to share their wealth, the large supply of food we brought, with others. Their children are playing between the kitchen and our building, tortillas in their hands. Located just outside our building, the kitchen is a cylindrical wall, about three-quarters of a circle, the last one-quarter an open doorway, with a sturdy roof of thatching big enough for one of the two cooks to stand and turn tor-tillas on the stovetop. A wood fire blazes under the barrel-top cook-ing surface, a second pot of coffee on the corner of the hot round stove, and several partially cooked tortillas sizzling in the front.

This breakfast is much larger than usual for me, and I am eating before getting any kind of exercise. At home, I swim on a com-petitive master's team and get a vigorous workout five or six morn-ings a week. Clearly I will not be swimming during these two weeks – I will be lucky to have water for showers – but will have to find some way to keep from turning into a slug. We are at fairly high alti-tude, judging from the consistently uphill drive to get here and the mountains surrounding the village, but nobody here has any idea what that altitude is. Walking and hiking may be a good alternative to swimming, providing some sightseeing as well as some exercise.

Since I am now feeling overfed, tired and still dirty from travel, I decide it is as good a time as any to investigate the shower. It was built especially for the medical teams several years ago and uses water from the new village holding tank a mile or so up the hill, piped in by gravity. There is only an on/off spigot and the water is whatever temperature the pipes are – warmer in the late afternoon, somewhat cold this morning. The shower building is about the size of a phone booth with a cement floor, enclosed on three sides with a curtain on the fourth. I walk across the same field of spider condos that I navigated in my middle-of-the-night outhouse quest, then head right and a few yards down the hill. I hang my towel over the curtain rod and step inside, take off my clothes and reach up to turn on the water. I am not alone. There is a moderately large tarantula above the spigot. I decide that it is a she, since I am now stark naked. After a quiet debate with my most rational self, I tell her that I am willing to leave her alone if she will afford me the same courtesy. I acknowledge that she was here first, but that there is room for both of us. She moves upward slightly, climbing to a somewhat more concealed crevice, but clearly not planning to vacate her spot just because I am below her and talking to her. I turn on the water and wash, quickly for several reasons: it is cold, water is a precious commodity not to be wasted, and I do not completely trust my shower mate. She stays there for several days and I begin to look forward to saying hello to her during my showers. I do not tell anyone about her for fear they will not welcome her company as much as I do. No one ever mentions her and I do not know if the others notice her.

△◆

Chapter Six

△◆

The "nurses" are ready to see patients and the word has spread that *"La Doctora"* is here. There is a file with charts on anyone who previously has been a patient. The chart contains demographic information, vital signs, medications, illnesses and past visit notes, everything necessary – I am impressed. These people are eager to run their clinic well. I am shown to my "office," a cubicle with a table about the size of a child's school desk, a chair and a cot. This is one of three rooms in this building, one of only a couple of cement buildings in the village. My office and the dental office are separated by three-quarter walls, the top open to the next room, so we always know what each other is doing. The pharmacy has a full wall and a door that locks, for obvious reasons. The entry to the clinic is a four-by-eight-foot area equipped with a scale, four chairs and a table for checking in patients and taking blood pressure, pulse, temperature and weight. The covered porch is enormous and a good place for waiting patients to get out of the merciless sun, or the regular and welcome afternoon rain. This building is used for community gatherings, meetings, educational projects for children, and a multitude of other things. In the five years it has been here, it has been used, cared for and treated with respect.

The medical teams before us have done a remarkable job of establishing relationships with locals, who are enthusiastic about learning and carry on the mission to the best of their ability between visits from North Americans. I am especially impressed by the "dentist," Eduardo. Several previous teams have included dentists from the U.S. They have trained this very smart and energetic local man to do basic "get the patient out of pain" dentistry. Eduardo has Novocain, syringes and a few very used but still useful instruments. He knows how to identify what is causing the pain, to inject numbing medicine, and pull the offending, always badly infected tooth. Nobody comes to see the dentist unless they have significant discomfort, usually an abscess or rotting tooth of many weeks' duration. He has gotten so good at what he does that U.S. dentists no longer come here. They cannot do advanced procedures as there is no X-ray or equipment for reconstructive dentistry, and the local man with the third-grade education can pull teeth as well as anyone. Eduardo also does preventive dental hygiene education and gives toothbrushes and toothpaste, supplied by groups like ours, to his patients. He is a fast learner and wants to learn from me when he is not busy with his own patients.

On our second day in the clinic, a man with a machete wound comes in. He has been in the fields cutting sugar cane and bananas and has cut his arm. It is wrapped in someone's shirt to put pressure on the bleeding and to keep it covered while he walks the hour or more to the clinic. I find a five-inch laceration on his forearm that has missed all vital structures, so simply cleaning it and closing it with sutures is all that is required.

Eduardo comes over and very politely asks if he can watch and learn how to put in stitches. I am already impressed by and very fond of this man, so I invite him to put on gloves and help me. My duties in my years of training and now as a part-time professor at the University of Colorado School of Medicine have always included teaching. In fact, the word doctor comes from the Latin "*docere*," a verb meaning "to teach." So, if I can teach enough people to be "doctors" and others to be healthy, maybe I can drive myself out of business in a few years.

Eduardo is thrilled. He knows about hand washing and gloving from working in mouths, so he gets ready to work quickly and without instruction. He helps me wash the wound and I show him how to inject Novocain into the skin edges. He is used to the mucosal tissue of the mouth, but quickly adapts to the different feel of subcutaneous tissue of the arm. After watching me anesthetize the first few centimeters of the wound, he deftly injects the rest. He has stitched mouth tissue when removing a tooth leaves a large gap, so handling a curved needle and suture material is not foreign to him. I show him how to approximate the tissue edges and put in a layer of absorbable stitches in the muscle. After I do several, he takes a turn and does a very respectable job, just a little tentatively, as with any-thing new. Together, we remove and replace a stitch we do not like. One of my teachers during my year of surgical residency, before I changed specialties to emergency medicine, taught me that it is al-ways better to remove and redo a stitch, or any other procedure that is not as good as I want. "If you don't do the best job you can, you only compromise yourself," said Fekede, a gifted surgery resident from Nigeria. My appetite for perfectionism is fed when I repair wounds. It is like putting puzzles together, lining up layers of tissue, sometimes tendons, then muscle, subcutaneous and lastly skin.

We finish suturing the skin layer, starting with a stitch in the middle of the five-inch cut, bisecting the laceration and pulling together the edges. We repeat this procedure with each two-and-a-half-inch section. In this way we line up the wound edges symmetri-cally, so we do not end up with a "lopsided" suturing job. The patient is still, feeling only the pressure of our hands around the wound, no pain as it is thoroughly numbed. Not all lacerations are so simple. Some involve tendons that must be identified and repaired in a spe-cific way, so they heal and regain function. Some wounds are through many more layers than the three this one has hit. Some ac-tually cut nerves, veins, or arteries and must be treated with very specific care. I discuss this with my dentist/student and promise to call him each time I have a patient who needs stitches. In a village with no doctor for most days of the year and that is a good three hours by car from medical care (and almost nobody has a car), this man with only three grades of formal education provides an enor-mous service. He understands my teaching, the basics of more seri-ous wound care. While we don't see a laceration that is more severe than this one, I have no concerns about his caring appropriately for future patients needing stitches. It is hard to tell who is most appre-ciative, the patient or the dentist who can now count laceration re-pair among his skills.

I have just practiced another medical school saying, slightly modified: "See one, do one, teach one." The dentist saw me do a few stitches, then did some, and now is prepared to do more and even teach someone else.

Not long after teaming up with the dentist to repair the ma-chete wound, I have a chance to let him return the favor. I actually have a few minutes without a patient, since word has not yet spread very far that a medical team is here. Eduardo works every day, so he has a constant flow of patients and I ask to watch and learn from him. We are both pleased at the opportunity to exchange knowledge and skills. He invites me to watch as he examines the mouth of a lady who has come in complaining of pain from a thoroughly rotten tooth. During my training at the University of Maryland and at Denver General Hospital, I saw a few people with similarly infected and painful teeth, usually homeless and alcoholic, or maybe just afraid of the dentist. All I have ever done is simply refer them to the hospital's "dentist on call." I have never thought about exactly what the dentist then does to provide treatment. Now I get to see. I watch as he gently examines his patient's mouth, and then speaks to her about what he will do. She is sitting in an ancient dental chair, paint chipped almost off, in front of an open window. All windows, our only source of light here, are open; there are no window panes or screens.

Eduardo draws up Novocain, and showing me every step of the way, injects it into her lower gum, just at the nerve root. She winces, but does not move. In a moment, he is finished and waits for her mouth to become completely numb before starting the procedure to remove the offending tooth. When he is sure she will not feel pain, he takes a primitive-looking instrument, sort of like a pliers, and grabs the base of her tooth. With expert twisting and pulling, he quickly extracts the infected broken chunk of dentition and smiles, holding it up for all of us to inspect. The bleeding in her mouth is minimal. He closes up the gaping hole the extracted tooth has left, and gives her instructions to rinse her mouth gently with water this evening and return if she has any problems. He then gives her a toothbrush and toothpaste and does his version of dental hygiene education. A very satisfied customer leaves the office smiling and out of pain.

I go back to my own office and take care of a few more patients before having another chance at the end of the day to join Eduardo. He is happy to see me come in to watch him with his last patient. He says something to her in Spanish, and then offers gloves to me saying it is my turn to pull a tooth! I am delighted, but a little intimidated. This is a turnabout of the "see one, do one, teach one" motto as I am the student this time. He helps me decide exactly where to inject the Novocain, explaining with sign language just which teeth are innervated by which nerve. Somewhere deep in the back of my brain, I recall the neuroanatomy of the mouth. I learned it when I took anatomy and dissected my cadaver as a freshman

medical student. With this memory, along with my minimal experience as a dental patient, it all makes sense. I will inject at the base
of the nerve and it will spread to numb the lower jaw, including the
tooth in question. When the patient is numb, Eduardo hands me the
funny looking tool, uh, instrument. With his help, I grasp the tooth
and pull, carefully twisting and turning. Eduardo helps me and together we loosen it, despite its stubborn stance. He lets me apply the
final tug and I have the excitement of actually removing a tooth! All
three of us, dentist, patient and student, are thrilled. The patient
will be out of pain for the first time in who knows how long (everyone
seems to wait until they have had pain for many weeks or months
before surrendering to actually coming in and getting help), the student has a new skill, and the teacher is proud. I remove several more
teeth under Eduardo's tutelage, until I get too busy with my own patients in the coming days. I am forever appreciative of my teacher
with the third-grade education.

On our third day in El Rosario, a retired doctor from Oregon
and his wife join us. They are awaiting paperwork so they can begin
a two-year term at a village three or four hours away by car. Somehow, they hear we have a team here for a few weeks, and ask if they
can spend their waiting time with us. They are both helpful and willing, so we put them to work. The night they arrive, Erik and I decide
on another candlelight kitchen table meeting. The retired doctor and
his wife wander in and respond affirmatively to the invitation to join
us. Louisa and Rick are already here. This new couple has an alcoholic son and has been involved in getting help for him, so they are
visibly moved at being in a recovery meeting. During the one week
they spend with us, they have many questions and express enormous
gratitude at finding some relief in our almost nightly meetings.

The next few days bring a steady stream of patients. At first
most are from El Rosario. Then word spreads that *La Doctora* is in
the village and people come from surrounding communities. I treat
ear infections, coughs, purulent tonsils, urinary tract infections and
many other uncomfortable, but relatively minor illnesses that people
have lived with for months. Anyone who is sick between medical missions either lives with the illness, dies, or manages to find a way to
get to town, find a doctor, come up with enough money to pay for doctor visit and medicine, or hospitalization if needed, and get home
again.

In recent years, however, another option is emerging. With
the training the "pharmacists" and "nurses" are receiving with each

North American team's two-week stay, they are learning to treat some common illnesses effectively. They know how to give an appropriate dose of antibiotics and are able to take blood pressures and adjust medication for treatment of high blood pressure and even seizure disorders. Clearly, part of my mission here will be to teach. If I can teach, anything I do will be much more far-reaching. Again, I am reminded of the origin of the word doctor – *docere*, to teach.

I am picking up Spanish words by the minute, now far beyond the ones I learned in my few weeks of "Spanish for the Medical Professional" classes. My mother was an English teacher and writer, so I grew up with awareness and love of language, at least the English language. Having never lived in a place where anything but English is regularly spoken, I do not actually speak another language. I do respect other languages and have a minute amount of recall of high school French and a few semesters of college German and junior high Latin. Yes, I really did go to a school that taught Latin. Of all the courses in all the years of school I have attended, I believe that Latin is serving me better than most. The roots of the words make it easy to pick up the Spanish vocabulary.

My patients are patient. My translator, Louisa, is available the first few days, and then leaves with the North American nurse on our team to go to outlying communities and do public health education and tell as many people as possible that "the doctor from the States" will see sick people for the next week. The patients just have to find a way to get here.

While working on a water project with some villagers, Erik is able to chat with them in comfortable Spanish and after a few days settles into using predominately the language of the land. While Louisa is gone, I am dependent on Erik to translate for me. He is able to do more than just translate, as he is trained in first aid and is very good with children as well as with adults. He can wear the hats of medical assistant, triage nurse, baby-sitter, or security guard if needed and is afforded the opportunity to be a combination of all of these with one of our little patients, Leonardo.

It seems that a visit to *La Doctora* has been used as a threat made by mothers to their children to get them to behave, something that happens in the U.S. too. We surmise this as Leonardo is brought screaming and struggling, tightly grasped by his hands, being dragged toward the clinic by his mother. He is about three-and-a-half-feet tall, whole body in fast motion, kicking hard at the air space between his body and his mother's. It is hard to believe that the volume of screeching that is piercing the relative calm of the clinic is actually coming from this diminutive being. We all, nurses, dentist, pharmacists, and I, go to the porch to see what the commotion is about.

At first glance it appears he may be severely injured and in horrible pain, but on closer look, this kicking, screaming blur is too active to have much of an injury. All fours are in motion, so nothing could be broken. His mother is doing her best to make forward progress toward the clinic with Leonardo in tow.

Erik descends the porch steps, walks to mother and son about ten feet down the dirt path, and kneels. He is now face-to-face with Leonardo and asking him, in Spanish, what is wrong. Leonardo stops screaming and moving and stares at this enormous, bearded, ruddy-blond man, now looking him in the eye. Leonardo responds to Erik with an explanation that he is afraid of *La Doctora*. We eventually understand that his mother has told him, over the few years since the clinic has been here, that if he is "bad" she will take him to the doctor for a shot. Ughhh! Now he has a cut on his foot. He has absolutely no reason to think that he needs to see a doctor and is quite happy to live with the cut and not risk the shot.

As I approach, Leonardo's motion and noise resume, so I back off toward the clinic and take care of the quieter, more receptive patients, letting Erik, who is very capable of assessing injuries, handle the little boy. After a while, Erik comes in to get a foot-sized basin of soapy water. Leonardo has consented to sit on the clinic steps, a safe five feet from the doorway and any possibility of a shot and an easy leap off the porch to escape down the road. The two, Erik and Leonardo, become buddies, older male reassuring younger that no shot is forthcoming, just washing and looking, maybe cleaning and bandaging. Since we don't have the capacity to give a tetanus shot anyway, Erik thoroughly cleans the wound, applies antibiotic ointment and lets him go, actually smiling.

The rest of the day fills up with routine patients. One is an elderly man who arrives on horseback. Taller than most Hondurans and very thin, he stands up perfectly straight with shoulders held back and head held high, making eye contact while maintaining a gentle appearance. He ties up his horse and walks into the clinic, removing his cowboy hat, steps onto the scale to be weighed, then has his blood pressure checked. When he is ushered into my office and sits in the chair in front of me, I am met with a kind, assured face, strength revealed in the wrinkles of many years of hard work in the sun and at high altitude. Folds of old gray skin, each ripple speaking of days in the fields, greets me with a depth of character I have rarely seen. There is a beauty about him, a calmness and seren-ity almost tangible. At eighty years old, he is almost twice my age and has ridden his horse four hours to see *La Doctora*. I am hum-bled. As if to compound how inadequate I feel, he says (through my interpreter, who has returned for the afternoon) that before we begin he would like to thank me for the help I am about to provide. He wants me to know how much he appreciates my coming to his coun-try to care for people. He has seen the other doctors when they have been here and their medicine always helps him. I accept his thanks and his praise for the doctors who have preceded me, and for their medicines, and I begin to take a brief medical history and find out just what it is that I can do for him that has already brought such appreciation.

This man is exceptionally healthy. He has a little arthritis and would like some ibuprofen. His chart (impressively well-kept and available moments after he arrives, without "appointment" of course, as there is no system of calling and scheduling) documents that he has had this previously, that his weight and blood pressure are stable, and that he has no other known illnesses. I do a brief exam, checking his ears, eyes, nose and mouth, listening to his heart and lungs, and examining his abdomen and extremities. We have no lab for blood work, or electrocardiogram machine and X-ray equip-ment, so there is not much else I can check. I reassure him that he is healthy and write a "prescription" for ibuprofen, to be filled a few steps away by the pharmacy. He is able to pay a few *centavos* for his medicine and seems pleased to do that. He thanks me profusely, fills his prescription and walks proudly out of the clinic, saying goodbye to all of the staff. Putting on his cowboy hat, he unties his horse, mounts up and rides off. Only a four-hour trip home, he should be there before dark. My heart is warmed; my trip is worthwhile.

△◆

Chapter Seven

△◆

This night we have a gratitude meeting. I cannot help but think of my not always grateful patients at home. None of them travel four hours on horseback to see me. Two doctors' wives once drove four hours from a small town in Kansas, so they could get confidential medical care and go shopping in the city.

The retired doctor and his wife, Louisa, Rick, Erik and I get our flashlights, candles and recovery books and head for the kitchen at dusk. Tonight the medical student decides to join us. She has had an intermittent alcohol problem and is visibly shocked at our lack of hesitation and our forthcoming information about our own recoveries. It is also the first night Rick speaks. He acknowledges his drug problem. He even lets us know that one of the reasons the church in New Hampshire sent him is to help him stay clean and sober, to do something positive and to realize he has potential.

I am glad we are doing this by candlelight. Someone gets up to find tissues as the retired couple talk more about their son. The darkness allows some privacy for those who want to conceal the degree of their emotions; tears fall quietly in the shadows. The absence of bright light, and perhaps Erik's gentle way of welcoming each individual and each comment, encourages openness. My directness about my own addiction and recovery seems to give the others permission to share their own struggles.

Why are we here? What is God's intent for us? How is He using us? Clearly we are supposed to be here, and not just to put in a few stitches and give out a few medications.

△◆

Chapter Eight

△◆

The next morning we start our clinic immediately after a big breakfast of eggs, tortillas and coffee. We are getting into the rhythm of life here and look forward to seeing the clinic staff and variety of patients. More patients are coming, and from farther away now, as word continues to spread.

One of the first to be seen on this day is a baby from our own village. Her mother has brought her in and reports that she has been increasingly listless and not feeding well for several days. She thinks that the baby has felt feverish but has no thermometer. We ask the mother to sit and open the lightweight blanket around her little girl. The baby is about ten weeks old and starts to cry when we handle her. Mother quiets her by gently rocking and speaking softly. We check a rectal temperature; it is alarmingly high.

The exam of an infant is difficult under the best of circumstances and in the U.S. we depend greatly on lab work, especially blood tests, and also on results of spinal taps to make diagnoses. An important lesson drilled into me when I spent my required months learning pediatrics at the University of Maryland Hospital is that a fussy infant with a fever has meningitis until proven otherwise. Great, now what? We are three hours by dirt road from any medical care other than what I can provide. And additional medical care is available only if the road is passable, if the family has a ride, money for the hospital in the city, and the willingness to make the trip. Not likely. As I have already noticed, some illnesses in this community, and many other communities like it, go untreated and the outcome is whatever the natural consequence is. An amazing number of ill-nesses resolve on their own; benign neglect, we say. Another large number of illnesses go on to become chronic, changing the life of the person for the worse, causing weakness, pain, fatigue, constant dis-comfort and often a shortened life.

I check the infant for neck stiffness or pain and do not detect any, but I cannot be sure as she cannot talk to answer questions about what hurts. We call this "veterinary medicine," having to get our clues from everything but words. I stop and take a mental break and briefly pray for the knowledge of what I should do.

The infant girl has bright eyes, despite being sick; a good sign. Her skin is warm and moist, not dehydrated. The mother is at-tentive, smart, emotionally connected and clearly concerned and adoring of her baby. I decide that we will keep this baby in her own home and treat her with antibiotics. I make this decision in large part because the mom is trustworthy enough to observe her baby and return quickly if there is a change for the worse. They live nearby, a few minutes' walk from the clinic. My quarters are about fifty yards from the clinic, so I can be called by a knock on the door at any time, day or night. I do not see any other choice.

We do not have setups for intravenous fluids, so we will have to administer the medicine orally, which may be difficult for this breastfed baby. The pharmacist is able to find exactly what I re-quest; the pediatric dosages of antibiotic and acetaminophen are ac-tually available in our little remote pharmacy. Mother, nurse and I work together to get a double dose of antibiotic into the baby; about three-quarters goes in and gets swallowed, not bad for a first try. In the States, the medicine would be given intravenously and absorbed more rapidly and efficiently, so I use higher doses to compensate for giving them orally.

The acetaminophen goes into her mouth with another group

effort, some of the syrupy red liquid spilling on her clean crisp white dress. Mother understands the importance of getting the medicine in, but may not be able to do it alone. The baby's father is in the fields and will not be home until dark, probably nine or ten hours from now. I decide to have mother and baby return every four hours to allow us to administer the medication. This way I can watch closely for changes in alertness, fever, hydration and other parameters. Mother seems not only willing, but relieved to come back in four hours to have us look at her baby again and give the next dose of medicine.

Another issue is that of mixing up the liquid antibiotic. Again, things are different here and there are problems I have not considered. In the States, or any other developed country, the entire course of medication for the week, ten days or longer, would be mixed by the pharmacist and kept by the child's parents in the refrigerator. There are no refrigerators in this community as there is no electricity. We have lights in the clinic and the team's sleeping quarters when the generator is running for a few hours in the evening. We use flashlights and candles most of the time if we need light after sunset. For the locals, life simply runs in coordination with sunrise and sunset. Our cooler ice, purchased in the city, lasted for the first few days we were here. We kept our chicken and a little fruit on ice for a day or two so they wouldn't spoil before the cooks prepared them. That ice is gone now, so I cannot even offer to keep the baby's medicine cool. Fortunately, much of the medicine we have access to is in the form of samples donated by the pharmaceutical companies. This means that the dose for only one day, four over twenty-four hours, is in each bottle. The pharmacist can mix up a new bottle each day and we do not have to worry about the medicine spoiling, or losing its potency, by sitting out in the heat over the next week.

Baby and mother return at the appointed time, early afternoon. The baby has a fever again, and is slightly more lethargic than early this morning. Mother reports that she has nursed a little, slept a lot and been somewhat fussy in the past four hours. We get another dose of both antibiotic and acetaminophen into her. There is no real change in my examination. I recheck ears, mouth, chest, abdomen and everything else I can see, hear, feel, or touch; no additional clues to the origin of the fever. We refer to this as an F.U.O., "fever of unknown origin," one of the puzzles of medicine. Sometimes the body produces a fever for reasons we can only guess; educated guesses, but no absolute diagnosis.

I am still somewhat uncomfortable with not doing the "million-dollar workup" on this little patient. I would be happier with a spinal tap, blood cultures and complete blood count pending. I acknowledge my discomfort only to myself, and later to Erik, but try hard to be confident when talking with the mother. I am encouraged by her promptness in returning to the clinic. It is obvious that she cares as much about her baby as any mother I have seen in my suburban Colorado office and is just as smart and willing to follow "doctor's orders." I encourage her to nurse more frequently than usual, as sick babies do not eat as much per feeding as healthy ones. I want to do everything possible to avoid dehydration; we have no way to treat dehydration except with oral fluids, tough with a breast-fed infant. We ask mom to return in another four or five hours, late afternoon. When she does, the baby is unchanged, no better, no worse. We get the medicine in, getting a higher percentage of it actually into the baby and less of it on her clean clothing with each visit. We ask the mother to make yet another trip to the clinic tonight, after dark, at about ten o'clock.

On this visit, both parents are present. The dad is quiet, has a worried look and is holding his daughter. I am happy to see nothing suggesting that the baby is worsening. Sick people, especially children and infants, are often worse at night. If this baby has early meningitis, she will likely get sicker each hour. I have not seen that over the past twelve hours. The frightening thing now is that I will let her go from ten p.m. until daybreak, explaining to both parents what to watch for during the next eight or nine hours. I also tell them to come to my room and wake me if needed. They understand and are so appreciative of the care and attention they are receiving.

I have a little trouble sleeping. My tired body and mind win for about four hours, and then I hear the roosters "tuning up" for their morning serenade, and the cows strolling past our bedroom window. I had gotten quite good at sleeping through their noises, deciding to interpret them as soothing, but tonight it takes only a little disturbance and my brain turns on. Okay, I surrender, I am awake. I think about the baby. Is she surviving the night? Is she getting rapidly worse, too weak to cry and alert her parents? I toss and turn, finally getting a few more minutes of sleep before the rooster chorus is in full swing. Why do they crow at three in the morning? I thought, until this trip, that they were supposed to be early morning alarms, not middle of the night annoyances.

Finally it is time to get up and start the day. I walk over to the clinic, meeting my nurse on the way. We both had agreed to come in early to see the baby before starting with the day's other patients. The mother is waiting on the steps; the baby is more alert than last night. She has only a very low-grade fever, and it has been more than nine hours without medicine – improvement!

Is it because of the high doses of antibiotic? Would she be better today anyhow, even with no treatment? Is this the course her sickness would naturally follow and our medicines are just giving us something to do while her body heals itself? It is possible. If her illness is a simple virus that has run its course without regard to anything we have done, the outcome would be the same. Maybe our medicine helped, maybe not. It does not matter; I am relieved and thankful. We continue to see her four times a day for the next few days to continue getting medicine into her, mixing up each day's dosage first thing every morning. She improves and is back to normal within another two days, but we give the full ten-day course of medicine, not wanting to take a chance on relapse. In this remote society, children so rarely get antibiotics that we do not worry about them building up resistance. In this case, the consequences of not using them are potentially much more severe than of using them even if they are not needed.

Later that day, between patients with abdominal pain, urinary tract infections, gynecological problems, upper respiratory disease and other routine medical illnesses, I see a very sick middle-aged lady. She is weak, febrile, and appears dehydrated. My Spanish-speaking medical student is with me and takes a detailed history. My diagnosis is dengue fever. I have never seen a case of this before, but it is an unmistakable, "textbook" case: rash, pain in her back, arms and legs, especially joints, and a fever. Dengue is transmitted by mosquitoes, caused by a virus, and something against which we visitors to this tropical paradise have to be on guard. It is not contagious from person to person, but possible to get only from mosquito bites. There is no treatment other than supportive: fever reduction, hydration and enough nutrition to boost one's immune system.

During the day, this lady has been staying alone in her hut and wrapping herself in layers of clothes and blankets mistakenly thinking that she should keep herself overheated in this hot, humid climate. We have seen this before, people with fevers thinking they should keep themselves bundled up more than ever. She has nothing to treat the fever, so is very flushed, skin hot to touch and dry from days of high fever and not drinking enough fluids. Her adolescent son is with her; her husband off to work in the fields. We treat her with ibuprofen and acetaminophen as well as fluids, explain that keeping cool will help her feel better, and ask her if she has any food. She does not. She appears very weak and almost falls asleep on the stretcher in the office. When her fever is down a little and she has taken as much liquid as we can get into her, we are ready to decide how to best care for her while the dengue runs its course.

My medical student agrees to go with her to her hut and as-sess the situation. When she returns, it is clear that we will need to be both doctors and nurses – "home health care nurses." So, senior student doctor Christine now wears several hats. She is attentive and does "hut calls" to our patient every few hours. We take her food from our supply, as we have more than enough, and she needs it more than we do. Most importantly, we keep her fever down and urge her to drink fluids. We both go to her hut to see her after our evening meal.

Erik has been chatting with her son, who, when asked if he had dinner, says, "No, there isn't any." It is just a part of life here; if there is no food, because the mother is too sick to gather or purchase it, or prepare it, everyone in the family goes without. Some people have extended family to care for them, but apparently not in this case. We are able to find some leftover dinner for this child, and re-assure him that we are helping his mother get well.

After what seems like many days of ongoing fever, rash and joint aches, she begins to improve. She spends more of the day awake, even starts getting out of bed and moving around a little. By the time our two weeks is over and we are ready to leave El Rosario, she is up and around, cooking again, and will undoubtedly recover from this episode. Many people die from dengue and all we can do is provide fever control, hydration and nutrition. This lady is healthy to begin with and recovers more readily than an infant or elderly per-son. I feel I have played only a minimal role in her recovery and am thankful for her healing.

Our team nurse, Beth, is out in the community, sometimes with our medical student, doing public health education. This is more valuable than anything I can do; I treat one patient at a time. She can teach whole communities about fever control, hydration, avoiding mosquito bites, hygiene, sanitation, nutrition, and so much more. We pray that the impact of this trip will include changes in practice of at least the supportive care of dengue fever victims and perhaps the prevention of it some day.

△◆
Chapter Nine
△◆

By the end of the first week, seven of us look forward to the spiritual support meetings we hold at the kitchen table most nights. The other two, Beth and her fifteen-year-old daughter, Julie, are the only ones who have not joined us. Approaching me together one afternoon, they ask about recovery; they want to talk about eating disorders. It seems as if these two, just as everyone else on the team, also have lives affected by addiction. Julie has been anorexic for the past two years; she is doing somewhat better now, healthy enough to leave the U.S. for a mission trip to Central America. As with Rick, perhaps something about helping in a developing country will also help her. After my invitation and brief explanation of our candlelight meetings, they join in for the first time. The quietest of the group, they just listen. Julie attends every night for the rest of the trip; her mother refrains. It is rewarding to watch this teenager develop an interest in recovery from her eating disorder using this type of support system. I pray that some of this group have gone on to develop strong recoveries and spiritual and emotional health. I know that they find comfort with us and each other for the two weeks we are together.

When Christine isn't doing public health education in surrounding villages, I listen to her talk with patients and gain new words for body parts, pain, itching, fever, a few specific medications and for seizure. I get along quite well, using nouns and adjectives, pointing at body parts and asking *dolor* (pain?), *quanto tiempo* (how long?) and other pertinent questions, never making a whole sentence. The words *"oreja"* and *"estomago"* are used regularly, usually preceded by *"dolor,"* as in *"dolor de oido"* (plural for ears, so it means earaches) or *"dolor de estomago"* (stomach pain). Seizures, or *"convulsions,"* spelled the same in English and Spanish, but pronounced very differently, are part of daily conversation, as this community has many people, including lots of children, who have seizure disorders. There is no known cause; it is epilepsy. Sometimes seizures are caused by trauma to the brain, tumors, or diseases. They can also occur from medications, withdrawal from certain medicines, or from alcohol. None of these causes has been identified in this village and surrounding area, but everyone knows somebody with a seizure disorder.

About ten days into our trip, with only a few days left to see patients, a father and teenage son arrive at the clinic. They have just gotten word that *La Doctora* is in town and walk six hours to get to me. I am humbled, speechless, although I manage to mutter a greeting and shake hands with them. They, like many others, have extended family in our village and will be spending the night before walking six hours back home.

Just after arriving at the clinic, the teenager, Juan, falls on the floor and has a generalized seizure. He loses consciousness and convulses for what seems like forever, really maybe up to one minute. His father cries and says he does this many times every day. He has had medicine in the past but has run out. Others in their part of the hills (it is not clear if they live in a village or just somewhere in the hills, perhaps in a cluster of half a dozen huts or so) also have seizures and he says his son has been blessed to have medicine some months of the year. When he takes the medicine, he does not have the seizures.

After looking at his chart and doing some investigating, I find that each time a doctor is here, he is able to get enough Dilantin, an anti-seizure medication, to last four to six weeks. He then runs out, goes back to having seizures and waits for another doctor to arrive. He is not able to work and his epilepsy is a great burden for his family.

I decide to give him enough medication for three months, until another medical team arrives. Actually, the way it works is that I write a prescription that his father purchases from our little pharmacy for very little money, but for at least a few *centavos*, so that the medical care, but not the medication, is free. The mission's New Hampshire parent group, the founders of this clinic, decided that each patient should pay something for the medication they receive. The point is to not provide charity, but to let the patients contribute something. The doctors' care is free. During the months when no doctor is here, the medication can still be purchased from the clinic. The pharmacists continue to sell supplies and do an admirable job of diagnosing, prescribing and refilling prescriptions in our absence.

There is enough Dilantin for a three-month supply for my teenaged patient, and some extra. We had brought some with us from Colorado, as we had been told that it was a needed medicine. Later that day, and each day until we leave, I see other seizure patients. I witness more generalized seizures in my time in this clinic than I have seen in my entire medical career. Word has spread in the community where so many have epilepsy that I am here and many of them arrive each day. I wonder if there is a genetic component to these seizure disorders, as it is likely that most of the people are related to each other, or if there is something in the environment that causes the preponderance of convulsions in this particular area of the mountains.

I evaluate and treat each patient carefully and decide how much of our precious supply of Dilantin, and in exactly what dosage, to dispense to each individual. This is truly a dilemma. How does anyone decide who gets the medicine? I am fearful that we will run out before we see everyone who has seizures. I wish I had brought an entire duffel bag with nothing but Dilantin. I want to give each patient a whole year's supply. It is out of my experience and comfort zone to know that most of these innocent people will run out and start having regular seizures again before they are able to acquire more medicine.

The patients accept it as part of life. They have had nothing to help, no way to halt the seizures for even a few days, until the clinic was established five years earlier. The range of frequency and intensity of the convulsions varies. The teenage boy is the worst; others may only have episodes once or twice a week. In the U.S., I have patients who have seizures once a month or less. There is no question that they are able to get enough medication and prevent their convulsions. Now I am faced with a whole population of people who have one or more convulsions every day! And they cannot consistently get preventative medicine. I am frustrated at not being able to help more people for a longer time and am also increasingly aware of how spoiled we are in developed countries. None of my patients at home walk or ride a horse to see me, much less walk six hours! None of them wait for three months between times that a doctor is available, then come in and say, "Thank you" before I see them. I have some very kind and appreciative patients in my practice in Colorado, but I do not think they, or I, realize how fortunate we truly are.

Our last night in El Rosario is here. All of our teammates attend our spiritual support meeting: Louisa, dealing with her childhood in an alcoholic home and her compulsive overeating and obesity; Rick, dealing with his drug addiction and how returning home will impact his life after two weeks clean on this trip; Christine, back to medical school and dealing with her alcohol abuse; the retired couple, staying in Honduras for two years and dealing with the knowledge their son is at home struggling with alcohol recovery; Julie and her mother, dealing with Julie's anorexia and something else nebulous and unspoken...is there some other dark secret?

We give contact information to each of them, encourage them to find appropriate support and meetings at home, and promise to send Adult Child of Alcoholics (ACA) literature to Louisa immediately upon returning home. We offer phone contact with anyone who wants to call and encourage continued recovery to each. We promise to keep each one in our prayers.

Departure day arrives way too soon. I feel as if we have just arrived, but I am so comfortable here I can imagine having always been here. I will miss my office, my opportunity to be dentist once in a while, my coworkers, and most of all, my wonderful appreciative, trusting patients. I will not miss the nighttime walk to the outhouse.

For a few weeks after my return to Colorado, my heart and thoughts stay in El Rosario. I look at the calendar every day, thinking about when I can return and for how long. Gradually daily life insists on taking over and my first medical mission experience is relegated to my memory bank. It will be five years before I do another similar trip – five years that pass in a blur as one daughter finishes high school, the other begins her senior year, my business grows, and our lives continue to be filled with family, friends, ongoing recovery and increasing joy.

△◆

Lessons

△◆

- ◆ Choices: I can uproot my family and move to Honduras. I, and they, would have to pay the consequences.
- ◆ I can live part of my dreams, tasting and testing them over a few weeks.
- ◆ It is possible to get comfortable and be productive in a new and different setting.
- ◆ Because I have healed, I am able to help and to hear God.
- ◆ You never know who needs and wants help.
- ◆ You never know what kind of help you might be able to provide.
- ◆ By being open and available, not secretive and withholding, we attract others who need, or want to hear and see what we have to offer.
- ◆ *Docere* – If I teach, I have more impact.
- ◆ Use what you have; don't focus on what you don't have.
- ◆ Be grateful and appreciative.
- ◆ Fresh eggs don't need to be refrigerated.

Dawn's Honduras office

Honduran "pharmacists"

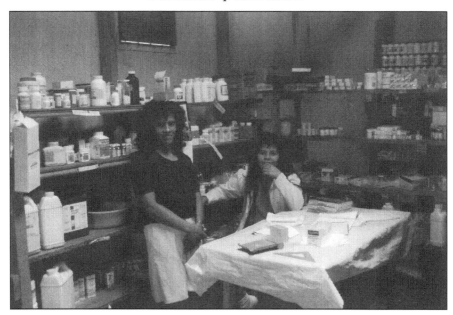

Leonardo

The dentist's chair

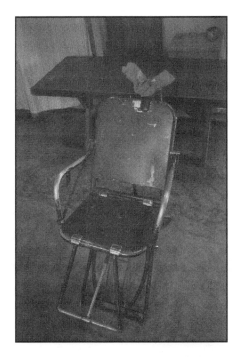

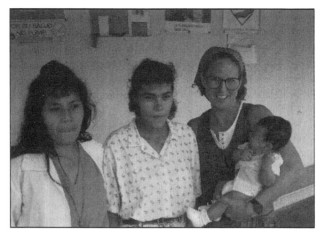

Dawn and clinic staff with the recovering baby.

A home for a family of six.

Medical team's quarters. One of the concrete buildings in town.

Part Three

Ecuador
1997

Our family trip to Ecuador gives us the opportunity to travel together as part of a larger church-based group. We are able to provide medical care as well as construction aid to a small community while enjoying a new country, culture, people and food. We also spend two days and nights in a second community on the edge of the Amazon Basin, where we are only the second group of North Americans to visit. We are profoundly impacted by the love and generosity of the native Indians. They appreciate our work and also want to give to us and share their own wealth, sending us home with gifts of hand-carved bowls and spoons and memories of eating cuy!

△◆

Chapter One

△◆

This adventure into another culture shows me a new way of looking at life. It begins for me one Sunday in church when I hear about an opportunity to travel to someplace I have never been. It sounds like a chance to provide help to a community in South America and possibly do some medical care – "rural" and "remote" are understatements when it comes to describing the area. Our small community church is putting together a team to join the ca-reer missionaries in Ecuador for a building project. The trip will take us into rural Ecuador to two different locations; in one area we will help build a church/community center, and in the other we will provide labor for whatever projects are under way while learning how a remote community has dramatically changed through the efforts of one man. My request to add a medical component to the trip is well received; the American missionaries in Ecuador will plan for this aspect of the trip. The collection of medical supplies begins again, building on our experience from Honduras.

I have never traveled with a group, unless you count a five-week trip to Europe with my husband and daughters, then ages thirteen and ten. While the Honduras trip involved six of us, we were not together much, worked and traveled separately, and ar-rived and departed on different days.

This trip to Ecuador will allow me the chance to observe career missionaries in action. I am interested in seeing and hearing what the lives of these "real" missionaries are like, as this is my "road not taken" – the lifestyle I wanted for myself decades ago when I decided to go to medical school.

We begin planning in the spring for an early summer trip and our nineteen-year-old daughter, Brie, decides to join us. She is considering a medical career and this will allow her to see a side of medicine not seen in the U.S. Besides, how many teenagers get to go to rural Ecuador and live and work with locals?

Departure day is exciting as we get to know the others, in-cluding some teenagers, with whom we will be living and working for the next few weeks. On arrival in Quito, Ecuador, the capital and largest city in the country, we are met by the local missionar-ies, Americans living in Ecuador much of their lives. We are only two time zones away from home, but have traveled for most of a day and night, and are ready for rest in a horizontal position. We attend to the basics: eat, shower, sleep and be ready to go the next day.

The directions to the first village, La Compania, are: Go north from Quito on the Pan American Highway and turn right at the Equator. Follow the dirt road and in an hour or two you will arrive at La Compania, altitude between eleven-thousand and twelve-thousand feet. No English or Spanish is spoken, just Quetchua.

We stop and get a group picture standing at the monument marking the Equator, all twenty-three of us, one foot in each hemisphere. The weather is warm during the day, but thanks to the altitude, it is not the stifling heat and humidity of other countries on the Equator. Surrounded by mountains, we see snow-covered peaks in the distance and feel right at home, as we live in Colorado's foothills and regularly hike and climb in mountains as high as fourteen-thousand feet.

I am enjoying the journey and am impressed by how organized this large group is, but anxious to get where we are going and start working. While the stated purpose of the trip is to build a church in a Quetchua Indian village, I find out that part of the agenda is to encourage our own relationships with God. I enjoy the group prayers before meals and the evening activities of sharing our personal stories, singing and listening to spiritual readings, as well as the quiet times. Grateful for the opportunity to focus more on my connection with God, I may get to be more of a human "being" and less of a human "doing" on this trip. As I get to know some of the other participants, I find that I enjoy them and respect their reasons for joining this mission.

Both of our daughters have traveled with us to Europe, Korea, Hong Kong, Thailand, Greece and Turkey, as well as extensively in the United States. Brie has also done some travel on her own in the U.S. and is comfortable with many different cultures and gets along well with almost everyone she meets. One of the joys of this trip is seeing her reap the benefits of some of the parenting decisions I have made. Her father and I divorced when she was seven and her sister, Kara, was four. I was a single, working mother for four years before we "got Erik," as the girls put it. I had many questions about what I was doing as their mother, and spent a lot of time and energy doubting my choices. I knew I had to leave their father; I knew I wanted what was best for them, including taking care of me. I had to be the healthiest possible example for them. Like most parents, I wanted to make their lives perfect, but clearly could not do that. I learned that if I took care of myself along with taking care of them, I could show them one possibility of how they could live their lives. Decisions like where to live, where to put them in school, which activities to choose, where and how much I should work, were all overwhelming at the time of my divorce. I was alone in making most of these decisions. Their father would usually pick them up one night a week and every other weekend. The rest was up to me. I had friends, other parents to talk with, some input from their dad about his preferences, but ultimately it was up to me to do the daily routine. I prayed a lot!

One major decision I am grateful for is the decision to keep them in our local public schools. They started at the school across the street from our new home (the one the three of us bought after the divorce), in kindergarten and third grade respectively. Of note is that I felt more at home and comfortable in this home than I had anywhere else I had lived in all of my thirty-five years. The choice I rejected was to send them to private school. Their dad wanted this, and I thought there were good points to this idea, but it would mean a full hour on the school bus every morning and every afternoon. If they got sick or injured and needed me to come and pick them up, it would take me at least forty-five minutes of driving *after* leaving an office full of patients. I could not count on their dad, a psychiatrist with his own practice, to be available to retrieve them. So, I made the decision that they would go to the public school across the street, walk with the other neighborhood children, and be a few blocks from my office. They could walk home or to my office after school if I was not finished with patients. I decided that the money we saved (private school was very expensive and would have been entirely my responsibility) would go toward other educational things like travel. For the past thirteen years we have had lots of extracurricular education, specifically lots of travel. So, watching Brie on this trip was a gift. We had invited Kara, sixteen, to join us as well, but some other activity had claimed her. Brie has been away in college for the preceding year, so the individual time with her was perfect.

Our stay in Cayambe, a town about an hour from the village where we are working during the first ten days of the trip, is comfortable. We are staying in government housing, but the cooks give new meaning to the term. They are terrific and go out of their way to take care of us. Every morning we have a new fresh fruit drink. I have never heard of most of the fruits and have to communicate with the cooks prior to every meal, as I have severe, life-threatening allergies to preservatives. I invite one of the bi- or tri-lingual missionaries, or Erik, to translate, asking for specific ingredients. Every day we are told the fruit drink is fresh, consists of only the fruit, no additives, and every day we think we've had the best juice yet. The morning meal also includes rich, strong Ecuadorian coffee, bread, eggs, hot cereal and more. The evening meal is just as good, always fresh and welcome after our days of physical labor. Lamb, chicken and fish, along with rice, potatoes, tortillas, salsa and assorted vegetables, all freshly prepared, are served to our large, hungry group.

Upon arrival at La Compania, we learn the process of building in this country. Thanks to Baxter, the American missionary who is hosting us, arranging our housing, travel and work experiences, the villagers are *allowing* us to visit and help build a community center/church. We are the first American work team to be invited here, and they did not really believe we would show up. Baxter had told them we would bring supplies and workers but needed a latrine. They had agreed to dig a latrine, but had not started on it as they expected us to back out. They start digging the latrine the day we arrive and it remains unfinished during our stay. Trees and shrubbery serve the purpose.

Supplies are purchased when there is money (often donations from the U.S.), and building proceeds until the supplies run out. Then the villagers wait. There is no such thing as a loan or mortgage, so it may take years to build one modest structure, like the one we work on. It sounds as if buildings are always "under construction," but this does not stop them from being used as soon as one part is usable. The structure we work on was started some months ago and has a foundation and the beginnings of walls. It doesn't look like a building to me, but I'm just a doctor and know nothing about construction. Fortunately, lots of team members do. We have a retired electrician, several experienced construction workers and lots of energetic, willing workers eager to learn, including me. Erik has done every aspect of construction from roofs to basements and everything in between. Over the course of the next week, I learn skills such as how to mix mortar, spread it on the bottom brick, and stack the next brick. I actually see the results – a wall is going up in front of my very eyes! The immediate gratification reminds me of suturing a laceration.

After lunch each day, many of us change jobs, so I decide that I want to learn what is going on upstairs (up ladder) on what is now the roof of the first floor. This "roof" is becoming the next floor. I have a patient and forgiving teacher who allows me to learn to tie and cut rebar, and measure and cut boards, as exactly as possible. This reminds me of times in the emergency room when I literally have put my hands behind my back and forced myself to watch and verbally coach a new medical student or intern putting in his or her first stitches. In those cases, it would be *so* much easier to just do it myself. Sometimes, when I believe the situation calls for demonstration, I put one stitch in first, praying that I can then allow the student to learn by doing the subsequent stitches. I empathize with my construction teachers and am grateful that they allow me to learn when it would be easier for them to do it themselves.

On this trip, our experience building ourselves spiritually is given importance equal to or greater than building the structure. I am learning more than how to cut rebar and stack bricks. The emphasis on acceptance, personal growth, relationships with each other and God is foremost the entire time. The conviction and commitment demonstrated by some of these big, burly men, as well as by the others, is profound. The strong faith I see is accelerating my own journey as I allow myself time and energy to listen, pray and absorb the positive energy around me. I am grateful that Erik, Brie and I all can share this experience. I am also aware that without years of recovery from my addiction, learning and growing in my spiritual support groups at home, I would not be open to the level of both spiritual and religious encouragement around me at this time. God's timing is perfect.

The local Indian men also learn more than construction from our team. Several of them acknowledge the lessons in humility from watching how our men treat the women, all of them, American and Quetchua, with such politeness and caring. In Indian culture, the women do the hard labor. We watch a pregnant woman swinging an ax, older ladies mixing mortar while Indian men wait to have it brought to them. Our men deliberately help women, taking the heavy brick loads from them, not sitting while they work. Some of the Quetchua men promise to treat their women better, wanting to follow our example.

△◆
Chapter Two
△◆

For two days Brie and I get to see patients. The public health team, including an Ecuadorian doctor and dentist, arrive in the village once every few months and time their visit to be here while we are. We have the ever-present duffel bags of medications and one-hundred toothbrushes and small tubes of toothpaste, a donation from a dentist in my office building at home. We set up shop in a small building cleared out for the purpose of holding "clinic." It is exceptionally dark, daylight coming only from the open door and tiny window. As in most Ecuadorian villages, there is no electricity in La Compania, so the team has brought a generator. The dentist is able to set up his light, drill and other dental equipment. On the other side of this small, dark room, we have medical patients and no need for electricity. In addition to our stethoscopes, we have otoscopes and ophthalmoscopes, each with its own battery-operated light. We also have a headlamp, the kind used for camping, that proves very useful.

Brie gets her opportunity to look into ears and check out rashes, and to help the dentist with basic procedures. She seems to enjoy all of it, clearly favoring the endless job of holding children. For most of this trip she holds the babies and toddlers during clinic, play time, church and at meals. The medical portion of this week is limited to helping the doctor from Quito, who is in the village for two days; donating some of our supplies to him, and distributing the toothbrushes and toothpaste we brought to the village children. It's a pleasure to watch the children with their new acquisitions as they stand over puddles and brush their teeth with such delight. With no running water in the village, dental hygiene is an outdoor activity. Having something of their own, being important enough to get a gift, is extraordinary for these children. They spend hours brushing their teeth with their friends, waving to us and thanking us each time we walk by a puddle turned sink.

The climate is extraordinarily dry and windy and the village is exposed and not at all protected from the elements. Situated in rolling hills with open fields, there are very few trees and no buildings to block the wind. The elevation is over eleven-thousand feet, but no one really knows exactly how high. There are only two seasons: wet and dry. With no snow or extreme cold, they are able

to plant three times a year. Crops include corn, fava beans, potatoes and more, grown on terraced slopes so steep that there is a
story about a farmer who fell from his farm to his death.

One consequence of the wind is windburn on the tender skin
of many of the children. Their cheeks are chapped and inflamed.
Some of them have ear infections, others have red, swollen tonsils
and many have rashes and minor skin infections. They all have dry
skin. We take care of their medical problems, promising follow-up,
as I will be here for another week. I can check to see that any medication we give has its intended effect, adding or changing something if necessary. I can look at ears, throats and skin to monitor
improvement, unlike the public health team who will not return for
another three months.

In many ways, this community is more primitive than
Oyacachi, our next stop a few hours over the hills at the edge of the
Amazon basin, where we will go in a few days. Even though we are
less than two hours by car from Cayambe, a small and very up-to-
date town, there is no electricity and no running water or indoor
plumbing of any kind. Women still dress in traditional clothing,
many layers of dark skirts, light-colored blouses, and bright
shawls. They each wear black top hats, sort of like a fedora.

Children as young as five have responsibility for infant and
toddler siblings. They carry the younger children, sometimes half
their size, up and down the hills in slings on their backs, imitating
their mothers. Fascinated by the bubbles our teenagers have
brought, children of all ages play happily on the makeshift see-saw
and in group games led by the American teens.

We accomplish more than I had thought possible, working
without electricity, just using hand tools. At the end of our ten days
when it is time for our departure, we are invited to a special meal.
Just outside one hut is a sort of outdoor kitchen with dirt floor,
stone benches and large wood-burning stove. We are served the national dish of Ecuador, *cuy.* We had noticed the chickens and
guinea pigs running around outside and inside of most of the huts
and were aware of the fields planted in various crops, but so far we
had only eaten sack lunches we brought with us each day. We did
not really know what the villagers typically ate. We did spend some
time helping them shell beans and knew that they had sheep in a
pen bordered on three sides by a rock wall. We thought that rice
and corn were part of their diet. Now we are passing around the
half-dozen or so plates and utensils, sharing platefuls of *cuy,* lamb,

potatoes, onions and beans. Everything smells wonderful, the wind taking away the billows of excess smoke and leaving behind an aroma somewhat like a backyard barbecue; slightly burned meat, combined with the scent of mouth-watering, sweet-cooked onions. The procedure is deliberate: the women serve plates for us, their guests, our men, women and teenagers, with the best cuts of meat and some vegetables. With half as many plates as people, we share, passing the plates of what they have to offer.

The lamb is excellent, the *cuy* interesting. The lean meat is a little oily, not fatty, and quite stringy with a high percentage of gristle, with the added interesting features of claws and an occa- sional tooth still attached to its roasted jaw. The *cuy* is guinea pig! Some of the little fellows we have seen scooting around on the dirt floors are now our lunch. They are a perfect food for these people: high in protein, easy to raise, multiply and grow rapidly, and easy to butcher and cook. Erik, Brie and I enjoy the flavor and the tex- ture, more game-like than domestic, in that the meat is lean and just slightly tougher than fatty domestic chicken or pig. The lamb is also exceptionally good, and more palatable to many of our team members.

Although they are discreet about it, it is clear that the vil- lagers serve much less meat for themselves, the plates for the men containing a small amount of meat and mostly vegetables. The women serve their own plates with only beans, onions and pota- toes. Meat is too valuable for everyday consumption, but they want to give it to us. The discrepancy in lifestyles between them and us is off the scale, yet they are sharing, beyond sharing, all they have. I pray I will remember this example of generosity and no apparent fear of not having enough. When we have all eaten, our Quetchua hosts and hostesses eat our leftovers, including gristle and claws. Nothing is wasted, yet there is no sense of greed.

During the informal closing ceremony after our meal, the villagers demonstrate even more generosity. Outside in the wind, the community gathers at the worksite and forms a circle for prayer and songs. We are shocked to find that they present each of us, including the teenagers, with hand-carved wooden bowls, each bowl with a Bible verse. Ours occupy a place of honor in our home today, and our daughter has hers in her home. It seems as if they cannot thank us enough for the work we have done, seemingly so little to me (although we did get a second floor onto the building). I am singled out by two women who had been patients several days

earlier; one presents me the bright red shawl she had been wearing, another gives me a roughly carved, unpolished wooden spoon,
about eighteen inches long and the bowl of the spoon five inches
wide. It is perfect for stirring large pots of soup or stew, but even
better as a reminder of the generosity of those who have very little
to give; they give proportionally much more than any North American I know. Their faces are the most joyful I have seen anywhere in
the world. The lesson is clear: there is enormous joy in giving.
These people, who live in huts that they share with their herds of
guinea pigs, want to give us, give me, a piece of their minimal
clothing and one of their few utensils. Again, I am humbled.

*Postscript: Since my trip to La Compania, others on our
team have returned. They described for me an exciting event – the
first-ever sixth-grade graduation. The school had one cap and one
gown. As each of the dozen children was called up to receive his or
her diploma, that student wore the cap and gown. After leaving the
makeshift stage, the special outfit was passed to the next student.*

△◆

Chapter Three

△◆

Oyacachi! It brings memories of *truchas*, hot springs, and
wind – rain and wind! Our first glimpse of this community at the
edge of the Amazon Basin is from the top of the mountain pass
traversed by the new road, barely one year in existence. Breathtak-
ing views include steep hillsides, equally steep waterfalls and jungle flora in a dozen shades of green dotted with multicolored flowers. This beauty greets us as we come over the pass, driving on a
road built on a portion of the old Inca highway used for centuries
by Inca natives.

A community at the edge of the Amazon Basin in the *ori-
ente*, or eastern side of the Continental Divide in Ecuador,
Oyacachi is the second of two locations included in this Ecuador
mission. Ours is only the second group of North Americans and the
first from the Covenant Church to visit. Ten years after our mission, Oyacachi has become a day-trip destination for tourists who
visit the hot springs.

For decades, maybe centuries, the only way into and out of
this remote community was on horseback or foot. Most of the mate-

rial goods have been brought in by horse, over rugged mountainous terrain and into the edge of the jungle. The elevation in these foot-hills of the Andes is 3,400 meters, about 11,200 feet, and the jungle is thick.

Twenty years earlier, this isolated Quetchua Indian commu-nity, then located about two miles downstream from its present lo-cation, was discovered (actually, the Indians were never lost, but they were not in touch with the outside world) by an Ecuadorian Covenant pastor from Cayambe, the large town on the other side of the mountain. The Indians, from the same Quetchua heritage as the natives we later meet in Bolivia and Peru, were living in pov-erty and poor health. The infant mortality rate was about ninety-five percent. Malaria-carrying mosquitoes added to the death toll and the population was decreasing; this was a dying community. Using the same water for cooking, drinking, bathing and refuse and not realizing that they were contaminating their drinking water, people often died from preventable disease. Lack of basic hygiene, no medical care at all, and more importantly, no education about basic health habits were all contributing to the impending demise of these people who had survived so much.

How did a group of people live in such isolation, remaining unknown to the outside world for centuries? What probably hap-pened is that they settled in this secluded valley to escape the Con-quistadors in the 1500s. Driving in our van, the historians in our group have visions of coming upon a lost city, wondering what they will encounter, perhaps archeological finds from hundreds of years earlier. The excitement and romantic fantasies increase as we top the pass now shrouded in a low-flying cloud and begin our descent. Mist, drizzly rain and a steep dirt road contribute to my apprehen-sion. What kind of people will we find? What level of civilization is here? If there had not been a road until a year ago, are there build-ings – where would the materials come from? Will we be camping outside in the rainforest? How can this be a useful time for us and for them? I am comfortable with many kinds of people and situa-tions, and here is another new one.

The Ecuadorian Pastor who found the community, Jaime (pronounced HI-me) went over the mountain into the Amazon val-ley on a narrow trail on horseback in the 1970s. Wanting to evan-gelize as he had done on the other side of the mountains, he real-ized that practical help was needed if there was to be anyone left alive to convert to Christianity. His own Quetchua heritage and command of both the Quetchua language and Spanish provided him with the unique ability to help. One of the first things he did was encourage the entire community, about three-hundred people, to move the short distance upstream to the hot springs, where the town exists today. Moving away from the area where there was residue from raw sewage to a clean location near hot springs made for a more hospitable home. The springs provided for natural bathing; they could obtain their drinking and cooking water from above the bathing area, and they learned basic hygiene. Almost overnight, the health of the Indians improved and the infant mortality rate dropped.

Realizing that nutrition was poor, Jaime helped the Indians establish trout-farming. The community is now famous for its trout, or *truchas*. We are presented with enormous platters of *truchas*, stacked six high, gutted, head still on, rolled in corn meal and fried, each night we spend here, with the expectation that we each eat several, and we do. They are fresh, flavorful, and abundant and provide an excellent source of protein, vitamins and minerals.

We can picture Jaime, whose hobby is woodcarving, coming upon this community, sitting with them and carving while teaching from the Bible. Imagine a setting where the people are casually sitting in a circle on the ground, Jaime preaching while he carves, telling stories about Jesus, and answering questions about being Christian and about woodcarving. He is simultaneously helping to meet spiritual needs while providing the beginnings of a way for his students to meet their own physical needs, to learn woodcarving as a profession. I am in awe that one man could do so much. I wonder if he had that sense of realizing that he was doing what he was meant to be doing. I have had that feeling a few times in my life, now and most of the time while I am taking care of patients anywhere in the world. It is a physical sensation to know deep in my soul that this is the way it is supposed to be.

Finding that many of the Oyacachi Indians were interested in learning woodcarving, and knowing this could be a way to trade with the outside world, Jaime asked his friends in Cayambe to donate tools they were no longer using. He then took the tools on horseback to Oyacachi, where he gave them to his protégés and continued teaching woodcarving and the Gospel. Now, a quarter century later, the town is known for its trout and wood carvings. Most men in Oyacachi are now accomplished artisans and Oyacachi woodcarvings are famous all over Ecuador and beyond. The carvings range from simple to elaborate, taking from hours to weeks to create. The skill taught to a few Indians and passed on to others, including the next generations, has provided a livelihood.

The infant mortality is now comparable to other Ecuadoran mountain communities, and the population is growing in spite of many leaving to connect with and live in other villages and towns. Those who stay have work and good health.

After Jaime's innovations took hold and the Indians became committed to change, many became Christian. Their love for the Gospel drove them to want a church, but there was no road to transport building materials. No problem. Walking around this high, wet valley, as well as enduring the drive here, gives us a glimpse of what it took to transport supplies prior to the existence of the road. The church was carried in, piece by piece, on horseback through the Andes and over jungle trails years ago and assembled after arrival. Just picturing what a daunting task that was reveals something about the ingenuity and persistence of the natives, and the willingness of Jaime and those who helped him to accomplish their goals and provide so much for these people.

After the church was built, the steel roof made too much noise, so the Oyacachi church members made the pilgrimage, on foot and horseback, back to Cayambe to rent a welder. They carried the tool weighing more than two-hundred pounds back to Oyacachi, welded the roof to the trusses and returned the welder. That's commitment.

Some time in the 1980s, a Christian Broadcasting Company, HCJB Quito, provided Oyacachi with a hydroelectric system to harness the waterfall's energy and generate electricity, allowing the community to become even more self-sufficient. Interestingly, power often fails in many parts of Ecuador. When the rest of this part of the country is without light due to poor electrical systems, Oyacachi, remote and isolated, has light.

The people of Oyacachi, predominantly Christian as a result of that first visit by Jaime, welcome our little band of missionaries like long lost family. With no large building here, we split up and stay in homes. The teenagers go together to one home, the women to another and the men to several others. Erik and I are one of two married couples on the trip, and the four of us are given the privilege of sleeping on cots in the church. It's very comfortable and quiet since the steel roof is now welded to the trusses, and we enjoy our roommates and "church mates," Vivien and Byron.

A soak in the hot springs following our trout feast, perfectly prepared fish six deep on the platter, makes us feel like we are on vacation at a spa. The moon and stars are bright, illuminating the dirt pathway from the houses and road to the springs several-hundred yards away. With no city lights and only a few lighted homes, I feel almost like I am camping. The crisp night air is clean and fresh, and there is no noise pollution, light pollution, or air pollution! I am in the middle of nowhere. No, I am here, in the Amazon, outdoors and feeling free and unencumbered by the business of my overly-civilized life. I cherish the moment, thanking God for allowing me this experience of new people, new places and of Him.

The next morning we all emerge from our respective accommodations, all within a few-hundred yards of each other, and crowd into the thatched-roof kitchen for breakfast, which includes juice made in the blender from fresh fruit. Question: How many Oyacachi natives and North American visitors does it take to run a blender? Answer: Four. One to hold the cord into the electrical outlet, just below the ceiling and attached to the single light bulb hanging over the table; a second to hold the blender in the air, allowing the cord to reach the outlet; a third to hold the lid on the blender; and the fourth to push the "On" switch. The teamwork pays off – the juice is marvelous!

Off to a day of seeing patients, as word has spread that a doctor is in the village. Public health nurses have been here, undoubtedly quite recently, since the road has only existed for about a year. The tiny room used as a clinic in one of the community buildings will accommodate the Oyacachi helper, one patient at a time, and me. Posters in Spanish, including pictures for the large portion of the population that speaks only Quetchua, depict good hygiene, nutrition, feeding and caring for infants and children, and prevention of disease. There is no evidence that a doctor or dentist has ever been here, but I am unable to find out for sure. At any rate, it has been a significant length of time since anyone at all has been in this room, as evidenced by the accumulation of dust and a film of fine dirt.

I see the usual array of minor illnesses and injuries. I am impressed with the overall health of the children and the adults, a tribute to basic public health knowledge, good nutrition and lots of physical exercise walking up and down hills at an altitude of more than eleven-thousand feet. They are appreciative and present me with a beautiful, small woodcarving of a fish – symbolic of a trout and of Christianity.

This two-week journey brings me to a place of living in the moment, allowing life to permeate me, instead of me attacking life with the mindset of having to "get through it." I am closer to God and to myself, the self I believe God means for me to be, the human being, not the human doing. I have an appreciation for these kind Indian men, women and children who live such a simple existence. I have an unexpected appreciation for my fellow short-term missionaries; I had expected to admire the career missionaries, but find the short-termers are remarkable as well. They are special people, each with their own reasons for doing what they do. On the surface they seem ordinary, with a sense of adventure and a strong sense of their relationship with God. They uniformly have a good work ethic along with a commitment to spending time with their fellow missionaries and other human beings, doing what they think God wants them to do, and helping where possible. Just these qualities make them extraordinary, or perhaps ordinary people living extraordinary lives.

Lessons

- One person can impact many lives, in Jaime's case actually saving an entire community. Part of this mission trip was for education about what this Ecuadorian Missionary did.
- Trust. Sometimes I have the sense that I am exactly where I am supposed to be, doing exactly what I am supposed to be doing.
- Ordinary people can do extraordinary things, dedicating their lives to helping others.
- Generosity. No matter how little they have, our new Quetchua friends find joy in sharing and giving. I want to be more generous and less fearful of not having enough. I get to receive and not focus on what I can give. Receiving may be more difficult.
- Balance. I need this different environment to learn more about myself. There is *much* more going on in the world than I see in my everyday life.
- Travel stretches my brain.
- Be present in the moment; I pray that I remember to do this.
- I can grow from times of being less goal-directed, allowing life to permeate me rather than grabbing at it.

- ◆ Flexibility. Work with the team.
- ◆ Working together for the good of many, physically and spiritu-ally, has a cumulative emotional effect.
- ◆ My journey in recovery is allowing me to receive more than ever before.
- ◆ Brie is a beautiful young lady, inside and out, adaptable, kind and insightful. She and her sister Kara have survived and thrived through my divorce, my addiction and my recovery and have formed an exceptional relationship with Erik, the perfect stepfather.

Brie with children from La Compania, Ecuador

Ecuadorian children enjoy their new toothbrushes

△◆

American teens meet Ecuadorian women and children.

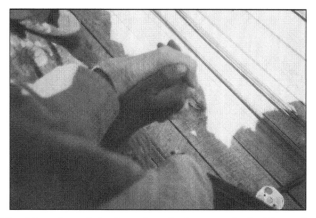

Working hand-in-hand to help people in Ecuador

A child stands in the doorway of his home in Ecuador

Erik and Quetchua workers construct a building

Part Four

Bolivia
April 1999

Our trip to Bolivia begins as a visit to my childhood friend and her family, career missionaries in South America. Erik and I rarely travel as tourists, but rather as visitors to friends and family living in other countries, or as volunteer workers. On this trip we provide medical care in several different settings, and my lifelong friend, Buff, and I experience a new way of relating to each other.

△◆
Chapter One
△◆

Buff calls me to announce her upcoming adventure. Friends since fourth grade, we have kept in touch intermittently since graduating high school together just a few years prior (okay, it's actually a few decades prior). Excited about a major change in her life, she relays that she and her husband, Steve, and their two young children are going to South America as career missionaries. They have been accepted to join South American Mission, or S.A.M., and change careers from writer and farmer to missionaries. I am thrilled for them and make that clear when she calls to tell me they are "selling the farm" and packing up the kids. A mixture of excitement and fear is apparent in her voice – she anticipates going somewhere, but has no idea where. She and Steve have told the mission committee that they will go anywhere they are sent.

I can relate! Fifteen years ago, in early recovery, I learned that I am not in charge of my life. I get to do the footwork and do what I think I'm supposed to do, but I cannot be in the results business. That is God's department. Sounds like Buff has the same attitude, which makes things a lot easier. Making a major life change is hard work and is usually associated with pain and agony. She and Steve are aware that there will be some difficulty and they can't anticipate the unknowns. They still make the conscious decision, as I did in recovery, to just go with it and trust God to do the rest. I respect them enormously for making the decision to listen to their hearts and follow through.

They head off to language school in Texas, then to parts very south, as in South America. A number of her family and friends are not so supportive, so she appreciates my interest and encouragement even more. Had she forgotten that I went to medical school to be a missionary doctor, or did I even tell her? She also doesn't recall that Erik had been raised in the mission field in Brazil, the son of Lutheran missionaries. Suddenly, after many years of being friends, Buff and I have even more in common than when we were classmates, and her career change at over forty years of age inspires me. Maybe I can do the same? With that thought, I immediately declare my support. Instead of sending money, I will send myself. I promise to visit her wherever she lands.

When Buff and her family get settled in Bolivia, in a very re-

mote town in the western part of the country near the Brazilian border, I periodically call them. They are adjusting and the children are
speaking Spanish like locals; she and Steve are speaking like foreigners, but getting better every day. She responds to my inquiry
about how I can help by asking for books for her two grade-school
children and for her. Now I remember who I am dealing with: Buff,
SAT scores in the 700s and curve-wrecker in our high school classes,
went to Smith College, reads during every free moment, and has had
brief careers as writer and librarian. She once told me she had to
limit her daughter's reading to only one book a day. So, I pack up a
large box of books, musing that I wish I was packing up myself and
mailing me to Bolivia!

A few more phone calls, conversations comfortably exchang-
ing questions and answers about our lives, and I am seriously considering a trip to visit. This time I discuss it with Erik instead of just
announcing that I am going. He is happy to plan a trip to South
America as he has not been back since leaving Brazil as a child to
return to the States. We tell Buff we are coming, find a time when it
will be convenient to visit (much of their work involves travel), and
buy plane tickets into Santa Cruz, Bolivia.

Santa Cruz is the closest city with an airport, still not really
close to their remote town of San Ignacio de Velasco. She and Steve
assure us one of them will meet us at the airport and Erik and I soon
discover new meaning to the phrase, "We'll pick you up."

△◆

Chapter Two

△◆

"Okay, now we'll plan for you to do some medical work in the
community near us where nobody gets any health care. Then maybe
we can spend a few days in… and then in…" She assumes I will be
happy to practice medicine during my vacation and she is absolutely
correct. We have been through lots together and communicate directly and honestly. Now I am even more excited about the trip, feeling much more of a purpose than just vacationing, and can begin
planning what I will need in the way of supplies.

Drawing on my experience from the two previous medical
trips, I put together a more comprehensive list of useful medicines
and supplies. Neither Erik nor I realize that we will be completely on
our own, not based in any kind of clinic or hospital, and will have no

help beyond Buff and Steve, non-medical missionaries. Interestingly, once again I do not need a copy of my medical license, no proof that I am actually a trained physician. There are so many places in the world where there is no doctor, no hospital, clinic, nurse, or medicine and there is no one to check to see if someone providing health care knows what he or she is doing. People are just grateful to have someone willing to help.

During the months of February and March, I collect pharmaceuticals for use in underdeveloped parts of Bolivia, which we learn is almost the entire country. I receive large quantities of an antibiotic used extensively in the U.S. The company had developed a 375-milligram dosage, between the normal 250- or 500-milligram doses, that did not become popular. One drug rep cleans out cases of it from her garage and happily gives us her entire supply. Another rep has cases of antihypertensive medicines to treat high blood pressure. She also has several extra digital blood pressure cuffs, a moderately expensive and very useful item that has her company and product name on them. She is very generous with these as well.

I idly wonder if any of the people we will see in Bolivia have high blood pressure. My expectation is that we will see the common infectious diseases that I had seen on my previous missions: poor nutrition and sanitation, lack of basic medical care including immunizations, and little or no health education, all contributing to a high rate of infection, including skin, ear, eye and urinary infections and other systemic illnesses. I had not seen any cases of hypertension in Honduras or Ecuador, perhaps because people are generally not overweight and get plenty of exercise as they walk everywhere they go. But we take whatever is donated. If we cannot use it, we will find a place in Bolivia that can. There are hospitals in the larger cities, and someone will be happy to have whatever we can give them. We remove excess packing from medications, and boxes from the sphygmomanometers and stethoscopes, and fill two of our six oversized duffel bags with blood pressure and other cardiac medicines.

Three of the other four bags have antibiotics, dermatological creams, gels and ointments, asthma and arthritis medicines, and everything else that is given to us. I purchase immunizations and medicine to treat worms, buying the entire supply of worm medication from several of the pharmacies in west Denver. Most children in developing countries have worms – yes, most. We rarely see children infected with worms, other than pinworms, in an urban or suburban practice in the U.S., so I had to learn about the diagnosis and treatment before I went on my first medical trip to Central America.

In addition to medicines and medical supplies, we gather shoes. Many people in other countries go without shoes, or with extremely old and worn ones. The children are at especially increased risk for certain diseases contracted from contact with worm- and bacteria-infested soil. I am a runner, so I ask my runner friends to donate lightly-used running shoes. One duffel is dedicated to only shoes.

We pack minimal personal belongings, just small carry-on bags, trusting that we can do laundry several times during the coming weeks and that there will be no need for more than a few changes of clothes. We also think we may buy from, or trade with, local Bolivian vendors since we enjoy coming home with native garb – although it somehow looks so appropriate in-country and seem so out of place here. We marvel at the enormous quantity of supplies we have been given: five duffels of medicines, one of shoes, each bag measuring approximately four-by-three-by-two feet, and weighing (for the most part) just under the allotted fifty pounds for international travel.

Departure day comes and Erik and I take our six large duffels and one tiny pack each of personal belongings to the Denver airport. At the check-in counter, it is obvious that we meet the definition of having "excess baggage." A very kind and somewhat amused agent listens as we say we are on our way to Bolivia to do medical work and have a few supplies. He could charge us a significant fee, but instead asks to see inside one of the bags. He looks over the contents superficially, sees that it is, in fact, medical supplies and then checks in all six bags without cost! With doors opening and obstacles disappearing, we are feeling blessed and have the sense that we are, once again, doing exactly what we are supposed to do. Thanking him profusely, we are relieved with each piece falling into place. I so appreciate this act of encouragement from a stranger, one in a position of authority concerning our travel. It is not the money, although that could be a chunk of our travel budget, but the kindness, acceptance and simple, direct help he offers that infuse our departure with the feeling that we are doing the right thing.

Both of our daughters are in college, but leaving the country and being unreachable, at least intermittently, is always at least a thought. As soon as we check the bags, my "mental switch" turns on. Now we are traveling and all the excitement of adventure kicks in – on the road to so much unknown. That brain chemistry that can be interpreted as either fear or excitement is definitely excitement.

Well, maybe a little fear, but not much. A dose of surrender seems to be part of my reaction to checking bags. Surrender for me is to stop fighting, second guessing and "shoulding" on myself. There is noth-ing to be gained by wondering if this is the right thing to do. I am doing it and might as well trust that the girls will be fine and that everyone at home and work will survive without us.

△◆

Chapter Three

△◆

The trip to Miami, then the long flight on to South America, is a good time to read about Bolivia, sleep a little and wonder what the next few weeks will hold. When we stop in Manaus, Brazil, we are not permitted to get off the plane; it is just a refueling stop and time for a few more passengers to board. The doors to the plane open and we get a spray of the humidity and heat. I have never felt any-thing like it, even in my travels in the southern U.S. and Mexico. The Carolinas, Florida, New Orleans in August, all are dry and cool by comparison. Erik has instant recall of the climate he lived in as a child in Brazil. I immediately want to plan a trip to the Amazon, as we are in the edge of it here at the airport in Manaus, in the middle of the night. By the time the plane doors close and we take off again, I am too excited to sleep anymore; we are really here in South America.

On arrival a few hours later in Santa Cruz, Bolivia, we see Steve as we deplane. He waves from behind a flimsy barrier and in-dicates he will meet us when we have our bags. We join the passport line to get our documents stamped and then get in line to retrieve bags, eventually collecting all six. We drag them to the next line to exit baggage claim and officially enter the country.

A stern-looking, short, round man is at the baggage X-ray conveyer belt. Meeting us with unsmiling eyes, he begins to question us about our supplies. We open the bags and he rifles through, never smiling. Erik uses his Spanish to answer questions and explain that we are bringing donated supplies to give to Bolivians in need of medical care. Still not smiling, the official wants to look in the next bag. As Steve appears, having found a way to enter the baggage claim area, he gives more explanation of our mission in this country. Another unsmiling official in full uniform, cap, nametag, polished shoes and too-tight belt, joins our growing group. They finally decide that we can have our six bags, but must pay a fee. Interesting, we get to pay to take drugs *into* South America. We get to pay to do volunteer medical work and bring donated supplies, which have cost us nothing to transport from the U.S., into Bolivia. Each official stamps several pages of documents multiple times and we are released, again in full custody of our bags. Steve assures us that the whole process is simply to provide jobs for more people by requiring many documents, all in either duplicate or triplicate, to be stamped by several different officials. I see that his temperament is perfect for his job and that I can learn tolerance and acceptance from him.

The next thing I notice is that we really are not in Colorado, which is still cold and having the occasional snowy day. I am hit in the face by a warm breeze, a dirt- and dust-carrying breeze, and remember what the climate in the south, as in South America, is like – hot.

We transport our bags to a tiny taxi, squeeze in as many pieces as possible, put some on top, and cram our big North American bodies (quite average for the U.S., but much larger than average for this country of short people) into the small interior. We decide we need two taxis for all of us and our bags. After rearranging people and luggage, we finally take off for the mission headquarters where we will spend the night after shopping for supplies and before traveling again the next day. Buff has stayed home with the children, some distance away, and will be looking for us tomorrow.

The mission is plain, clean and quiet. The few people in residence speak English, among other languages. We have access to a computer and can email our daughters and friends from our church and Bible study group informing them that we have safely arrived. We even get email responses later that night, assuring us that all is well in the U.S., despite our temporary absence. It is especially rewarding to get an immediate response from daughter Kara, a college freshman who not long ago had been in a phase of not necessarily having time for us. Her upbeat email ("Hi Mommy and Erik ...!") is so loving and encouraging that we feel connected to her over the miles.

After a most welcome shower and change of clothes, we are off on a fascinating excursion to the farmer's market for fresh fruit and vegetables, and some household supplies Buff has requested. The market is enormous and packed with shoppers, so I am careful not to lose sight of Erik, who at six-feet-two-inches tall and blond is easy to track. The smells, hustle and bustle of sellers and buyers, and the unusual produce are wonderful. The meat products include some that are quite unfamiliar to me, startling, yet interesting. Whole carcasses of pigs and chickens hang just inches away from the narrow aisle, barely out of the way of my head as I walk trying to dodge other shoppers and display cases, and the not-so-occasional dog and toddler.

After buying supplies and some mouth-watering meat-filled pastry for lunch on the go, we return to our room. For a donation of a few dollars to the mission, we have dinner, a shower, bed and breakfast. So far, this is one of the great bargains of the trip.

It's always a challenge to figure out the exchange rate for the U.S. dollar in other countries. I have found that the dollar goes amazingly far in all parts of Asia, including the shopping district in Hong Kong. Likewise, it goes further than I realize in South America. It takes only a few transactions before I am comfortable eyeballing and guesstimating the value in Bolivian currency of anything I consider buying. At this time, the dollar is strong. Traveler's checks are useless this far south and in small villages. No one takes credit cards except a few places in big cities, and there are only two cities of any significant size in Bolivia. We are in one of them, but not for long. A trip to the bank to change some dollars is high on our priority list.

By the time night comes, I am ready for sleeping in a horizontal position. The plane was great transportation but horrible sleeping quarters.

The next morning we are ready for more travel. After one last email, and a wonderful breakfast of strong South American coffee, papaya, *maricuja* (passion fruit), banana, pineapple, guava, eggs and toast, we load all our luggage onto a bus and head for the airport. Fortunately it's not necessary to go into the international terminal again; we go to a separate area and board a military plane. The only ways to get to San Ignacio de Velasco are by road, perhaps a twelve-hour drive if the roads are not washed out; by the twice-weekly military air transport; or on an occasional missionary air transport. Today, Steve has arranged for us to fly military. The plane is huge and equipped for lots of baggage, but only for a few people and we are lucky to be aboard. The plane is meant for transport, not comfort, and the flight is rough. The view takes in landscape more remote and closer to jungle than I have ever been. The adventure is on! A short time later, no worse for the wear, we land safely and drive a very few minutes to Buff and Steve's house; everything in tiny San Ignacio is close and most travel is by foot.

Erik hears familiar words in Portuguese mixed with the Bolivian Spanish of the eastern part of the country. That afternoon he discovers a shop, really just a miniscule room attached to a small house, selling snacks and the soft drinks that he remembers from his childhood. Another look at the map and we realize we are only a few miles from the Brazilian border, which explains the accent and random Portuguese words. He is excited to be this close to Brazil.

Erik is comfortable and so am I. Buff and Steve make us feel so at home, giving us a comfortable room and asking about our food and drink needs and preferences. We are adventurous and willing to eat and drink in Bolivia as the Bolivians do. We enjoy *Guarana*, the soft drink Erik remembers while growing up, excellent coffee (even though Buff and Steve are tea drinkers), *lumbo do puerco*, the pork dish Erik recalls being his favorite in Brazil, and all of the wonderful native fruits and vegetables: papaya, passion fruit, a variety of citrus, coconut, and fresh potatoes and beans.

Settling in, we get to know Buff and Steve again, and their children, who at ten and twelve are much younger than our young adult girls. As children do, they have easily mastered the local language and have no problem flipping in and out of English and Spanish with no foreign accent, or struggles with "chatting" which is more difficult for their parents. Erik merges easily into Spanish, also with no foreign accent, but again gets the occasional strange look when he inadvertently slips into Portuguese. We are close enough to Brazil that it is not uncommon, but most people here speak only Spanish. The languages are similar, but distinct. Not dialects of each other, they are separate languages. Several years later when we are in Portugal, he gets the same quizzical looks from locals as he speaks their language with a strong Brazilian accent.

I, on the other hand, feel like the dumb American. I speak one language and I speak it well and often. I can call up a little French and German when in those countries, can order from a menu, and ask a few basic questions, sometimes even understanding the answer, but I have almost no Spanish, just the medical words I learned before going to Honduras.

Besides getting settled in with our hosts and catching up with the happenings in our lives over the past however many years, we compare where we are spiritually. I love this about our friendship. We can be open and honest about our beliefs, sharing without fear of being judged, criticized, or otherwise thwarted in conversation.

Buff is clearly Christian, a Christian missionary believing in evangelism to the extent that she is dedicating her life to teaching the doctrines of Christianity. I am not there. I definitely have a relationship with one God. He works in my life and I talk and listen to

Him all day. I am not interested in preaching, but will share my beliefs with anyone who asks. I know that my Jewish friends have the
same God that I do. When I came to believe that Jesus is the son of
God and is God at the same time, I still understood that God the father is the same God my Jewish friends worship. I never get the feeling Buff is trying to change me, but she is interested in where I am
with my beliefs, and where my children are spiritually. We started
these honest and open conversations in grade school and they continue today. I am grateful to have someone to communicate with,
however intermittently, about my evolving beliefs and relationship
with God.

△◆

Chapter Four

△◆

We are in a tiny town with dirt roads. That means dirt everywhere; in the air, on our clothes and skin, in homes and cars. Thankfully, we have a shower awaiting us. As we walk around our temporary neighborhood on this first day, Buff introduces us to acquaintances, neighbors and local shopkeepers. I smile and nod, not able to
speak their language. I feel handicapped. We also visit the local hospital. The nurses are dressed in white uniforms and stiff caps, reminiscent of nurses from decades ago in the U.S. Equipment is primitive by my standards and I wonder about the quality of patient care.
I am really a tourist and just walk through the hallways, smiling as
Buff chats with the nurses, explaining that I am a visiting doctor
friend from the U.S. and just want to tour the hospital. The hallways
are lined with patients in wheelchairs, some in regular chairs, some
tied into their chairs, and children in portable cribs. The scene looks
so depressing and antiquated to me. I have no authority or invitation
to make change, as if I could in the space of one brief trip to this part
of the world. But I can provide care for a few of Buff's friends and
acquaintances, perhaps making a small difference in their day, if not
their life.

Soon we return to Buff's home and discuss plans for the next
day. She had decided weeks earlier that we would go to Santa Marta,
a small Christian community about an hour's drive outside of San
Ignacio de Velasco, unless we get stuck on the alleged road – then it
could turn into a day's drive. Santa Marta is smaller and more remote than the town we have just completely toured, on foot, in fif-

teen minutes. I guess we haven't seen anything yet. They are expecting us, or rather, they are expecting *La Doctora*.

I spend the evening sorting through the supplies we have
brought and repacking what I guess to be a day's worth of a variety
of medications. I have somewhat of an idea of what ailments I will
see and want to be sure to take the appropriate supplies since we
will not be able to just run back and get something we neglect to
bring. Besides medical equipment, we decide this is as good a place
as any to donate most of the shoes, so that duffel comes with us.

The trip to Santa Marta in Steve's pickup truck is interesting. The whole concept of what constitutes a road is entirely different
from what we have in the U.S. and I am reminded of my previous
trip to Honduras. A road is any pathway through the brush almost
wide enough for your vehicle, always with many holes and pits, most
passable if you are going very slowly. After several stops to check out
the "pathway" ahead and an hour or so of bumping along at very few
miles per hour, Buff, Steve, Erik and I arrive with a small pickup
truck full of medical supplies and shoes. A few stray locals have
hopped in the back of the truck to catch a ride to this outlying community, making themselves valuable by helping us push and pull the
truck over the frequent muddy sections of absence of road. How familiar! Far safer than the road we survived in Honduras, we are also
with locals. Buff and Steve and everyone but me speaks the language. This is very civilized compared to previous experiences. I relax even more, already feeling very comfortable with my role as *La
Doctora*.

Once safely in Santa Marta, we are greeted by a few adults
and lots of smiling children and directed to the one-room cinderblock
building in the center of town. Similar to the "clinic" in Honduras
with rectangular openings for windows, cement floor, and sparse fur-
nishings of table and a few chairs, it is perfectly adequate for our
needs. The building is used for school, church and any other community events, our presence being a very important "community event."
It seems as if I have always done this and it feels natural and normal to be practicing medicine in a language I don't speak, pulling my
minimal medical equipment and supplies out of duffel bags, and being paid with smiles and 'thank-yous.' I don't take extensive medical
histories, only gathering the most pertinent information necessary to
treat the immediate problem. There is no chart for family history,
immunizations, past medical diagnoses, or medications; no one is on
regular medications. I also don't spend time writing down anything I

do, as there is nowhere to keep it and no one interested in preserving anything we do today. There is a certain freedom about this. We are not providing comprehensive care, just dealing with a few-dozen villagers with minor medical issues and providing comfort for a few.

I am reminded of the "Starfish Story." A little girl is walking along a beach taking the starfish that have washed ashore and throwing them back into the sea. Soon she meets a man who asks what she is doing. "I'm saving some starfish," the girl responds. The man responds, "Look at this long stretch of beach. You'll never be able to throw them all back into the sea. What you're doing can't make a difference." Unfazed by his negativity, the little girl reaches down to pick up another starfish, throws it back into the sea and says, "It did for that one."

So many people are so thankful. They are used to living with pain, infection, fever and other discomfort with no help. What we provide is enormous to them.

I accept without hesitation that there is no backup, no hospital, no specialist and no other doctor with whom to consult or confer. I am it. Some part of me is functioning so automatically that I wonder if I was a full-time missionary doctor in a past lifetime. All the pictures Erik and Steve take during this mission show me to be happy, excited and smiling. This is truly how I feel while seeing patients. It is so different from my daily practice in suburban Colorado. I love that, and those patients, too; this is, oddly enough, somehow more familiar. How strange.

We make our way from the truck to my new "office" through the crowd of villagers, which has grown logarithmically. We are clearly the most exciting happening in recent memory. Assessing the space, Buff and I rearrange the furniture, putting the table in the middle of the twenty-by-twenty-foot room, lining one wall with the dozen or so chairs, and setting up the duffel of shoes near the doorway, medicines closer to the table.

By now the room is full of local Santa Marta children and a few adults, smiling and watching us, helping move furniture, finding corners to occupy, giggling and shyly retreating when we look directly at them. I am impressed by the obvious happiness and healthy, well-nourished appearance of these people. The community is far enough from San Ignacio de Velasco, the closest town, that villagers rarely go there, or anywhere else for regular medical care. As far as we can tell, there were no vehicles in the entire village, so travel to town is not routine. I am reminded that there are places in the world where medical care is the exception, not the rule that it is in most of the modern-day U.S., and that many people in these place still live long, healthy lives, especially if they have good nutrition and hygiene.

With Steve and Erik's help, we establish enough order to line up those who want to be patients, separating them from the throngs of onlookers. My first patient, a little girl nine or ten years old, climbs onto the "examining table." Her mother stands beside her as Buff begins to translate my questions. "What is bothering her? How long has she had this earache? Has she had anything along with it; fever, sore throat, stomachache?"

Just before Buff asks if it's all right if I look in her ears and throat with my "ear-looky" (child speak for otoscope), I notice something a little out of the ordinary: the room is still full of people, really full, as in packed with quiet, staring, villagers. Everyone is watching me examine this child! I make an executive decision to clear the room except for the person being seen and his or her immediate family. Buff asks everyone else to leave and wait for their turn. They file out easily, without protest through the doorway as I return my attention to the little girl sitting on the edge of the table. A moment later, heads start popping up at the two windows, uncovered openings at the back of the building. The onlookers have found a way to comply with our request to wait outside and still not miss anything. I surrender. I cannot change local custom or expectations. They just don't have the same sense of privacy we expect.

The little girl is the first of many children with minor complaints. After examining her and finding ear and throat infections, both there for weeks – much longer than almost any child in the U.S. would wait for treatment – I dispense antibiotics and acetaminophen, give instructions to her mother, and give them each a pair of shoes. Next.

Several-dozen more children and adults with minor complaints come into my "office." Their ailments would cause most North Americans to rush to the doctor. People in this South American country live with sickness unless someone like me arrives, or they become extremely ill. Everyone makes a point of thanking Buff and me profusely and while some seem more excited about the shoes than about the medical care, all are appreciative of both. Hours later, I think we must have seen a high percentage of the people who live in this village. Thankfully, I have anticipated and brought the medical supplies I need, spending the day treating skin and stomach ailments, urinary tract infections, arthritis and a multitude of typical child-hood illnesses. I'm ready to say goodbye.

On the way out of the village, I wave to some of my patients and watch a mother sweeping the dirt "patio" in front of her one-room thatched-roof hut, laundry hanging on the line, children beside her. These people are indeed very clean, healthy and seemingly happy with what they have. I can learn from this.

The next day is Sunday and we attend church. Buff has in-formed me we will be holding "clinic" that afternoon and evening at her house. Steve makes the announcement to the whole congregation – free medical care all day, just come to their house. I smile as he introduces Erik and me, not understanding what he is saying. Later we laugh that I am just standing up there, smiling and nodding, not knowing Steve is volunteering my services to the fifty or sixty people smiling back. I do notice they are very friendly; unaware it may be because they are going to be my patients later that day. No problem, I am much happier being a doctor, seeing the real side of life in Bo-livia, than being a tourist. I don't do "sit around and hang out" kinds of vacations, nor do I like "Americanized" hotels, tours, travel with other tourists and superficial looks at other countries. I understand this is the more comfortable way for some to travel and have no judg-ment about that; in fact, I am grateful there are traditional "tourists" to feed the economy of remote corners of the world. I simply enjoy having the opportunity to do it differently. I like to be in the middle of reality; either as doctor, friend, athlete, or in some way a partici-pant in the lives of the locals. Sunday afternoon gives me just that opportunity.

Buff and I set up clinic in her living room. The house they are renting is perfect: it has a courtyard with plants and trees around which are the rooms, each with its own doorway off the courtyard. Our bedroom is adjacent to the kitchen, but to get from one to the other, we have to go outside and walk a few feet in the courtyard, then re-enter the inside portion of the house through the kitchen door. The same applies to the living room – it has its own entrance. This allows us to bring one patient at a time into the clinic room, em-ploying Erik, Steve and their two children to entertain subsequent patients in the kitchen waiting room.

Today's patients are much more sophisticated than the villag-ers we saw yesterday. The people from the church (and their friends, family, neighbors and anyone interested in free medical care) are more educated than those in outlying rural areas and receive occasional, if not regular medical care from one of the two local doctors. Those we see appreciate not having to pay part of their small and hard-earned salaries to see a doctor. I don't know how many patients we see, but it takes most of the afternoon and evening. Buff knows almost everyone and assures me that we are providing a service they simply cannot otherwise obtain. None of these patients are wealthy enough to pay local doctors even though they have jobs and live in this larger town. All make it clear how thankful they are, especially since we also provide medication in addition to diagnoses. We see lots of children, all basically healthy, many with easily treatable minor illnesses. We also see a number of women who seem to be especially grateful to have a woman physician.

Buff does a terrific job of translating even though she does not know many medical or anatomical terms. I am able to do a lot with the few Spanish medical terms I remember and a good bit of "universal sign language," such as pointing and grimacing.

By the end of the evening, I have used two of the six duffel bags of medicines and have given away dozens of shoes. Buff and I look at each other and burst out laughing. Who ever would have thought when we began walking to school together as eight-year-olds that we would one day be in her living room in Bolivia seeing patients together? It is a very satisfying few days.

The next day we rest and do laundry, washing out some of the few personal items, underwear, socks and shirts that we allowed ourselves to include with all the medical supplies, and hanging them on the line in the courtyard. While Buff holds school for Sam and Sarah, Erik and I enjoy walking around town, he practicing his Spanish. He also enjoys talking with Buff's children, who learned Spanish mostly playing with local children. Buff is using the Calvert home schooling program, which I find amusing since she and I attended Bryn Mawr High School in Baltimore and were rivals of the Calvert school in rural Maryland. Again, we look at each other and burst out laughing. As believers that God is in charge of our lives, we just shake our heads and look heavenward.

Another travel day is upon us already. Our clothes are clean and dry enough to repack, and we consolidate the remaining medications, still carrying around a variety, but predominantly the blood pressure and other cardiac medicines and equipment. I have needed very little of that so far. If nothing else, I will give it to a hospital before leaving the country. I have no idea how we are traveling today, just that Buff and Steve and the children are all going with us back to the city of our arrival, Santa Cruz. They want to spend a few days at the mission, see other missionaries, go shopping and introduce us to another medical project.

We head back to the airport and tiny landing strip where our military flight arrived, and on to the next adventure. There is a pilot and plane designated to fly missionaries from place to place in Bolivia, as in many countries. Erik knew this from his childhood experience, but I did not. When we arrive at the airport, the only plane visible is a high-wing, single-engine, "station wagon" type of Cessna – the 206. We have four adults, three of us small, and two children. We also have lots of luggage. There is also another man, besides the pilot, going to Santa Cruz. After some comparing of our respective weights, we cram one child and me into the far back of the plane, Erik in the front beside the pilot and the other three adults, a child on one lap, into the middle seats.

This is one of the many times in my life, especially in my travels, that I have an exceptional opportunity to trust. There is absolutely no choice about how I could continue this trip; there is no other way I can reliably get back to Santa Cruz. The roads are not passable and there is no one to drive anyhow and no vehicle big enough for all of us. I trust that we will be safe, that people do this all the time and that the gray hair of the pilot means that he has experience and has lived to tell about it. Most importantly, I trust that God is in charge – always a good thing for me to remember. I just get to put one foot in front of the other and do what I think He wants me to do, and leave the results to Him. If I thought there was a great chance of disaster on this flight, I would just decline. The truth is that it's just a surprise to me to see the small, single-engine plane. There's no reason to believe it's more dangerous to fly this day than to drive, had that been an option. At one time Erik and I both had pilot's licenses and flew our own single-engine plane, smaller than this, so the whole concept is familiar to me. Erik is thrilled to be in a small plane, especially in the front seat. The views are fabulous; trees close by, sun and shadows stunning. I would repeat this flight any time.

△◆
Chapter Five
△◆

Our arrival back in Santa Cruz and off to the mission housing feels good. Returning to a place and a few people we know makes
us feel like real missionaries and we are rapidly getting comfortable
in our roles. The next day, we join two young Bolivian physicians, a
married couple both still in residency training, at the site of their
"mission." Buff is friends with the family of one of the doctors, and
when she mentions our visit, they line up a "day at the mission" for us.

Toni and Placido spend one day a week in a slum on the out-
skirts of the city and are the only doctors the inhabitants, Ayore Indians, ever see. With the minimal training they have, they try to provide care for this group of outcasts. The Aymara and Quetchua are
the large groups of Indians who live mostly in the Altiplano, though
many have moved into the lowland area because of lack of work in
the highlands in the last thirty years. The Indians, a minority who
are shunned by other Bolivians, live in poverty, scraping a living
from the sale of their crafts, and sometimes finding menial jobs in
the city. The Ayore are still relatively uncivilized, and are not accepted by most of Bolivian society. They were killing missionaries
and other non-Indians who entered their territory with spears as recently as the 1950s.

I grew up in Baltimore and did my own medical training in a
very poor part of that city. I have seen poverty – but never anything
like this Bolivian slum. The location is an empty dirt lot, much of it
muddy. The "houses" are pieces of cardboard propped together and
covered with scraps of anything available – slabs of tin, canvas, or
other material, all undoubtedly scavenged from garbage.

Children are playing in the mud, others peek out of the
"doorways" of their homes, and soon we are surrounded by children
and adults. There is a concrete platform in the middle of the
"neighborhood," apparently a start at a community center by some
philanthropic organization. It has three walls, no roof and is fur-
nished with several plain, old tables and chairs we use for examina-
tions, now our routine and expected "office furniture."

After appropriate introductions, I arrange my supplies. Opening the duffels, I show Placido and Toni what I have, including the
digital blood pressure cuffs and entire bags of blood pressure medications. I watch Placido's eyes get wide as he whoops like he just won

the lottery. Looking at the contents of the duffel, he then looks at me, his jaw dropping. I am baffled by his excitement but glad he is happy with the medications. The mystery of his enthusiasm is solved when his wife, Toni, tells me that the primary disease among the Ayore is hypertension. It is apparently genetic, undoubtedly aggravated by their poor diet. I am not sure exactly what they eat but know they have very little access to protein and fresh food, which leaves them with only cheap carbohydrates and fats. A very high percentage of the adults and some of the children are hypertensive.

Now I see. Several months ago while in Colorado, we were given blood pressure medication and new, up-to-date blood pressure monitoring equipment to take to Bolivia. We didn't know why; we didn't need huge quantities of these medicines in Honduras or Ecuador. We had no knowledge of this genetic disease among Ayore Indians and didn't even know we would be providing medical care to them. Again, I am reminded that I am not in charge; that it is completely a God thing that we were given the medicines and opted to bring what we were given, trusting there would be a use.

Like a child on Christmas morning, Placido asks me to show him how the digital cuff works, explain each of the medicines, starting doses, and everything else I know about hypertension. We proceed to check blood pressures on everyone: patients, bystanders (always the "audience," wherever we are), each other. Placido starts many of the adults on low doses of medicines. Even though the medicines take several days to have an effect, and he knows this, he is so excited that he returns the next day, instead of waiting until his regular trip a week later, to recheck their pressure. We spend the rest of the day seeing infections, abdominal pain, arthritis, headaches and dental infections. I am struck by the obvious length of time some of the infections have existed. There are children with bilateral ear infections, drainage from noses and ears, fevers, and sores on faces and arms, and painful dental decay, so I am grateful for the supply of pediatric and adult antibiotics and pain medicines.

I am also grateful for these young local doctors, still in training, who are eager to tap into my knowledge and experience and share theirs with me – again, the meaning of doctor, to teach: *docere*. I am here for one day; they come every week, an hour from their home and hospital, and do what they can for these people. In the U.S., indigents have access to care, minimal or imperfect as it is, but in Bolivia these people, poor and a minority, are literally turned away from medical facilities.

When we finish, I give my doctor bag, the one I got as a third-year medical student in the 1970s, to Toni. She is thrilled. I am both happy to see my first equipment get passed on and know it will be used, and somewhat nostalgic to see it go. I am overcome by her gratitude for such a small gift. We also leave all of the rest of our supplies with them, knowing they will be used.

Tomorrow we will leave the area and begin a week of vacation travel, no itinerary, carrying only our tiny packs. Unbeknownst to us, there is more to our "mission." We think we are now going off for pure vacation, not dreaming that we may have more opportunity to be of service to anyone else, just wanting travel and adventure. We board a bus to Cochabamba, then to La Paz, the largest city in Bolivia, similar in population to Denver.

△◆

Chapter Six

△◆

In Denver, there is a large population of recovering alcoholics and addicts and about two-hundred various recovery group meetings a day with more being started every week. In La Paz, there are only five meetings a week. Recovery is very hard to find in South America, especially in Bolivia. There are no recovery meetings specifically for drug addiction, as possession of drugs is illegal and punishable by lifetime imprisonment or death. No one admits to using drugs, even if he or she is at the point of wanting to stop using. Consequently, there are only a small percentage of addicts who ever have the opportunity to hear about recovery. The few who do, who want to get well, attend the "more acceptable" alcohol recovery meetings, a much safer place as alcohol is not illegal. I am again grateful that in the U.S. we are allowed privacy in our recovery meetings, assured that we are not under surveillance, and are able to talk freely without fear, in our meetings and elsewhere, about past drug use. Also, people in recovery meetings are careful to keep the meeting locations safe, not allowing anyone still using drugs to have them on the premises.

During all our years of recovery, Erik and I find continued support by joining other recovering people on a regular basis to discuss life without drugs and alcohol. For us, it puts us more in touch with our gratitude for being alive, clean and sober, and healthy. More importantly, going to meetings, like church for some, puts us in touch with God and encourages our evolving relationship with Him.

Part of our experience in La Paz is looking for a recovery meeting. None of the phone numbers I had taken with me from the States work. The number in the La Paz phone book is disconnected. We are not worried about drinking; we just like to attend recovery groups at home and when we travel, the way many people like to attend church. The groups are the foundation of our spiritual health and we enjoy connecting with others who are similar in their emotional and spiritual beliefs and growth. Walking into a recovery group away from home, especially in another country, is like finding family. As foreigners, we are always asked about ourselves, usually invited to speak at the meeting, and often are invited to socialize after the meeting, frequently to join others for a meal. We find that we get more than we give, but we always try to contribute something positive when we are visitors at a meeting.

After eating lunch in a second-floor café on our second day in La Paz, we walk out onto the street and look up to see the familiar symbol of recovery, indicating a meeting location. I am sure it had not been there when we went into the restaurant – or had it? We look at each other and just smile, looking up and saying "Thank you, God." An immediate sense of belonging comes over me. We will get to meet with "friends we have never met" tonight. Our experience at the meeting is worth the whole trip. It is a small group, six people; the man with the longest-term recovery this evening has eleven months without a drink or drug. Erik and I each have been in recovery, without drink or drugs, for well over ten years at this point. We are so appreciated and welcomed, and are able to encourage others and be examples of healthy, happy life without chemicals. One man asks Erik to meet and discuss his recovery; they arrange a time after the next day's meeting.

Many more people, perhaps twenty recovering men and women attend the next day's meeting and they welcome us as warmly as the people the night before, thoughtfully deciding that after each person speaks, they will stop and allow Erik to translate for me. I feel a warm glow as I see two of the people from last night's meeting and realize we are not alone in a big city; we are part of an underground spiritual support system and are getting to know people in less than two days. We command a great deal of laughter when, after one member goes on and on, for more than ten minutes in rapid-fire Spanish about his wonderful life since he has stopped drinking, Erik turns to me and says simply, "He says he is grateful." The others wait for Erik to say more, and then laugh as it becomes clear he has distilled ten minutes of talking into one sentence.

After the meeting, Erik and the man we had met the night before, Jorge, find a place to talk in private. I get to explore the city, primarily the market district, on my own. Erik and the young Bolivian discuss recovery in a mishmash language of Spanish, English, and a few Portuguese words thrown in when Erik cannot find the right word in Spanish and Jorge cannot understand it in English. This is part of our mission: sharing our recovery with anyone who wants it; reminiscent of our Honduras trip seven years earlier. Upon our return to Denver, we send a large box of Spanish literature to Jorge to be distributed as he sees fit.

Since that trip, we have always taken recovery tapes and books to give away anywhere we go, leaving a dozen or more tapes in Kuala Lumpur, Malaysia on one occasion.

The rest of our vacation in South America includes a trip to Lake Titicaca, on the boundary between Bolivia and Peru, and a trip to Macchu Pichu. We hike and run the trails, visit the natural hot springs, and stay in tiny hotels, meeting locals and fellow travelers, and sampling local foods.

It is just about the perfect trip, with a perfect combination of medical work, visiting friends, helping some recovering people, and being travelers.

△◆

Lessons

△◆

◆   Trust God.
◆   Participate. Combining work and visiting old friends is a great way to travel. The best part of travel is the people we connect with; friends, locals, patients and fellow travelers.
◆   If we teach and share our experience and knowledge with others, we can help many more. Be open to helping and encouraging anyone who is in front of you to share their knowledge, to pass it on, to help in their own way.
◆   Trust. Accept gifts and don't question why they are given; they will be useful.
◆   Remember to help people from your heart; never mind that you do not speak the language.
◆   Needs will be met.
◆   Every little bit helps (even if it's one starfish).

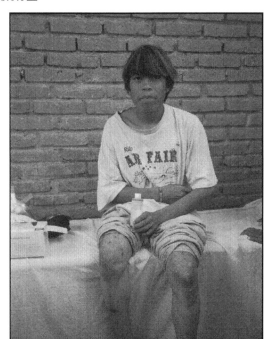

An Indian boy with skin infection

A slum outside of Santa Cruz, Bolivia

Doc Dawn with patients in Santa Marta, Bolivia

△◆

An Indian baby with worms, possible diabetes and poor nutrition

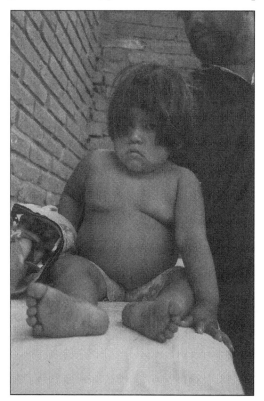

Fueling up before flying over the Bolivian jungle

△◆

Dawn and Erik in Bolivia with Buff and Steve

Part Five

Viet Nam
2001

Our excitement at going to Karen's birth country is thwarted almost immediately by the unkindness of the people in the hospital. The Vietnamese nationals, nurses especially, are militaristic and often rough and uncaring with the patients, and rude to us, the foreign volunteers. An emotionally disturbed American physician on our team contributes to the negative atmosphere, even suggesting Karen and I not make our planned visit to her family in Danang. The love and kindness of Karen's family is a welcome contrast to what we leave in Ho Chi Minh City. We are treated like princesses; in fact, some of the children asked if I am a movie star. We feel good about being able to provide medical care and donate food and supplies for the needy in that community, salvaging some of the trip.

△◆
Chapter One
△◆

In accepting this offer to join a medical mission venture to Viet Nam, I have no idea just how different this trip will be from the others.

A momentary glitch: Erik, who has been with me on all previous trips and is supportive of anything I want to do, is at a place in his real estate business where he decides against taking several weeks off. Do I consider going to Asia without him and with people I do not know?

This is primarily a surgical trip; I am not a surgeon, but am quite comfortable in the operating room and capable of performing minor procedures and assisting with major ones, as well as doing non-surgical medical care. Having had one year of general surgery residency before changing my specialty training and completing an emergency medicine residency at Denver General Hospital in Denver, Colorado, one of the first of its kind to exist, I am comfortable with every aspect of medicine. I was in the first class of E.M. residents at what is now Denver Health and Hospitals. There were three of us: a biker from New York, who still heads a small hospital emergency room; a former hippie and avid kayaker from New Mexico, who is very well-respected in the field of E.M.; and me. We ran the Denver General E.R. as it had never been run before; working well together and opposite each other, we improved the care in the E.R. during our years there. Learning a great deal from us, the residents in other departments and the E.R. nurses respected our expertise. That program has remained one of the best in the country. All of these memories, especially my one full year of surgical residency, come back over the first few hours after being told about the possibility of joining this trip to Viet Nam.

As soon as I see some of the before and after pictures of surgeries, children with repaired cleft palates, adults with disfiguring cancers removed, I am hooked. I daydream about some of the experiences I had at the University of Maryland Hospital and School of Medicine in 1975 as the first woman in the four-year surgical program. I had the opportunity to get to know the surgeons, both professors and senior residents, while I was a medical student. I had worked with most of them during those last two years of school, when students are finished with most classroom work and spend all of their time in the hospital. These last two years of medical school are much more fun than the first two classroom years. As juniors and seniors, we function as "student doctors," spending time with patients, and learning by working alongside the more senior interns, residents and attending physicians. This hands-on learning is imperative, as the day after we graduate from medical school we are "real" doctors, M.D. degree in hand.

Everyone familiar with medical training knows not to get injured or sick enough to go to the hospital in July, as that is when the new doctors begin working. Interns are on the front line, usually the first to see patients who show up in the E.R. and clinics. No matter how smart they are at this stage, interns have minimal experience. I feel safer when I see a little gray hair on doctors, indicating book-learning *and* experience.

My thoughts return to the possibility of travel with a group of surgeons, nurses and technicians I do not know, and without Erik. Not known to be easy to work with, "the surgical personality" is tolerable to me and I have always experienced mutual respect between medical specialties. Erik and I object to being apart for several weeks, but we both will be busy and the time will go fast, plus I am excited about the possibility of another adventure. I am confident enough with new cultures, new customs and new situations to accept this offer. I cannot possibly know the strength this trip will require and how much I will wish for Erik's presence and support.

Hearing about this opportunity seems to be coincidence – again, that alias. Karen, the young Vietnamese medical assistant in my medical office, will be more than interested. Although her parents have visited their homeland, she has not had an opportunity to return to Viet Nam since coming to the States twenty years earlier as a baby. Before mentioning that I am going, and the possibility of her joining me, I inquire of the trip leader and find it is open to anyone who is interested and qualified. He is thrilled to have someone bilingual in English and Vietnamese. Karen, who has grown up in Colorado and lives in an English-speaking neighborhood with her Vietnamese-speaking family, is fluent in both languages. Escaping Viet Nam on her father's fishing boat when she was an infant, she has never been back to visit her elderly grandmother and other relatives in Danang. A city north of Ho Chi Minh City, Danang seemingly is not far from where the trip is going, especially when compared to the distance between Viet Nam and the U.S. I soon find out just how great that distance is, not just geographically.

Within a very few days, Karen decides to join me. We arrange to work with the team for most of the two weeks and then travel to Danang, where she can meet her relatives for the first time in her adult life.

My office is doubly excited for this trip since Karen is going. The whole staff sets about asking all the pharmaceutical representatives to donate medications, equipment and money toward our cost. As always, volunteers pay for their own flight, hotel and other trip expenses. Some people find this strange, as we also are taking our vacation time to do this, but who else would pay? The countries we go to are poor and unable to bring us there; we are going to help, not to be paid. There are usually no "parent" organizations sending us and we are not working for anyone. We are just with a group of medical professionals who want to spend vacation time serving in a capacity to which we are uniquely suited. Some organizations, such as *Doctors Without Borders,* accept medically-trained individuals as employees for full-time work, but we are not looking for a career, just a short-term volunteer experience. So, we fundraise, acquire medications and prepare emotionally and logistically for this trip. Karen is apprehensive and excited; so am I. This will be my first international volunteer experience without Erik, and my first time to a communist country. I am relieved and happy Karen can translate for me.

△◆

Chapter Two

△◆

The trip halfway around the world is exhausting. Some people sleep for part of the trip; not me. I attempt to sleep but am completely unsuccessful. We are all wide awake on arrival in Ho Chi Minh City, known as Saigon before 1975, the same year I began my year of surgical residency.

On arrival at the airport, we are met by some of the Vietnamese medical team from the hospital, people with whom we will be working. With near perfect English, they welcome us and take us to our comfortable hotel, which is modest by U.S. standards and conveniently located across the street from the hospital; and then to dinner at a very upscale restaurant. Both professionally and in accommodations, this trip is not like my previous experiences. We are in a city, have a hotel room instead of a cot in a hut or dormitory, and are working in a hospital, not a makeshift office setting under a tent or in a schoolhouse. And Erik is not here. There is an established sys-tem for medical care, including the hospital fully staffed with doc-tors, nurses, pharmacists and techs, unlike some of the places I have been. One of the problems is that the care is not available to every-one, especially those living in rural villages. Nevertheless, we are able to provide a service, teaching Vietnamese doctors and nurses up-to-date procedures, including post-operative care, and introducing some of the newest medications and other supplies.

Perhaps the most innovative if not most important member of our team is the prosthesis technician; she is the one who makes an eye for the woman who has lost hers to cancer, and constructs an ear for another woman who had hers destroyed in an accident. These change the patients' lives because they can show their faces, make eye contact, and let go of some of the shame their disfigurement brings. They regain the opportunity to be part of society and no longer wear scarves over half of their faces.

Things go well for a few days. We are enjoying the city as well as the hospital, which is across the street from our hotel in busy, loud downtown Ho Chi Minh City. The first time I attempt to cross the street, traffic takes on new meaning. Wide enough for at least eight lanes of cars, the street does not have lane lines! Cars, trucks, bicycles and motorcycles of all sizes zoom past, weaving in and out of each other's pathways with no apparent order. My jaw drops as I stand on the curb observing this chaos. Reminiscent of traffic in San Pedro Sula, Honduras, I now remember the absence of traffic laws in some countries. The big difference now is that I am on foot, unprotected by the truck that protected me in Honduras, and I want to cross the street and live to tell about it.

Over the subsequent days we find a way to deal with this sense that we are risking our lives to get to the hospital. We discover that if we wear our white coats and stand on the curb in a group in-stead of alone, it's easier to get to the other side alive. I'm not sure whether this is because any of the drivers defer to us and slow down (they never actually stop), or simply because we are braver in a group.

Our hotel is plain, but luxurious compared to the quarters I am used to on other mission trips. Karen and I enjoy being room-mates, sharing the new experiences and talking until falling asleep late at night, using our tiny sink to wash the few clothes we have brought, and marveling at the opportunity for inexpensive massages available in the hotel. There is even Internet access in the hotel lobby, although it takes me an hour to get a two-line message sent to Erik to inform him of our safe arrival. Not like home! Every afternoon when we return to the hotel, there is fruit, along with a knife to cut it, in our room. This daily treat is perfectly displayed on a tray sometimes surrounded by tiny blooms from brightly colored flowers. The first day the fruit is large and almost round, slightly smaller at one end than the other. It has a greenish skin, thinner than an avocado and smells faintly citrus-like. Upon cutting into it, a burst of the strong, sweet, tangy citrus fills the air. My mouth is watering before I even taste it. It is similar to pineapple, but softer and sweeter. Neither Karen nor I know its name, but we happily devour it. One day we find a papaya in our room, larger, softer and sweeter than any I have had in the U.S. before or since, and another day a guava. Each day it is different. Most days we find something we have never seen or heard of, all of them exquisite and delicious, and presented perfectly as if part of the decor, or for a photograph, not really meant to be eaten. Each evening when we return from dinner, the plate, knife, peel and seeds from the fruit have been removed and our room is again tidied, beds remade, bathroom again cleaned.

Medical care in this communist country is archaic by our standards, but more than that, patient care, patient rights and respect are almost absent. Patients are expected to deal with pain, postoperative and otherwise, with little if any medical attention, much less relief. Families provide food, bathing and "luxuries" like pillows, sheets and soap. Family members wash the patients, comb their hair and change their bandages. If one is not lucky enough to have family, or if family is in another town and not able to get to Ho Chi Minh City, the patient may not get meals, bathing, clean clothes, or any other care beyond the strictly medical. The nurses are disciplinarians, requiring visiting family members to leave at certain times, dispensing prescription medication with harsh rigidity, walking through the patient wards and talking among themselves, never smiling and paying no noticeable attention to patient comfort. There is something vaguely militaristic about these women, a feeling I encounter in other areas of the city where there are so many armed military. The nurses are harsh and their attitude smacks of "consequences if not done our way," even consequences to the volunteer American doctors and nurses. While the only consequence they actually can enforce is to snub us, there are some who appear to wish we are not there, as if we are intruding, and they would clearly like to see us leave. We definitely feel unwelcome by some; do some of these nurses feel threatened by our expertise, our caring about post-operative comfort for the patients, our way of doing things differently? We are careful not to criticize them while demonstrating how we do things in the U.S., yet some seem to hold on to resentments.

Neither Karen nor I are able to determine how the other Vietnamese women, and men, react to the fact that she is Vietnamese-born and has grown up in America; we have no idea how they feel about her having escaped twenty years earlier. Are they envious, curious, resentful, or secretly proud of her? I am overwhelmed with pride for her, young and inexperienced, entering this culture that is both hers and not hers, in such a responsible capacity. Easily going back and forth between both languages, Karen is invaluable for her translating ability, medical skills and for compassion that is evident in all she does. She and I are both uncomfortable with the low status of women in this country. The concept that throwing acid in the face of "the other woman" is a usual and even accepted event leaves us speechless. The lack of education for women and the general thinking that they are second-class citizens is so archaic and incongruous with our thinking.

The patient ward has about twenty cots, separated from each other by twenty-four inches or so without curtains for privacy, and is nowhere near as clean as the oldest and dirtiest of hospitals in the U.S. The operating rooms are connected to each other, allowing easy communication, but no privacy, which is not an issue unless the patient happens to be awake, as in some minor procedures. One of the three operating rooms is a double where we run two procedures simultaneously. No one seems to worry about sharing germs or contamination and nurses even go from one patient to the other. I think they change gloves between most cases, but I don't observe this every time; this disturbing reminder of where we are would be unacceptable in the U.S.

Three years later, I actually have an opportunity to experience being a patient in a similar, but slightly more advanced hospital in Malaysia. I became very ill twenty minutes after finishing the Ironman Malaysia triathlon, vomiting several times, and requiring I.V. fluids and blood testing. The air temperature during the race was approaching 100 degrees, and the humidity almost equal; brutal. About a third of the racers dropped out, a third of finishers needed I.V. fluids, and many of them needed hospitalization. I was in good company. In the medical tent at the finish line, I was diagnosed as hyponatremic, as were about thirty percent of finishers; my electrolytes (body salts) were way out of balance and did not equilibrate after receiving fluids intravenously for more than an hour. I rode in an ambulance to the Malaysian hospital, where I was reminded of my Viet Nam experience of almost no medical or nursing care. Other patients had families "camped out" in the hallways cooking for them and tending to their needs. I was lucky to get in and out of the hospital in about twelve hours and not need anything but I.V. fluids. No nurse or doctor came in to check after my arrival and at one time during the night when my fluids were running out, I had to get out of bed, hold the gown around me and walk down the hall holding my I.V. tubing and empty bag of fluids to find a nurse to change it! Definitely different from the regular, sometimes hourly nursing checks we are used to in this country. On a positive note, the whole hospitalization cost me only forty-nine dollars including lab work, and I won my age group in the race, qualifying for The World Championship Ironman competition in Hawaii in 2004.

In Viet Nam we spend the first week and a half at the hospital, helping in the operating room, recovery room and on the wards. Our medications are really needed and appreciated, useful in the recovery room for pain control (a seemingly new concept to the Vietnamese doctors and nurses), infection control, and a variety of other things. My time is divided between assisting in the operating and recovery rooms and providing general medical care.

Many of the patients are children with deformities. Cleft palates are common in Asia and the Vietnamese surgeons have become expert at repairing them, doing these surgeries every day. They save the more complicated cases for us and are eager to learn new surgical techniques. There is an especially poignant case of a young woman whose face is partially destroyed. The victim of an acid burn, her vision was gone in one eye and diminished in the other. Another woman had thrown acid in her face when she discovered the woman was seeing a man she liked. This apparently is not uncommon – a jealous woman throwing acid in the face of the other girlfriend. The surgical repair of the deformity and scarring was dramatic and afforded this woman a chance for a more normal life and possibly eventual marriage.

Karen and I are finding we can be helpful in many areas, especially in the wards with patients who are still sick enough to be in the hospital, but who have no family to care for them.

△◆
Chapter Three
△◆

After a few days, the atmosphere rapidly deteriorates. An emotionally-disturbed American doctor creates chaos by being verbally abusive to Karen and trying to be verbally abusive to me as well. I refused to allow it and shut her down, eventually removing Karen to protect her from this woman. Karen is only in her early twenties, not used to such harsh demands, intimidated by this unkind woman's anger and inappropriate behavior. She is in tears when I rescue her.

Even though "Witchy Doc" has not practiced medicine since finishing school fifteen years earlier, she insists that she will be in charge of the recovery room. She does not even recognize some of the medicines Karen and I have brought and pushes them aside with a scowl. Later that week, she acknowledges that the hospital pharmacist has said he is thrilled to have some of the relatively new tramadol (brand name Ultram) for patients who are in pain, as well as some newer antibiotics and other medications. He is very familiar with them and thanks us.

On about day four, the doctor aggressively requires that Karen stay with her, by her side all day in the recovery room, to translate. Willing to do whatever is needed, Karen joined the trip to do a variety of things and while she doesn't mind serving as a translator, she wants to use her medical assistant skills as well. She soon tells me that the real problem is the doctor's rudeness to her and to the patients' families, giving orders instead of making requests and being unresponsive to families. The Vietnamese families are used to being at the bedside from the moment their family member leaves the operating room, especially if the patient is a child. The doctor objects to this and scolds them for bringing the whole family into the recovery room. As the families comment on her persona of fear, anger, negativity and anxiety, Karen chooses not to translate everything they are saying, fearful of provoking more anger, undoubtedly directed at the messenger, Karen herself.

One evening back in our room, Karen tells me the doctor said, "You didn't pay to come on the trip, so you are working for me." And that this trip is paid for by "blood money." I never have been quite sure what "blood money" means, much less what she means in this case. Lots of people back home in the U.S. made donations and maybe she thinks they were somehow made to the detriment of those who contributed. My office took care of the finances and arranged with the organizer the amount we would pay for the two of us to join the trip. Weeks ahead of our departure, we paid the agreed-upon amount, having worked out all of the financial dealings months earlier. Karen was going at my invitation, so my office covered the cost for both of us, a package deal, and it was none of this nasty woman's business.

I watch Karen emotionally retreat from this increasingly demanding and rude woman and a week into the trip I am worried about her. She is making regular calls to her fiancé and parents in the U.S., is tearful much of the time and clearly is not enjoying the experience. When I ask, "How are you, what happened today?" her responses include "She doesn't let me go to the bathroom without asking"... "I did not get a lunch break"... "I want to see the patients on the ward and she won't let me leave the recovery room"... "She is scaring the families by making a big deal out of recovery care. The patients are fine, and she won't let the families see them."

I never learn many more details, as I had already stopped working in the recovery room due to this doctor's inappropriate behavior, but I get the picture.

This invasion of personal space and lack of respect parallels the lack of respect I feel in general with the Vietnamese medical staff. Working with a group that includes more than the usual number of intrusive and disrespectful physicians and nurses, and having to live with them, is difficult. The most difficult physician, Witchy Doc, disregards everyone else's expertise and experience and does whatever she wants, essentially becoming so controlling that I, and anyone else who can, leave her alone. She demands Karen's presence at all times to interpret, and then treats her harshly and rudely to the point that Karen is often in tears. This doctor also wants to prevent Karen from leaving, as we have planned since agreeing to join the mission, for the last few days of our time in this country to visit her grandparents in Danang. As soon as it becomes clear that this unkind woman's behavior is not going to change, I pull Karen out of the hospital and instruct her not to return. The situation has become abusive and I stop it, as Karen is too young and fearful and not able to protect herself from this woman.

The deteriorating mood around the hospital, primarily in the recovery room, matches Karen's feelings, and I tell her to take the day off. When Witchy Doc stops me in the hallway and demands,

"Where is she?" I respond, "Doing something for me." Looking at me with disdain, she again shouts, "She didn't pay to come on this trip. I want her to work off what she owes and be with me every day!"

I have had enough, so quietly, very close to her face and making serious eye contact I say, "Karen is not your property. Karen paid what everyone else did and has been working at least twelve-hour days. Where she is and what she paid is none of your business." I inform her that she will not continue to have the opportunity to be unkind to Karen and it is not okay for her to treat anyone with such rudeness. In spite of my sky-rocketing heart rate and bubbling rage, I keep what I say calm, clear and concrete. "Karen is finished working here and we will be leaving for Danang as soon as possible." She even suggests that Karen visit her relatives, "the next time!" The absurdity of coming to Viet Nam for the first time in twenty years and *not* visiting family a few hours away escapes her. I decline to participate in an argument with her, refuse to stoop to her level or tell her what I think of her and what she should do. I only say what I will do, and that is to protect Karen. Then I simply walk away, declining to engage further. I am a mix of emotions; angry, scared, and sad.

Significant conflict is the last thing I expected on an alleged "Christian Mission," so this interaction makes me feel extremely uncomfortable. Some of the physicians and nurses who joined the trip from another state are actually Jewish, so the only part of the trip identified as Christian is the group from Colorado. I refrain from shouting, name-calling, or even accusing Dr. W. of anything. I do not tell her to go work on her control issues. I don't "You" or "Should" on her by saying things like, "*You should* be kinder and more flexible to patients and staff." For me, the basics of recovery and healthy behavior in any relationship define "You-ing" and "Should-ing" as not useful. I thank God for my years of recovery, years of learning better ways to handle my own anger and not display it inappropriately. I have learned to communicate directly and not say things that are unkind, yet not collude to accept the unacceptable.

One of the tragedies is that Dr. W. professes to be Christian. Karen is Buddhist and this is her first close exposure to a group of Christians. She and I talk about individuals not necessarily representing an entire faith and Karen knows other Christians who are kind and caring, but it is obvious this experience has an impact. The Jewish contingent, two doctors and a nurse, are very kind and contribute much of the laughter and positive atmosphere of the trip while also being very focused on work and somewhat emotionally distant.

At this point in my own spiritual journey, I have a strong, close relationship with my God and know that the God my Jewish friends pray to is the same one that I know. I have become Christian, although a bit non-traditional and very liberal. Having moved from being agnostic in the 1980s – from "Okay, maybe there is a God, but I don't care," to "There is a God, but this religious stuff is not for me," in 1990 – I have progressed, kicking and screaming all the way. In the mid-1990s, I began to attend church for the first time since the 1970s, feeling that if I were to find out the beliefs, sure to be rigid and judgmental, of the church-goers around me, I would not return. At that time, I was unable to accept a number of the basics of Christianity, including the concept of the Trinity. In spite of this, I accepted the invitation to join a small group Bible study at the church I attended (I did not belong to the church, just attended it). I invited Erik to join the small group, even though he was not attending church. Through the next several years, we provided frustration, entertainment and skepticism, as well as an introduction to our deep faith in a God working (hard) in our lives, to our small group's members. They provided us with love, acceptance and education about Christianity. They found us to be rebellious and questioning and at times not only tolerated us, but enjoyed the lively conversations we provoked. Somewhere in the late 1990s, after both education and soul searching, but not much struggle, I became Christian, allowing my relationship with Jesus to develop. I have maintained many of my liberal and non-traditional beliefs, sprinkled with occasional conservative pieces, while growing in my relationship with a God who is ever present in my life.

The next day I buy our tickets to Danang. We tell the trip leader we are leaving, in large part because he is unable to effectively deal with this angry, controlling physician. He has not seen the level of her rudeness, as he has been in the operating room for most of every day, and is undoubtedly unsure about how to handle it when we tell him the magnitude of the problem. The big issue for him: the disturbed physician is his wife! Two days later, we leave our group and Ho Chi Minh City.

△◆
Chapter Four
△◆

The next few days we spend in Danang, easily the most wonderful part of the trip for both of us. When we originally made the decision to come to Viet Nam, we raised money for food for needy villagers in Karen's family's town. Karen's parents had been in ongoing communication, visiting every few years and talking regularly to their relatives. When we asked what the greatest need was, the answer was food. When we give the hundreds of dollars donated by our patients, staff, friends and business associates to Karen's aunt, she sends someone to buy dozens of fifty-pound sacks of rice and quietly distributes it to elderly and needy neighbors. She knows everyone in the community, knows who is the poorest, who goes with very little to eat and is dependent on handouts and help from others. We trust her to distribute the rice to those most in need, not to families with young, healthy men and women who work and have plenty. I am surprised at the number of single mothers and the very elderly, most living in extended families. In the U.S., we often put our elderly in nursing homes; in other parts of the world they are cared for at home.

Karen's aunt very kindly asks if it would be acceptable to give some of the rice to the local Buddhist monastery since I am Christian. Of course this is fine with me. I am just grateful to have someone local who knows where help is most needed. Our U.S. money buys many hundreds of pounds of rice; it's amazing how far money goes in poor countries.

Karen, known as *"Na"* to her family, is greeted and treated like the long lost niece, cousin and granddaughter that she is, and so am I. I feel like family. It is so comfortable to be wanted and cared for and not treated as a tourist or outsider. And, having had my first negative experience on a volunteer trip, it is a relief to be away from unkindness and anger, and welcomed with love and caring.

I can still smell, almost feel, the aroma and warmth, in temperature and in love, contained in the enormous bowl of noodle soup that is offered to us as soon as we arrive. This is not like our noodle soup. It is more like a stew, full of vegetables, the stringy bits of eggs cracked into the boiling broth, and tiny pieces of some kind of meat.

Someone in the home where we are staying surrenders their bed for us; a large mattress in a loft, clearly the best part of the hum ble house. Others sleep on smaller, less private mattresses, couches, or at the homes of neighbors. We are fed well, even savoring a chicken dinner the last day we are there. Chickens run wild in the "streets" in this part of Danang, as I suspect they do in most parts of the countryside and smaller towns. They feed on what they can; bugs, food scraps, unlike the grain-fed poultry we eat. The taste is stronger, the texture lean, dry, almost stringy, more reminiscent of game birds than domestic chicken. I enjoy my piece very much, noting that it is far less fatty than chicken in the U.S. Karen tells me that her family doesn't like the U.S. chicken because it seems "mushy" compared to the substantial and flavorful Vietnamese birds. Some of our meals, especially breakfasts, are the large bowls of noodles with a variety of vegetables, seasoning, and sometimes egg or tofu. Everything is made with fresh food absent of any fat or grease, and has a wonderful aroma and flavor of spices I don't get at home.

People everywhere in Danang are kind and helpful to us, some even attempting a few words of English. Again, I am grateful to have my personal interpreter even though Karen gets an occasional strange look, as her command of the language is different from the locals and her vocabulary limited to what she has learned in her home. Having left Viet Nam before she was old enough to talk and having attended an English-speaking school in the U.S, she hasn't learned some of the colloquial words and expressions she would have heard from Vietnamese school children.

Soon word is out that there are visitors from the U.S. who are medical people. Neighbors start coming to Karen's aunt's house to see us for their illness or injury. One asks us to come and see his father, who is bedridden with stomach pain. The easy diagnosis of gastritis is also easy to treat with some of the common antacid medications we have. Another very old neighbor has back pain, most likely osteoarthritis. He might do well with some of the nonsteroidal anti-inflammatory medications we give him, but I am concerned that I will not be here to follow up with him. I wish he had access to physical therapy, or massage therapy, and an ongoing medication supply. I demonstrate some easy stretches; a little more movement, rather than sitting in his chair trying to avoid pain, might help. We have so little to work with and no capacity to follow up and there is no further care here in this tiny section of the city, at least not for those who cannot pay and cannot travel to local facilities.

This part of my medical mission experience is enjoyable and easy, giving me a different perspective on how to help. The money for rice is one of the best things we do; I am so thankful Karen's family thought of it. The medicines I have to distribute to the patients I see are useful. And, since we had only planned to visit, not to see patients, I am glad some patients find us.

Exploring the neighborhood, we use the extensive pathways, jokingly referred to by some as "streets," to navigate through the residential section where we live for a few days. Sometimes a motorcycle will come down the path, often a bicycle, but most of the traffic is on foot. The climate is perfect. We walk everywhere, even to make house calls to our patients, and always have a throng of children following us.

We do get out of the neighborhood for a few hours one day, on the back of two motorcycles driven by Karen's cousins. The ride through the real streets of Danang is an adventure. No helmets, of course, and no lanes of traffic. The most interesting vehicle is a bicycle with a very large tree on the back. It appears as if the tree is rolling down the street on its own.

The brief three days is over too soon and we split up for our return to the U.S. Karen flies directly home as planned, while I rejoin the rest of the group for two days of "rest and relaxation" in Kuala Lumpur, Malaysia. I feel as if I have been away from the U.S. for much longer than two weeks. Experiencing Viet Nam in such contrasting settings and being part of such a difficult trip will take some emotional recovery and processing.

I am sorry for the painful experience Karen has. We talk about it some during the weeks after returning home. I am also sorry for my own negative experience, finding it necessary to stand up to a very sick and unkind woman. I pray this doctor does not join in on other trips and repeat her performance. I am thankful she does not practice medicine in the U.S. I also hope she gets some help. She is the daughter of at least one alcoholic parent, perhaps two, and has clearly not done any work on her own recovery. I discuss this with her husband after our return when he asks for my input on the trip, explaining to him where her behavior probably comes from and offering to point her toward some recovery options. So far I have not heard from her. I wish I had been able to speak to her while on the trip about her anger and fear. I would love to have helped her see herself; to have helped her (magically) change. I work with adult children of alcoholics and with adults who have been abused as children, and I recognize her behavior.

I feel sad and angry that I had to take care of both myself

and Karen because the trip leader did not do his job and deal with the problem. Yet, I am grateful that I am able to be a responsible adult and handle problems, protecting myself and others. Most of all, I am grateful I recognize abuse and stop it when I can. I expect positive lessons to come from this trip. I trust there will be personal growth for all of us, positive change and increasing closeness to God.

Lessons

- You cannot know what to expect from your own team, much less the people in the country where you are going.
- The most difficult person, often the one in the most pain, may be the person sitting next to you.
- I cannot always be helpful; sometimes I am too close to the problem, and sometimes the other person does not want help.
- I am grateful to be able to incorporate many of the things I have learned in recovery and in daily growth and use them at difficult times.
- There are times when I need to take a stand, protect myself or someone else, refuse to allow abusive behavior, and not collude to make the unacceptable okay.
- I can see control issues and fear in others because I have had them and have had the opportunity to at least partially deal with them.
- Traveling without Erik allowed me to recognize some of my own strengths and depend even more on God.

Dawn visits with Karen's family in Danang.

△◆

Residents selling goods on the street in Danang.

Danang villagers

Sacks of rice for the Danang villagers.

Part Six

Brazil
May 2003

The reasons for our trip to Brazil does not include medical work; we go so that I can participate in a race and so Erik can visit his childhood homes. We also plan to see our former exchange student and meet her family, and visit my friend Buff, now a missionary in Brazil. The race goes exceptionally well and I use the time in Buff's town to recuperate. As typically occurs when we visit Buff, she arranges for me to see patients one day. I have the luxury of a clinic setting and lots of medications and supplies, all donations to the mission.

△◆

Chapter One

△◆

Ironman, Brazil. My first International Ironman competition is in the resort town of Florianopolis, Brazil. I have been training since taking a few weeks to recover from my first "iron distance" race last summer. The Ironman trademark is reserved for races sanc‑ tioned by the Ironman organization – other races can be the same distance, 140.6 miles, but cannot use the name "Ironman." Complet‑ ing this distance race had been on my "to do" list for a relatively short time, about two years. I began racing shorter distance triath‑ lons almost eight years ago, at age forty‑six.

The journey from cigarette smoking, heavy drinking and drugging child of the 1960s to competitive athlete had been un‑ planned and a daily surprise. In contrast, the journey from finishing my first 5k run in 1996, immediately followed within five weeks by my first sprint distance triathlon, to being a top‑ten age group fin‑ isher in the Hawaii Ironman World Championships in 2004, was straight, direct and intentional. The jobs of doctor, wife and mother had all fit into their places and I had received consistent support to pursue the added goal of amateur age‑group athlete. Ironman Brazil was one stop on the way to Hawaii.

On arrival at the airport near Florianopolis, three days before the race, I immediately feel weak and scared – no, terrified and over‑ whelmed, intimidated by the crowd of beautiful bodies. Hundreds of other competitors arrive on every flight. What was I thinking? I am just an ordinary middle‑aged woman, wife and mother of two, way out of place mingling with these incredibly tanned, toned and buffed athletes waiting for the large, awkward pieces of luggage that con‑ tain our bikes.

Oh, wait – I am tanned, toned and buffed, also a competitive athlete, just a tad older than the average, but not at all out of place. The age range for international Ironman races is late teens to early eighties. Most of the older athletes do not look older, do have lots of experience, and are amazing human beings. The younger ones look up to the older ones, admiring their continued strength and ability. I am somewhere in between, but minus the experience of most of the older athletes who may be competing in their tenth or fifteenth inter‑ national Ironman.

My mind is a mix of thoughts and emotions. I am excited and

scared (physiologically these two emotions are the same, what matters is how I interpret it). I am overwhelmingly happy to be part of this group waiting in baggage claim for bikes, then finding our way to the vans and buses to the race hotel. Most of the racers at international events stay in the main hotel; part of the fun is seeing each other in the hallways, elevator and dining room. I am suddenly aware of Erik chatting with another athlete in Portuguese. He is home, all six-foot-two-inches of him, blond hair and fair skin, of Norwegian heritage, and not looking Brazilian, but definitely sounding like a native. After all, this is the country where he grew up. Speaking with no "foreign" accent, having learned the language as a child, others assume that he is a local.

Erik's familiarity with the language, customs and overall feel of Brazil puts me at ease. My comfort zone is when I am taking care of patients, no matter where, or under what circumstances. I am at ease in my role as doctor, but this is different. My first International Ironman race is in an unfamiliar country and everything is different, from the cobblestone streets, to foods, language and the ubiquitous cigarette smokers. As an aside, my favorite Portuguese word is "*paralelepipido*" which means cobblestone streets.

Erik is instantly comfortable here and it rubs off on me. In addition to the practical aspects of his simply speaking the language and helping me with the bike box, there is the intangibility of his comfort level which helps me to stay as calm as possible. I've always considered myself to have attention deficit disorder and while I'm able to focus intently on most things, I still find it difficult to sit still much of the time. The fact that I have been off of caffeine for three weeks, part of my race preparation, may be helping me to stay calm, too. As a staple at recovery meetings, coffee is one of my best friends and the smell of the incredible Brazilian coffee does *not* help. There is no such thing as decaf here. I can't even have a cup of decaf! The smell will have to suffice until race morning. A small amount of caffeine can be helpful during a race, and is legal, while large amounts are not. The caffeine is more helpful if one is not desensitized to it by regular use.

I can't believe we are really in Brazil. And my bike made it, too. Nine months earlier, in August 2002, coming across the finish line after more than twelve hours of racing in Boulder, Colorado, my first words to my waiting husband were, "We're going to Brazil!" I did that race to see if I could actually go the distance before traveling out of my home state. I felt terrific! It had been a perfect race day.

The Colorado climate, dry and cool, is excellent for endurance racing. I was, at fifty-three, the oldest female participant in that race. I was, by far, nowhere near the oldest racer to have finished other larger Ironman competitions; at least two men in their early eighties have competed at this distance. The fun part about being the oldest woman that day, in a small field of racers, was that the announcer provided that piece of information every time I went by the part of the course near him. As a "viewer-friendly" event, the race course crossed the start-finish area several times. Each time I approached that area, and at both of the transitions, from swim to bike and bike to run, I could hear my name, home town of Golden, Colorado, age and other information, including "oldest woman in the race." Energizing! The monotony of putting one foot in front of the other again and again, hundreds of thousands of times, was broken as I heard this announcement. After dark, hearing my name became especially valuable as motivation to continue.

Erik knew that I was considering racing internationally. He knew that I was avoiding saying it out loud until finishing Boulder – one race at a time. We had talked very minimally about going to Brazil for my first international race and using the trip for visiting his childhood homes. Or was it that we had briefly talked about visiting his childhood homes and getting a race in on the same trip? We also had a former Brazilian exchange student from a town Erik had actually lived in decades earlier – lots of reasons to choose this country for my race. And my friend Buff was now living in Brazil.

So, the plans for Brazil in May 2003, nine short months away, begin to take shape. I find some outstanding coaching. My first coach several years earlier was for shorter Olympic distance triathlons. It was very helpful to work with her, but now I want help preparing for longer distance races. I met her when I was in a study on the cardiovascular health of amateur athletes and she was doing research as part of her Ph.D. requirement at the University of Colorado. I underwent extensive testing of lung and heart function, arterial wall flexibility, oxygen use efficiency and performance capacity while charting everything I ate and drank over several weeks. The comment from her that I remember most after she reviewed my obsessively-recorded food and drink consumption was, "You ate all of this?" I have always liked to eat, just never looked at it all on paper before. It is all really high nutrition value, "real" food. One day I ate an elk burger for one meal and tofu for the next, all with lots of vegetables. I eat fresh food, almost nothing processed, as I am allergic to preservatives, dyes and most food additives – allergic as in several near-death episodes.

In the past I have also worked a little with a world-renowned Ironman triathlete made internationally famous by winning the Hawaii World Championships six times in the early years of that race, primarily the 1980s. He lives and coaches in Boulder, and is helpful to me intermittently over several years. I attended his triathlon camp for a week a few years ago and have seen him individually to develop a training schedule and work on my race nutrition. He coaches mostly professional athletes, so I am grateful I have access to him.

The coach I use for most of my long-distance training helps me prepare for Brazil. I swim, bike and run many hours, many miles, every week, over many months, lots of the cycling miles with her in the foothills and canyons outside of Boulder. I am blessed to be able to work part-time and also fortunate to have lots of friends to train with. I rarely do a workout alone. I am thankful to Barb, Jeanne, Laurie, Heidi, Roger, Rex and all the others with whom I spend so many hours moving forward. I have found that if I can swim, ride or run at Denver altitude, a mile high, while talking with friends, I can feel confident about racing at lower altitude – sea level in most cases.

Ironman Brazil is at sea level. From the start of the race I am thankful for all the extra oxygen at this elevation. During my short training sessions in Brazil immediately prior to the race, I notice immediately that each sport is just a little easier than at five- to eight-thousand feet, where my training has taken place.

The days in Brazil just before the race are filled with pre-race meetings, short workouts, obsessive bike care, going over each part of the bike, deciding exactly what pressure to have in my tires and exactly what equipment to carry on the ride. The less weight on the bike the better, so there is always the trade-off of how much water, food and repair equipment to carry versus what to leave to chance and to the aid stations. My decisions are colored by the fact that I am allergic to so many of the race foods, energy bars, dried fruit and sport drinks containing dye – so I carry most of my own. I also carry two extra tire tubes, a tire-changing kit and carbon dioxide cartridges for rapid tire inflation. A flat tire, and no way to change it, means the end of the race. For me this is the scariest part of any triathlon, the possibility of technical problems. I figure I can survive a body breakdown and walk to the finish, but a bike breakdown means it is over. All the other racers, new and experienced, young and old, male and female, are going through the same thing in the days and final hours before the race.

I hear lots of languages in the hotel and outside with lots of people switching between several. Most hotel guests, in fact, most people in town, are either racing or are support crew, or are somehow related to the race. It is a big deal. Vendors from all over the world are here selling everything race- and fitness-related.

Encouragement and support from home arrives in emails from several friends including my training partner Barb and my coach Bettina, and in phone calls from daughters Brie and Kara. My daughters and I have always had a telepathic connection, seemingly able to sense when we are thinking about each other, or when one of us is about to call. I had this with my mom from as early as I can remember and often have it with close friends. Hoping to ensure an uninterrupted nap one day prior to the race, I turn off my hotel phone. When I wake up, I immediately think of Kara. We had not planned to speak on the phone during this trip, not knowing how easy and inexpensive it would be, but we had told both girls how to reach us if necessary. The moment I reach over to turn on the phone, saying to Erik that Kara might call, our phone rings and it's her. We have done this so many times in the past that Erik just smiles at my intuition. Ever the encourager, Kara is calling to check on me and continue her constant support.

The climate is perfect; we can walk comfortably everywhere in the small town. The breeze from the ocean, where the race will begin with a 2.4-mile swim, keeps the temperature from being as hot as many other places in this country and it is winter here.

The hotel is open to the air, with enormous doors on every side. On that first day, Erik and I settle into our room, a seventh-floor suite at the quiet end of a long hallway. It is equipped with kitchenette, living area, bedroom and bath and easily accommodates us and all of my gear, even my bike. On our way back down the elevator to the hotel lobby to check out the pre-race schedule, we meet another woman racer. I smile at her and Erik says something in Portuguese. This prompts a friendly barrage of rapid and animated Portuguese in close quarters and directed at me, apparently because Erik has told her I am the one racing. I am sure my mouth inadvertently drops open, expressing my bewilderment, at which point she intuitively says, "Oh, English? English is fine," and resumes happily chattering away to me in English, never missing a beat. I think my mouth is still open when we get to the first floor. We continue talk-ing and discover that she is the one person out of eight-hundred rac-ers and hundreds more support crew that Kara has told us to find! She is the mother of a friend of Kara's, a Brazilian who lives in Rio de Janeiro, Brazil and in San Diego, California.

Off to check out our neighborhood, we find a bakery. Inside there are wonderful concoctions clearly able to provide me with the additional carbohydrates I am consuming in advance of the race. Erik translates my many questions to the grandmotherly lady be-hind the counter. After a few words, she winks at him, gestures to-ward me, and says something in Portuguese. Safely out of the bakery with our treasures, Erik tells me that she was congratulating him on going to America to get me, thinking he is a local! More "foreign lan-guage" encounters add up by the hour. At one point while Erik is standing around with a group of guys chatting in Portuguese, a Bra-zilian lady hands him a business card and tells him his business will go better if he learns to speak English. Her card is from the Wall Street Language Institute. Without hesitating Erik says to her in English, "What's wrong with my English?" She is not amused and takes back her card.

We spend a lot of time smiling, helping to keep my nerves in check as the pre-race hours pass. The hotel provides breakfast and dinner buffets, perfect for racers – convenient, lots of good food, and a great place to talk with other athletes. One American lady is dis-traught because she cannot find peanut butter anywhere. They do not have this product in Brazil. Long-distance athletes commonly eat peanut butter because the high-density fat provides energy for many hours. Foodie that I am, I have brought some and offer to share. Rarely have I seen such a relieved and appreciative person – she clearly is counting on eating peanut butter on race morning. I give her some of my plentiful supply, declining her offer to pay some exor-bitant price.

Race morning finally dawns. I am surprised when I awaken and realize I have actually slept six hours. I can hardly wait to have coffee, my first in Brazil, as I have resisted it for three days despite smelling it every time I enter the dining room. The challenge now is to put one foot in front of the other and remember that God is in charge. I have less trouble remembering this when I am not so nerv-ous, but I need it more now. As I have become more secure in my re-lationship with God, I have felt more secure in myself and have taken more risks. The dangerous risks have been minimal – a few mountain climbs and fast bike rides – but I am very cautious physically.

The real risks for me are making the commitment to try new, difficult and scary things. I decided to try to get to the Ironman World Championships and told some of my friends and family, so if I am not able to I will be disappointed and maybe a little embarrassed, which is an emotional risk for me. I sold my business, an enormous risk financially (What will I do for a living now?) and emotionally (What will I do with my life now?). We are talking about moving out of our very comfortable home and neighborhood to a rural area outside a tiny Colorado mountain town. I want to be a writer, but I don't dare say it out loud for fear of failure. All of these things could be emotionally painful, yet something is pulling me to do them. I have a long-time friend, a Jewish doctor from Chicago, also a member of my recovery/spiritual support group, who told me more than twenty years ago, "Go ahead and have your fear, just don't let it paralyze you." At the time, we were climbing one of Colorado's fourteen-thousand-foot mountains together, so it was applicable to our physical activity. What he meant, of course, was grow emotionally and spiritually – don't let fear hold you back.

The more risks I take of any kind and the more fear I walk through, the more I find myself asking God for guidance. I really have to work at trusting Him and when I do, I feel closer to Him. Then the results cease to be so important; what becomes important is God's presence in my life and the peace I feel when I remember He is here. The external stuff is just noise to keep me separate from Him. There is a wonderful bumper sticker that says "Turn It Over" with the word "Over" printed upside down. I always need more practice in turning it over to God.

Busy with race preparation, we do not look for support group meetings these first days in Brazil, but pay attention to maintaining conscious contact with God. In our chatting with other athletes and their families, we discover several other recovering alcoholics and addicts; people in recovery just seem to be attracted to each other. While riding in a race bus with several-dozen athletes to check out the course, we say something, probably a comment or phrase often used in recovery meetings, which triggers another athlete to ask us if we are also recovering. That night we eat dinner with this person and several other members of the same support group, further reminding each other that as recovering people, we are blessed to be alive and doubly blessed to be able to participate in this event.

Race morning! I am amazingly peaceful as I rack my bike in its slot next to the other older women athletes (an advantage, as we can tell which of us is out of the water and on the bike first by seeing whose bikes are still here). Placing my cycling shoes exactly where I want them, I line up my helmet, gloves, sunglasses and sports drink so they are ready to go. There is an indoor changing area and volunteers assigned to help us change clothes, take a sip of water, and put on sunscreen between the swim and the 112-mile ride, all preceding the 26.2-mile run. Into my full wetsuit, as the water temperature is sixty-two degrees, and I am on the beach and deciding how to place myself among eight-hundred other athletes for the best start in the ocean swim. I don't want to be in front and get "run over" by the younger, faster professional men and women, but I am faster than many amateur swimmers, so I don't want to be held up behind them.

Finding a place close to the front, but out to the side a little, I run into the water as the starting gun sounds. Beginning a swim that usually takes me about an hour and a quarter, I pray for safety and for God's protection, now and throughout the day, expanding into asking for safety for the other athletes and for our entire trip over the next three weeks. My prayer is quickly curtailed, as I sense that my heart rate is not slowing down as much as I would like. Heart rates are expected to be elevated at the start of any race; the goal is to settle down to a reasonable rate, get into a comfortable breathing pattern and find a rhythm for the swim; easier said than done with eight-hundred other swimmers around me, very cold water in my face and on my hands and feet, and rough ocean water. My other races have been in lakes; the ocean is rough today, and the waves are big and rolling. They stay this way for the entire distance. I never pray for a result, other than safety, believing that whether I finish, win, or lose is unimportant; it is the journey and my relationship with God that counts.

My unspoken prayers are more than answered when I begin to play in the waves. A gift from my past is my father up there (he died in May 1987, a few months before his eighty-seventh birthday) reminding me what fun we had playing in the ocean when I was a child. I remember him taking me out past the breakers and onto a sandbar where he could stand. I was five and loved the water and I especially loved this time with Dad, a wonderful human being in spite of his disease of alcoholism. At night he was always drunk and not available to me and he was rarely sober on weekends except for a few hours in the mornings. He worked all week, long hours selling dog food at The Obrecht Feed Company in Baltimore, so having some time with him sober and playing was a special treat. Part of how he taught me to swim was that he would back up as I swam toward him, playfully pretending that I was only going to go a few feet and encouraging me to swim farther as he backed away. He never let me feel threatened or afraid that he would not catch me; he just made it a game and taught me how to keep swimming farther than I thought I could. We played in the waves, up and over, floating with them, then going under and diving through them. Now in Brazil, I am playing in the waves, up and over, into a rhythm that propels me forward with minimal effort. I am a little girl and Dad is in front of me, helping me swim farther and faster.

I am among the first swimmers out of the water, the first in my age group as I can see by the bikes still racked. Not expecting me so early, Erik misses me emerging from the water. The "stripper," a volunteer waiting for the racers to run up the beach to the transition area, helps me out (strips me) of my wet suit (I still have a swim suit on), then under a fifteen-second shower to rinse off a little of the salt water. In less than three minutes I am into and out of the transition area, swim suit and goggles off, cycling shorts and gear on. The rest of the day and into the night goes well; I remember to thank God often for the privilege of being here, here in my life, health, fitness, capacity to travel, and being here with Erik at this stage of our lives together.

Each racer has packed an aid sack to get at mile fifty-six, the halfway mark of the bike ride. Locals, often children, help with handing them to us as we slow down at the turnaround point, a very exciting and loud part of the race, as volunteers shout out race numbers when they see us coming toward the turnaround while other volunteers find our bags and hand or throw them to us. They do this for eight-hundred racers and somehow always get the correct sack to each cyclist.

Finishing in the dark, having had only had a few episodes of stomach upset and minor body pain, I am directed to the massage tent. The volunteers at the finish line assess each athlete as he or she comes across the line, directing some to the medical tent for I.V. fluids and other measures, and others to the massage tent, with our finisher's medal around our necks! I am pleased with my time, under thirteen hours, and with my overall race, and remember to continue to thank God for getting me through safely and with no mishaps. Later, I hear about others being pulled from the rough ocean, one near death; and several-dozen others disqualified for missing a turn buoy they did not see due to the waves, inadvertently cutting some distance from their swim.

I come in second in my age group and am thrilled, as at fifty-four I am at the older end of the group. My coach is worried that I will be devastated at missing first place by only a few minutes. Some studies show that people who place second often go into a depression, or become very discouraged, much more so than third-, or of course, first-place finishers. To the contrary, I am delighted with my race and already planning to compete again at the younger end of the age group next year.

Allowing ourselves a recovery day before leaving Florianopolis to travel in other parts of the country, I eat, sleep, eat, go for a short run to loosen up, eat and get a massage, then eat again. Off to be a traveler now, and leaving my athlete mask behind, I am excited to stop being "on." I can just be, not having to perform, for the next few weeks. This is especially true since Erik does most of the communicating, knows the country and is willing to take over. We are able to find a very kind athlete from Colorado who takes my bike box, containing bike and other gear, home with him. We are each left with one small pack, making travel simple. I am happy to say good-bye to my race gear including a wet suit, goggles and cap, bike, racing wheels, extra tubes, tiny repair kit, cycling shoes and gloves, helmet, running shoes, sunglasses and clothes. And this is just for one day! Getting ready to travel for the next few weeks is exhilarating and freeing. For now, no strict training schedule looming over me – and I can drink coffee again!

△◆

Chapter Two

△◆

Visiting Erik's childhood homes in several different towns is fascinating and healing for him, fascinating and an adventure for me. The combination of dust from the dirt roads leading to and in the small towns, and blooming vines, trees, bushes and flowers are reminders of why his family left this country: his asthma. Wonderful smells, very tickly lungs.

It is astonishing to both of us that Erik remembers so much from early childhood. In one town we see his former next-door neighbors and have dinner in their home, walk around town and visit familiar landmarks including the church where his father was pastor when Erik was eight.

In the town where they lived for the next three years, Taquara, we track down the parents of some of his childhood playmates. Several of the older women remember him, exclaiming how wonderful he looks, how big he is, and how well he speaks Portuguese. We easily find the church where Erik's father was pastor in the 1960s. The current pastor is interested in hearing Erik's memories about the church in its earlier days and invites us into his study and then to the evening choir practice that will begin in a few hours. His father's picture is still hanging in the back of the church with pictures of other men who have been pastors over the years. That evening at choir practice, Erik introduces himself and many of the older adults remember him. They ask him to stand at the podium and speak, updating them on his family. He does so in Portuguese, prompting many questions about his parents and siblings. In turn, some of them tell Erik about his former playmates, now men in their forties; their jobs, marriages and children. All who remember his parents ask to send messages to them. One lady even sends a written note with us to take to Erik's mother. The Bible study that was started by Erik's mother thirty-five years earlier is still going strong, still meeting every week. The impact his family had is clear.

The next morning, walking down the main street, cobblestone as most streets are in small Brazilian towns, Erik has a déjà vu experience. When we stop for ice cream, he feels that he has been here in the past. Remembering this store as the home of one of his childhood friends, with a watch repair shop instead of ice cream parlor in the front room, he asks about it. Yes, this is the home he remembers.

After these heart-warming visits, we travel by bus to another town, Campinas, to visit our former exchange student. Erik lived here when he was a very young boy and the town he remembers is now a city with a population of more than one million. Carol, who lived with us when she was fifteen and in high school, is now a twenty-one-year-old college student. She greets us as the family we were to her during the time she lived with us in Colorado. Her family treats us as family, organizing a large outdoor party so friends and other relatives can meet us. We are again humbled and astounded at the gratitude they express for their perception that we helped Carol through a very difficult year.

As I accept hugs and words of gratitude from Carol's mother and grandmother, I realize they think we did something extraordinary while she was living with us. Until now, it had not occurred to me that we were much of an influence in her life. While Carol was with us, her father died back home in Brazil. We comforted her, helped her arrange a flight, packed for her and sent her home on very short notice. After the funeral and a week at home, she decided she wanted to return to finish the last few weeks of the school year in Colorado. We did everything we could to help her through this painful time, mostly just treating her with love and support, doing the best parenting we could. I guess that is what she needed, as now her family profusely thanks us for our help.

There is an interesting "God story" that goes with any mention of Carol. My older daughter, Brie, answered a phone call from someone asking us if we wanted to have an exchange student. Brie responded in the affirmative, allowing the agency representative to believe they were speaking with me. Then Brie left for college. When I received the next call asking for more information, I declined to take a student. No problem, there were plenty of homes. Three weeks later we received another call stating a fifteen year-old girl was in a living situation that was not working and would have to go home if the agency couldn't find another place. Before I could get the word "No" out of my mouth, I asked where she was from. When the answer was Brazil, I knew we had to meet her. The director of the agency brought her to our home that night. Sad, dejected, looking down at her shoes and not making eye contact, she sat with us while the director asked questions about us and our home. When Erik began to quietly speak to her in Portuguese, she was stunned. His gentle manner and perfect command of her language gave her the courage to look up and meet his eyes. We liked each other and decided that she would immediately move into our home. If Brie had not been trying to play a joke and impersonate me with the agency, we would not have been on their list and Carol may have had to miss her year as an exchange student. There were the usual issues to resolve with her school and the tragedy of her father's death, but overall it was a good experience for her and us. She and Kara, who was a senior in high school that year, acted like sisters, getting along sometimes, not others. Now ten years later, they email and talk on the phone regularly.

△◆
Chapter Three
△◆

The third week of the trip we will be staying with Buff. Since we last visited them in Bolivia in 1999, she and her family have been relocated by the organization they work for, South American Missions (SAM), have learned Portuguese, and are now working in Brazil. I had no plans to do anything medical, so I had not packed any medications or supplies, or even thought about working after the race. Of course, Buff knows she can recruit me any time, and she does.

Rest, friends, no schedule, freedom! On to visit Buff in the western part of this huge country and we are at the airport again. Hearing Erik's accent from the south of Brazil, a flight attendant asks where he is from. He explains that he is from the city of Taquara and has returned to visit after living in the States since age eleven. He is welcomed with compliments on his command of the language after not speaking it for thirty-five years. Again, we are made to feel welcome by everyone in this country.

A week in Buff's town, Chapada in the hills above Cuiba, is perfect. We stay in a bed and breakfast two blocks from Buff and Steve's tiny home and are treated like royalty. In this higher elevation, we have left behind the intense heat and humidity of the middle of the country. Located about an hour from Cuiba which is possibly the hottest place in Brazil, Chapada is resort-like, and is in fact where many Brazilians come to escape their summer heat, our winter, in December and January. It is May, so there are not many tourists and we get special attention, clearly foreigners in this town where the locals all recognize each other.

Without hesitation, Buff asks if I will see some patients at the Agricultural School where Steve teaches. She assures me it is only a few people, and that we will have access to supplies. No problem, I love being a doctor and enjoy meeting new people.

The next day, Buff, Erik and I visit the school. Previous mission teams have left some supplies, a common practice in rural areas, but nobody who is medically trained or can actually see patients and make use of the medications has been here for months.

We see a few patients from the mission school, almost all Indian and underserved for all of their lives. There are the common ailments like children with ear infections, a woman with abdominal pain and some people with skin rashes. Buff translates for me again, with perfectly adequate Portuguese, a larger vocabulary than Erik, but not with his fluency and absence of accent. This medical work with Buff providing patients and translating for me is getting to be a routine. Little did we know as fourth-grade classmates or high school friends that we would still be friends, much less working together under such unpredictable circumstances, *thirty-seven years* after our high school graduation.

Buff and Steve are interested in where our spiritual journey has taken us since we spent time together in Bolivia four years earlier. Having both returned to Christianity, independent of each other, but at about the same time, Erik and I are happy to share our progress. We think our current beliefs have come about in large part from some recent education; we have been in a Bible study with a group of adults from a church we attended for several years and have learned a great deal. The most recent part of this journey has been gentle, resulting from many previous years of struggle. It feels comfortable and right to have my relationship with God expand to include the trinity of the Father, Son and Holy Spirit. The crucial part for me is my personal relationship with God whatever that looks like at the moment. Buff and Steve are obviously pleased.

I do not bother to tell them about all the non-Christian friends we have and risk disappointing them by sharing my belief that these folks are not doomed to hell and that I do not try to convert them. I know there is one God and I am not it. That is the important piece. I am also fully accepting of my friends with alternative lifestyles and do not believe they are going to burn in hell. I have a great deal of difficulty with Christians who are judgmental about others whose beliefs are different. So I will continue my own spiritual journey, trying to draw ever nearer to my God. My spiritual support group says religion is for people who do not want to go to hell and spirituality is for those who have been there and do not want to go back!

A 2008 update on medical care for Indians from the area surrounding Chapada and at the Agricultural School: They have their first full-time missionary doctor. Previously, the little care they received had been sporadic and by minimally-trained, non-physician health care providers. For anything serious, they would either go a long distance to the city or simply not get treatment.

△◆
Lessons
△◆

- I acknowledge the many gifts of my Brazil experience. I get to do my race, travel with Erik and meet people who remember him as a young child, and do a little bit to help a few people who have limited access to medical care.
- God is everywhere, even on the race course. It's up to me to be receptive to Him.
- If we don't get to meetings to connect with other recovering people, God will bring them to us.
- Mom and Dad, even though they have been gone for many years, are still major influences in my life, perhaps more now than when I was younger.
- Taking risks is frightening, but not taking risks keeps us stuck.
- Simple kindness, such as caring for a teenage exchange student, has more meaning than we know until years later.
- Starting something positive, perhaps a Bible study, may impact people for years to come.
- People remember kindnesses, friends and much more.
- Visiting places where we grew up can prompt memories that teach us more about ourselves and each other.
- Some friendships last for a lifetime.
- As the years go by, it's more fun than ever to be with Erik, this time in a new setting.

Triathlete Dawn is marked with her race number before the start of Ironman Brazil in Florianopolis

Decked out in her wet suit and swim goggles, Dawn awaits the start of the 2.4-mile swim to be followed by a 112-mile bike ride and 26.2-mile run.

Twelve hours, 51 minutes later, Dawn, 54, crosses the finish line second in her age class.

Dawn and Erik with Buff and Steve in Chapada, Brazil.

Erik speaks in Portuguese to the congregation at his father's former church in Taquara, Brazil.

△◆

Pictures of the pastors at the church in Taquara. The portrait of Erik's father is on the bottom left.

Part Seven

Indonesia
2005

After the tsunami of December 26, 2004, I think about going somewhere in Asia to provide medical care for victims. An opportunity presents itself and I make plans. Erik, of course, is willing to participate and we put together a small group from the Denver area to join a larger Texas-based team. We travel to a remote island, Nias, in the Indian Ocean. The team, consisting of three doctors, three dentists and support crew, sees about 3,000 patients, many quite ill or severely injured. It is exhausting, frightening at times, and life-changing.

△◆
Chapter One
△◆

The tsunami hits Asia on December 26, 2004. Like many people, I remember the moment I heard the news: Erik and I were driving through the Midwest on our way home to Colorado after spending Christmas with his parents in Minnesota. It is the worst disaster to hit Asia in my lifetime. The death toll will grow to well over 250,000. The destruction is beyond my capacity to imagine. For weeks, the TV news stations all show video of the waves, with people, vehicles and parts of buildings being tossed around like toys. The stories of personal loss and survival keep me riveted.

A few days after the disaster I am struggling to push back the increasingly strong sense that I must go. Eventually I allow the jumble in my brain to gel and actually verbalize the thought that I would like to go to Asia and help. I was in Malaysia last year for an Ironman triathlon, and Viet Nam three years earlier with a medical team. I have traveled to Japan, Korea, Thailand, and Hong Kong, and have a strong love for Asia.

At Erik's urging I call *Doctors Without Borders*. Their pre-recorded message says they have enough doctors for this event, even enough monetary donations, and refers me to the online application – for "next time." In fairness, it is appropriate that they not take just any doctor off the street, but screen their physicians carefully. For me, though, I take it as an indication that I am not meant to go to Asia at this time. Being an "everything happens for a reason" kind of person, I almost immediately say, "Well, maybe in a few months I'll get a chance to go. There will be enormous need then, when the long-term consequences of this disaster are present. I'm pretty busy now anyhow." Resigned to not going to Asia, I sleep well.

Twelve hours after my call to *Doctors Without Borders*, at about eight o'clock the next morning, I get a call from someone who has overheard a phone call about a group forming to go to an island in Indonesia on a medical relief trip.

So, once again in my comfortable Colorado home, that constant reminder about who really is in charge of my life. I had just surrendered the prior night and decided not to look further for opportunities to get involved with tsunami relief. Then, an opportunity is simply offered to me. The connections with this group, based in Texas, seem so random that I am sure "random" is another one of

God's aliases.

After talking to the trip leader in Texas, I decide that I want to go, especially since this relief trip is not going until the end of February. Hadn't I said just the night before that there will be a need for help in several months?

Erik is completely unsuspecting when he returns home that evening and I greet him with, "I'm going to Indonesia, want to come?" Similar questions have been posed to him over our sixteen years of marriage and are not unacceptable, or even especially surprising. I have a lot of processing to do to make the final decision. We have to raise money, especially if two of us are to go and having recently sold my medical practice, I have to justify not working at any of my part-time endeavors during the weeks I will be gone and while I'm preparing to leave. There are also all the usual scheduled events to deal with, from paying the mortgage and other bills, to attending various professional and social engagements.

The noise between my ears is getting louder, not yet organizing. I know it will change from the initial overwhelming feeling like my thoughts are all in a mixer being whirled around and splattered out. I fondly refer to this state as "Blender Brain!" Soon my inner scientist will kick in and I will be on fast forward, methodically doing what needs to be done, doing my part to put pieces in place.

I think I know from the first minutes of hearing about the opportunity that I will go, but I have to allow myself to actually choose, giving myself permission to either go, or not. And I need to gather more information. Am I the only doctor on this trip? In my initial conversation with the trip leader, that is the case. He will be looking for others, though, so there could be several. Who else is signing on and how many? Will I have any support such as nurses, medical assistants, equipment? What about safety? How much money do I need? Erik is not committed to going and questions taking time off from work, especially since we have just returned from a twelve-day road trip to visit his family in Minnesota for Christmas. And one of my daughters questions the safety: "Another wave could come."

I do get immediate support from lots of people. Several say that when they heard about the tsunami they figured I would go, although they didn't know to which country since many were hit by this one disaster. They all suspect I will find a way to get there and be of some service and none are surprised to hear that I am about to sign up for a trip. My friends and family know me so well – their comments are rays of warm sunshine on my face.

One comment, however, stands out because it feels more like a punch in the gut. The speaker is an overweight physician who has a medical practice in weight control! And while he camouflages his borderline obesity well in work clothes, it is obvious at the gym. The irony is that he takes money from people who go to him for help. To be truthful, I know a number of people who have done well in his program, undoubtedly due to the structure of any program and his excellent nutritionist. This aside, I have no idea where his fear comes from, when he responds, "Why would you want to do that? They don't like little white girls over there. You'll come home in a box!"

I am stunned at his sick thoughts, his fear and poor judgment in saying out loud something so negative, prejudicial and distorted. I am embarrassed for him, ashamed of a member of my profession, a member of the human race for that matter, for being so myopic, close-minded and judgmental. I can picture him at the gym where we both work out and feel sad for his self-absorption and self-righteousness. I thank God that I have the ego strength to consider the source.

That evening I process his words in my regular Thursday night spiritual support group. Random people, representing a wide range of ages, educational and socioeconomic groups, are uniformly shocked that anyone can be so insensitive and negative. Often feedback from this group includes people sharing their own experiences, strengths and hopes. One twenty-six-year-old, who has been in this group for more than ten years and is a single mother who has gone back to school, is especially appalled and says, "You know you're going to be so fine over there!" I retain her voice to drown out his.

My twenty-seven-year-old daughter, Brie, who is in graduate school in Connecticut and on a tight budget, sends one-hundred dollars. More important than the money is her strong show of approval, permission in a way, to go on this trip to the other side of the world. One of her longtime friends asks her how she feels about Erik and me going and if she's worried about our safety. When she responds that she doesn't like not being able to talk to us to know we are okay, her friend, Tonya, a young mother, and her husband, Jack, rent us a satellite phone for the trip – an amazingly thoughtful gift! We had never even considered it, assuming that we will have little or no communication with anyone after leaving the States. Now we can call any time.

Family members keep helping. Erik's sister in Chicago sends

a large donation and tells her church about it. The Sunday school class one of her sons attends does a fundraiser, raising more than seven-hundred dollars for us. Their confidence in us is overwhelming and Erik and I vow to be good stewards of the money; to be respectful of the gifts so freely given. One nephew calls and in a quiet, gentle voice says, "Uncle Erik, I am praying for you every night." That says it all. We are doing the right thing and are meant to go.

Individually and quietly, other members of Erik's family send support. Each of his other two sisters, neither of them wealthy, immediately mail substantial monetary contributions. His parents and several aunts and uncles, all retired and living on small, fixed incomes, also send money. We are especially touched by two checks from a married aunt and uncle, Susan and Arne, who are in their sixties and seventies and each managing their own retirement income. In one envelope they mail two separate checks, one from each of their own accounts. This same aunt is among the first to call us when, eight days after our return, another quake hits the exact spot where we have been stationed. It is clear that she is very involved in our trip on every level. I feel humbled by her awareness and her concern for how we must feel.

Several ladies from the locker room at my gym are really interested. Some make donations, others say they will keep me in their prayers; others just want to hear about the trip before and after.

One unexpected offer of money comes from Buff. I know she will be encouraging, but she and her family of four are career missionaries and live on very little money. Currently back in the States from South America for a year of furlough, she and I have been able to speak on the phone over the past year. Just the thought, the offer, the consideration of actually sending money to help gives me a sense of warmth. It confirms what I know more each day – that we are doing the right thing.

My friend Martha is a high-energy, redheaded retired high school art teacher, fifty-eight years old and going on thirty. One of my swim team friends for twenty years, we still see each other at the gym. A gifted artist, she is illustrating a "work in progress" we are doing together – a "daily inspiration" book with a reading for each day of the year, about physical health, getting the workout done, eating well, etc. She is all energy and often twinkles like an adolescent getting away with something. So, when she makes a short announcement about our plans at the end of a service at her church, she inspires people to get involved. They hand her cash and three-hundred-and-fifty dollars later, she hands it to me.

Another dear friend, Lori, asks what she can do to help. I don't know how she knows about my trip plans because I don't talk with her regularly, but I just love seeing her when I do, usually at some spiritual support group or another. Lori insists on helping and sends an email flyer to all her contacts, some of whom also are friends of mine. The next day I get a check from her and her husband, the day after that another from a mutual friend, and the next day, four more checks. She also sends the flyer to her husband's law office that he shares with other attorneys and accountants.

Doors start to open wide. I email Lori's flyer to most of my contact list and print off some to take to local businesses. I never get around to actually posting any after getting some strange vibes from the first two businesses I approach. Email seems to be the better route since it can be either deleted or responded to so easily, and everyone will either know me or know which of my friends is sending the note. It's much more personal than a flyer posted where only strangers will see it.

Even my daughter's in-laws in California send money. Her brother-in-law, Ole, tries to get his donation matched by his company but our trip is so spontaneous that it appears there is not time to do so, and our organization is not officially tax-deductible. We ultimately find out from other potential donors that businesses will only match organizations on a specific list; the biggies like *Red Cross* and *Doctors Without Borders*. Our little group, still without a name, does not qualify for matching funds. Ultimately we join forces with a "parent organization," allowing contributions to be tax-deductible through a circuitous process. Five of my contributors who make large donations send checks through this parent organization.

The support keeps coming in and each day there is something in the mail or by phone. I even get several checks from people I don't know. One for ten dollars from Indiana is from a friend's father. Another for one-hundred dollars is from someone in Alaska I can't track down. I have the name from the check, but no address or connecting information.

Some people are just not into it. They hear we are going, but cannot relate and are not interested. That's okay, a little grounding is good. Other things happen in the world when I am preoccupied with my own life; not everyone is going to care what I do, or be in a position to help.

Lots of donations and consistent verbal support come from

people in our recovery and spiritual support groups. While meeting topics are about recovery, we also talk about what is going on in our lives, so when we start discussing our opportunity to go to Indonesia on a relief trip, we get enormous interest. People want to know details about where, when and how they can help. More donations just pour in, unsolicited. The recovering community is made up of people from all walks of life and in all stages of change, from addicts still using drugs to those who have been clean and sober many years and are extremely productive. Two things most of us have in common are gratitude for getting a second chance at life and desire to help others. This is never more obvious than during our preparation for this trip. One recovering nurse who works in the operating room of a large hospital brings me a huge trash bag full of intravenous supplies; needles, tubing and other equipment worth many hundreds of dollars. One friend gives me a prayer on a piece of paper. I carry it with me every day on the trip, a concrete reminder that people back home support what we are doing.

Since we haven't actually purchased our plane tickets, we are not officially committed to this trip. We could bail, send all of the donations to the group and let them go without us. Final decision time; time to "fish or cut bait," "poop or get off the pot." The expense is a big commitment; the time an enormous commitment; the danger, while minimal, is not zero. I know from past experience that I will get lots more than I give and decide that I am going. Erik is not so sure. Last year he went to Malaysia with me and had to refer a big sale to someone else, losing a significant amount of income and disappointing his client. Eventually he surrenders and decides to go for two weeks and return when half of the team will also be returning. I remember how far it is to the other side of the world and decide to stay for the entire three weeks.

I realize that while I'm there I will celebrate twenty-one years without a drink or a drug: March 9, 2005. I usually acknowledge my sobriety anniversary by attending a few more meetings than usual, seeing friends who attend other meetings across town and having a "birthday" cake at my main weekly meeting. On this trip I will not be going to meetings because there are none on the island, possibly none in the rest of the country. As a Muslim country, Indonesia is unlikely to have groups of recovering alcoholics, or especially drug addicts, congregating to talk about their past behavior and developing a relationship with a God who keeps them clean and sober. Of interest, though, is that last year we attended a recovery meeting in Kuala Lumpur, Malaysia, a country close in proximity but very different from Indonesia. This year I will celebrate without a meeting, but Erik will acknowledge the day.

Once I commit to going, I start collecting supplies; medical, dental, physical therapy and a few items of clothing and toys for children. We receive lots of samples of antibiotics, analgesics, blood pressure meds, and many others from my former office and the offices of several of my doctor friends. Even expired medications are useful. The expiration date almost never means the medicine won't work, but in the United States it is illegal to dispense outdated medicine, so we get a lot of recently expired samples. My podiatrist friend makes a large financial donation *and* sends us a box of medications, including lots of ointments. Several people donate their leftover prescriptions, medications they do not finish for one reason or another. One family gives us the narcotics not used by a family member who died of cancer several weeks earlier. My physical therapist friend collects and donates used braces, ace bandages and slings. Everyone wants to help.

Having learned in Honduras how to pull teeth from the local "dentist," a man who had only a third-grade education and learned how to do basic pain-relieving dentistry from other medical missionaries, I had not had the chance to do so in the U.S., of course, as a non-dentist, and with liability such a big deal. I need a refresher course for Indonesia. You just never know when the need to put a local anesthetic into someone's mouth and pull a tooth might arise. So far, there are only one dentist and two other doctors signed up for our trip and I might have to function as both for part of the time. I ask my friend, Dr. Jack, to let me observe in his office, especially to remind myself where to put the anesthesia to numb up different areas of the mouth. Dr. Jack has been to Papua New Guinea on dental mission trips at least five times. He is good, precise and fast. I even have the chance to practice on one of his patients, who is willing to let me inject the Novocain. Dr. Jack and his wife, his main office employee, send me off with renewed knowledge, lots of supplies donated at their expense, and the promise to keep a candle burning in the office to remind them to pray for me each day I am gone.

Days fly by as I communicate by email and phone with the trip leader in Texas, and with my ever-growing Colorado contingent. My friend Patty is an environmental geologist and the tsunami is of particular interest to people with her knowledge. She decides to go on the mission when she hears that returning after just two weeks is an option. Another friend who has been fundraising for me calls with a question about a friend of hers who would like to go. Nancy has no medical skills and no official job at this time either, so consequently no money to pay for the trip. What she does have is experience doing more things than any of the rest of us have so far. She calls herself a "caretaker," caretaking ranches, homes, animals and sick people. She has worked as an emergency medical technician, massage therapist, carpenter, fisherperson in Alaska, and in lots of other professions, and seems perfect for this trip. The money will come – and it does, from donations made on her behalf by people in her small mountain town, especially from one of the churches. Our Colorado team grows more with Gail, a nutritionist who, when asked to donate says, "I don't want to donate, I want to go!" She joins us, as does our main fundraiser's husband, Larry, an English teacher at an independent school. Lots of parents at his school donate and some of the students do their own fundraisers. We now have a Colorado contingent of six.

My living room and front hallway are walltowall medications. Most of my hours and days are now spent collecting supplies, researching what we will need and where to get the best deals. A wonderful organization, the faithbased Medical Assistance Programs, MAP International, sells nearlyoutdated medications, donated by pharmaceutical companies from their overstock, to medical missionaries who promise to take the medicines out of the country. Keeping them here would compete with new medicines being manufactured every day, and dispensing them is illegal anyhow. I am able to get eight *thousand* dollars worth of medicines and supplies, packed especially for tsunami relief trips, for only eight *hundred* dollars. These, and other donations, start to fill up my home. By now I know the routine well – combine these small quantities of pills or capsules into appropriate doses, a full course of medicine in each container. Friends who visit me during January and February sit on my living room floor and pack pills – I am *such* a good hostess.

Packing personal items is an afterthought. I will need some clothes, shoes, my personal medications (asthma inhalers, thyroid medication, maybe some Tylenol). I will take a toothbrush even though we have had hundreds donated for distribution to the Indonesian people. A bathing suit might come in handy, just in case we get a few hours off, and a few nonmedical things to read, especially on the plane. We will be on the Equator, so it will be hot and humid. I will take loose, lightweight clothing and respect the custom of

women covering their legs – shorts will be acceptable around the hotel. I will also need to pack food for the flights and decide to throw in
crackers, cheese, fruit and several-dozen of my special homemade
oatmeal-raisin-chocolate-chip-pecan cookies to share with my new
best friends – I am confident that most of the team members will become friends. Living with people twenty-four hours a day is a sure
way to get to know them, so we'd better all become friends. All my
personal items for the three weeks will go in my carry-on bag – I
save the entire weight allowance for checked bags containing medical supplies. No problem, I am small, my clothes are small, and if it
doesn't fit in the bag, I probably don't need it. Erik is another story –
he and his clothing and shoes are big. We determine that we can
throw our extra shoes in with some of the medical supplies and retrieve them in Indonesia.

△◆

Chapter Two

△◆

Most of the team members are from Texas and several have
worked together on medical mission trips to Belize. This team to Indonesia becomes the "TEARS" (Tsunami Earthquake American Relief Services) team. The trip leader has been able to get very inexpensive flights on China Airlines because there are more than twenty of
us. China Airlines has also agreed to not charge for excess baggage,
our more than six-thousand pounds of equipment, especially heavy
dental equipment. At the last minute, two Philippine dentists commit to meeting us in Indonesia. They have been in Sri Lanka doing
tsunami relief work and are willing to come straight to Indonesia.

In spite of being seemingly disorganized (but who knows just
how much work he is doing on short notice; all things considered, he
is probably very organized), our trip leader accomplishes an enormous amount in a few weeks and has some amazing contacts. Still,
he is unable to give me flight information from China Airlines, specifically whether or not the flight stops in Seattle for possible boarding, or if it's just refueling, or if it stops in Seattle on the return
flight. If the flight stops in Seattle, the Colorado group could go from
Denver to Seattle, obviating the need to go Denver-Houston-Seattle,
and saving us almost a day's worth of precious time. The outcome is
that our six from Colorado have to fly to Houston the morning of our
departure and wait there for an evening departure to Asia, then fly

over Denver on the way from Houston to Seattle, our last stop before crossing the Pacific to Taipei. We are all so excited and full of energy for the trip that no one cares we are spending this extra day by going to Houston.

It turns out that the day in the Houston airport is okay. We are able to help tag the hundreds of pieces of equipment and get to know our team members a little. We also eat dinner in the airport, our last American meal for three weeks. We make the last of the phone calls to family in this country; Patty is worried about her dogs because one of them is sick and she even considers not going on the trip. We reassure her that her sister and father can take care of the animals for two weeks. Erik and I talk to our daughters and tell them we will use the satellite phone to call if we can, but to not worry if they do not hear from us. We may be so remote that we will have no contact at all.

At last we're at the gate for our China Airlines flight, where we have a team meeting and each do formal introductions, saying how we got involved with this group and relating our experience and credentials. The twenty-some people make up what seems like a huge group, in part because I only know the six from Colorado. Even more group members, Indonesian nationals, will join us when we get to Medan, the largest city on the island of Sumatra, Indonesia. I share my cookies and make friends immediately. These are my special cookies – the secret ingredients are love and all the memories of making them as a medical student with my former roommate, Carole who is now a psychiatrist and still a close friend. We used them to get through sleepless nights studying, exams, breakups with boyfriends, and parties. I fed cookies from the same recipe to my children and their friends at every stage of their growing up and my now adult children still ask me to make them. They work every time, in this case as an easy introduction to my teammates.

The others on the team have varied experiences; nurses, engineers, a young couple married two months earlier – she is a teacher for special needs children and he works in construction. Anyone willing to work, and be flexible, can be helpful on a trip like this.

We will be joined in Indonesia by additional team members including several American missionaries who have lived in Indonesia and who will serve as interpreters. Our trip leader, Jim Karl, having lived in Indonesia for several years, has connections with many locals. Some of them have lived in the U.S. and will translate and negotiate everything from transportation on buses and in cars, to pur-

chasing supplies. Jim also has connections with Indonesian government officials and will be signing a contract to use and staff a pre-
World War II hospital for the next twenty-five years. We are off on
an adventure that may have far-reaching consequences over many
years. I am having a sort of "out of body" experience. I feel like I am in
another lifetime, living the "Albert Schweitzer" life of a jungle doctor,
caring for people in another culture. Am I twelve again? I am so excited!

    The flight is like any other over the Pacific – very long. Most
of us sleep at least a few hours, some read and we all talk to each
other and begin to form friendships. Erik and I enjoy the Chinese
food on the flight and are looking forward to eating a variety of Asian
foods over the next few weeks – the newer and more different, the
better. We have never had any problems with food anywhere else in
Asia, choosing smaller, family-run restaurants and freshly prepared
dishes. Often we see the fresh vegetables and fish or meat through
the open space between kitchens and dining areas in these tiny es-
tablishments. I don't know what the food situation is since the recent
disaster, but I'm not worried. I expect there will be enterprising people starting up restaurants from nothing, or acquiring vending carts
and starting a business as soon as the last wave is gone. I have been
in Asia enough to know the work ethic and creativity of the people.

    There are people in our mission group who have never been
outside of the U.S. and only a few have been to Asia. I feel like an
old-timer as this is my fifth trip to this part of the world; once to Viet
Nam on a medical trip, to Malaysia for a triathlon, and two family
vacations, one to Thailand and one to Japan, Korea and Hong Kong.
The whole family, all four of us, were in nearby Perth, Australia, in
2000 when I was on the U.S.A. Triathlon team competing in the
amateur World Championships. I've been to other parts of the world,
too, but none have my heart the way Asia does. The beaches in Thailand and Malaysia are incomparable. The islands are all slightly different from each other. The people have a special energy, a desire to
be with us and help us feel welcome. I have memories of almost everyone on my previous trips being friendly and helpful. Most assume
we want to be with them, to spend our time with them, perhaps seeing part of their country, doing some activity, but always with them.
They are so proud of their country, their families and their few possessions. They have so little and want to share it all. The cook in the
Malaysian hotel where I stayed came out of the kitchen every time I
came to the dining room for meals. He talked me through the buffet
line during every lunch and dinner, helping me to understand all the

ingredients of each dish, so I was not fearful of eating something with preservatives.

The next day, more than twenty-four hours after leaving Colorado, we arrive in Taipei, Taiwan. China Airlines is giving us a twenty-four-hour layover here including a hotel stay and tour of the city. The friendliness and willingness to help that the airline demonstrates is very impressive: the free excess baggage is a huge savings, and now the free tour of Taipei. Since Erik and I have spent many hours in the Taipei airport and never seen the city, we are looking forward to this part of the trip. Taipei is the regular refueling and crew-changing stop for most flights from the U.S. to Asia. The usual deal is that all passengers disembark, in what is the middle of the night for the biological clocks of anyone who sleeps nights in the U.S., take all carry-on items with them, and get confined to the airport. No one has Taiwanese money, so buying anything to eat is almost impossible. If someone either finds a place to change money, or talks some vendor into taking U.S. currency, the next issue is to find some recognizable or at least palatable-appearing food. All the while, either leaving someone else with the luggage or lugging (wow, I just realized this must be where the name *luggage* comes from) everything up the escalator and down the very long corridors. On most of our previous stops, this was all too frustrating to deal with, so we sat in the waiting room in those fold-up chairs that are attached in groups of six, like the type that used to be in old movie theatres. I remember one trip when I found myself a corner of the waiting room and was able to lie down on the floor and get almost comfortable during the two-hour layover.

This time, we go to baggage claim and actually exit the airport. Finding coffee in the terminal on the way to our bus, we begin the process of changing our internal clocks to daytime – it is noon in Taipei, midnight at home. The experience of Asia is so familiar to me. I feel like I am back to a place I have come to love and appreciate; a place that occupies a spot in my heart that is starting to warm up again. Taipei is an enormous city, in many ways like Seoul, South Korea, the bustling international port of Hong Kong, and the still-communist Ho Chi Minh City, South Viet Nam. Although unlike the small Thai villages we had visited ten years earlier, Taipei feels like all of these Asian places from my past.

The hour-long bus ride through the city to the hotel selected by China Airlines provides a feast for our eyes. Signs in Taiwanese, some with English subtitles, announce every possible store, shop, industry and eating establishment. Some are similar to those in the U.S.; and some are just different enough to attract our attention. There is a fried chicken restaurant with colors similar to an American chain, but looking just enough different to provoke laughter among the Americans.

Once settled into our hotel rooms, we fight off sleep and decide to go for a walk. Maybe daylight and movement will trick our bodies into believing that it is afternoon, not early morning. The bus tour is anticlimactic, but a nice gesture; and we do get to see the attractions of the city, including the Chaing Kai Shek Memorial. The history teacher in our group and Erik, with his political science degree, have some conversation about this. I am just so glad to be back in Asia and almost to Indonesia that I don't have much of a reaction.

Next morning, off to Indonesia. Another eight hours of travel, a layover in a Malaysian airport, and on to Medan, the large city in northern Sumatra, Indonesia. Here we are met by several Indonesian team members. We change money into Indonesian *rupiah*, about nine-thousand *rupiah* to the dollar. We are rich, with millions of *rupiah*! Our American dollars will go a long way, but we have a long way to go. It does feel good to know we can spend as much as we want on food, even extra clothes, and not have to worry. The most expensive meal in this country, at least in any part we will be in, won't be more than a few dollars. We see all of our supplies get unloaded from the plane and put onto a truck. The truck will leave tomorrow, escorted by two of our Indonesian teammates, for the overland trek of at least a full day to the ferry on the west Sumatran coast. From there, an overnight ferry will bring supplies and people to Nias, our island destination. Some of us volunteer to go overland with the supplies, but are told that it is not the safest for American men, totally unsafe for women (not to mention that the overnight ferry has no bathroom facilities), and only marginally safe for our male Indonesian team members. They are going with the supplies anyhow. Belongings are sometimes known to *"hilong"* or "evaporate" in Indonesia. We have valuable medical and dental supplies and do not want them to *"hilong."* Andrew and Margunda manage to guard themselves and our supplies and all arrive safely in Nias.

△◆
Chapter Three
△◆

Dizzy from three days of travel, running on adrenaline, and suspecting I look like a wide-eyed child, I am excited to see this country and its people, to meet our Indonesian teammates and just be here and in the moment. I have not seen any of the wreckage from the tsunami yet, don't have to think medically yet, and am able to just feel the reality that we are finally here.

Organizing which bags go where is monumental; what do we take for clinic the next afternoon, will we have the quantities and types of medicines we need for the illnesses we will see, or will some valuable item be somewhere in northern Sumatra, in a duffel bag on a truck, when we could use it now? We do the best we can. We have been traveling for three days; have only the personal items and clothing we packed in our carry-on bags; and are twelve hours "upside-down" in time.

The evening in Medan is the last time we are sure we can communicate with home. There is an Internet café in the hotel and it's possible to buy phone cards. Our satellite phone works! Our daughters are glad to hear from us and all is well at home. Lannie, an important Indonesian team member who speaks perfect English as she has lived in Texas for eight years and is married to a Brit, has planned an evening in Medan for us. She takes us to a shopping district, then to a "food court" or fair in the street for dinner. Vendors sell local delicacies such as fried rice, noodle dishes, and python. The atmosphere is party-like; friendly people, twosomes holding hands, parents with children, teenagers telling secrets to each other and laughing, many stopping at carts smelling of hot oil and chili. Larry and Erik try the python – of course, they declare it tastes like chicken. I taste several delicacies, some spicy, some sweet.

Patty and I, swimmers to the core, want to use the hotel pool which closes at eight, so we decide to go back earlier than the rest of the group. Nancy wants to come with us. We find a local taxi driver to take us, in his version of a taxi; a three-wheeled, open vehicle attached to his motorcycle. The "taxi" is old enough to have some rust, but everything in island countries does. Deciding the cart is stable enough to be safe, just a little rickety, and the motorcycle functional, we agree to ride. The bench is made for two riders, but we are determined to get all three of us in. I crouch on the floor in front of the other two, holding the front railing. This is the perfect position for me to imitate those guttural car sounds that Erik is really good at making. As we leave the quiet side street and enter the six lanes of traffic on the main highway, the only appropriate response is to *"nyewww"* and *"rmrrmrmmum"* along with the motorcycle, leaning in the direction dictated by the lean and turns of the "taxi" and waving to other motorists. Erik would be so proud. He will be even prouder, and definitely happier, if we get back to the hotel safely.

As in most Asian cities, there are no lane lines. I don't know how they have so few accidents. We weave in and out of traffic, riding within inches of the much larger vehicles next to us, never actually touching them. Our driver is not only very cautious, but clearly enjoying attracting lots of attention with three silly American women (in our forties and fifties), laughing, waving and making motor noises.

I am aware of a new layer of city grime on my skin. I can't separate the feel on my body from the gut-level sensation I get from the sounds, sights and smells of the city. Dank, sticky aromas of wonderful spices, cumin, chili, soy, peanuts and more, mix with motorcycle, auto and bus fumes. The city lights are bright as darkness moves in, and we hear horns, screeches and shouts of drivers in pretend fury at being cut off by a smaller, faster vehicle. The *motos*, small motorcycles, sound like enormous metallic mosquitoes, zipping in and out between vehicles that could squash them instantly. Ah, an Asian city. I am happy to be here, even knowing I am inhaling sulfite-infused air from the traffic. It's only for a day; my lungs will tolerate it and soon I will be in a small town without pollution, ocean air filling my lungs. Our driver grins and looks at us in a paternal sort of way and delivers us safely to our hotel.

After a refreshing swim in the outdoor pool, Nancy, Patty and I go to the hotel restaurant and, coincidentally (God again) meet up with Dr. Derek from New Zealand. He is in the hotel for a night on his way back to the hospital where he works on Nias. This is our first contact with a physician who is actually working with the people on the island. He has devoted his career to Third World medicine, caring for people who live in places where there is no access to regular medical help. He currently goes to several different islands in this part of the world and plans to be on Nias intermittently for the next two years. We learn from him about the needs of the people, some specific problems since the tsunami; respiratory and other infections, dermatitis, untreated or poorly treated and poorly healing injuries,

but more ongoing issues of untreated illnesses such as thyroid disease, massive infections of feet and legs, asthma, ear infections, lack
of medication, lack of iodine in the food resulting in goiter, poor nutrition, lack of prenatal care, infant mortality, lack of treatment for
accidents, and on and on. We will be on a different part of the island
from Dr. Derek, but hope to maintain contact with him as he is
clearly the best resource we have.

It seems like we have been on the "Never Ending Journey."
Stop, start, wait and do it again. We have come to expect regular de-
lays of an hour or more on arrival anywhere. On finally arriving on
Nias, where we are going to set up medical/dental/eyeglass clinics,
we wait for Jim to fulfill his leadership role by schmoozing with Indonesian officials and continue his goal of making our group known
and accepted. The outcome of this hobnobbing will be a twenty-five-
year contract to work in the hospital in Hilisamaetano. So, twenty-
some American adults and a half-dozen Indonesian team members
hang around in a building without air conditioning or cold drinks
after three days of start-stop travel while Jim does his political stuff.
Then we get into buses and go to the hotel. After another hour or two
wait while the hotel staff stalls about our rooms, we learn they do
not have the reservations Jim made on his scouting trip in January.
The hotel has only three rooms available with air conditioning, several more with fan only. Jim scrounges for another hotel only a few
miles away that has more rooms with air conditioning. It is ninety-
five degrees and humid, still oppressive heat, mosquitoes already
starting in on me. I am among the six percent or so of the world's
population described as "mosquito magnets." They come after me
when no one else seems to be of interest. They bite me through the
ninety-nine percent DEET contained in my Jungle Juice. Erik and I
are also both asthmatics. His entire family left the mission field in
Brazil when he was eleven years old, returning to live in Minnesota,
a better climate for his asthma, and with better medical care. He cannot tolerate the pollen in tropical cultures without asthma medications,
something he does not always need in clearer breathing conditions.

Five of the single women work out a way to share one of the
air-conditioned rooms by creating a dorm room-style arrangement
with two sleeping in the double bed and three on mats on the floor.
Five of the single men copy their idea and one couple gets the third
room with air conditioning. Several other individuals opt for a single
room with fan only. All agree that the conditions are not ideal but
tolerable. Along with four other couples and two additional women,

Erik and I move again after dinner to another hotel, again to wait and sort out who gets what room. Grateful we are able to obtain an air-conditioned room, I find this other hotel to be very pleasant and quiet, with the bonus of lots of geckos, mosquito-eating machines! Each room is simple with its own entrance along a pathway, attached in groupings of three or four, wicker furniture, plain bed, thin but comfortable mattress, and old but clean towels and bedding. Our new hotel welcomes us.

△◆

Chapter Four

△◆

Day number two on Nias and the team splits up. My group goes to a refugee camp on the northwest coast, an area hit hard by the tsunami. The other team members travel south, holding an impromptu clinic in one community along the way, and then arriving at the hotel where we will spend most of the next two weeks. Our group, heading across the island, will return this evening to spend one more night in the hotel in the city of Gunung-Sitoli. This means, of course, that those of us who were in the secondary hotel get to move back to the initial hotel since half the team is gone and now some rooms with air conditioning have opened up. By tonight, the fifth night I have been gone from the United States, I will have slept in five different places.

My group boards the bus for the trip across the island and I climb into the back with four others. Erik is up front, six rows away from us, where he has unwisely chosen a seat with leg room designed for an Indonesian. At six-foot-two, Erik is about a foot taller than most Indonesian men. There are disadvantages to each seat. In the back, the two seats facing each other have lots of leg room between them. This area is also used for some of our smaller packs and boxes, while most of our supplies are on top of the bus or in a pickup truck that goes with us. The disadvantage to the back-of-the-bus seating is the bounce. The island vehicles are old and appear even older due to the heat, humidity and very rough, predominantly dirt roads, and a large measure of overuse. The bounce, the most noticeable part of bus travel, is far more pronounced in the back. Anyone prone to car sickness finds it is aggravated in these seats, especially for those sitting in the rear-facing seats and riding backward. The major issue in the back is that passengers bounce so much that the taller ones hit their heads on the ceiling when we go over bumps. The road to Sirombu is essentially one bump connected to the next. Two of the taller men in the back manage to be repeatedly jarred vertically into the ceiling, their heads connecting with a loud thump, and even louder expletives.

After about an hour and a half, we stop to check out a part of the road to see if it is passable. "Patty, let's find the ladies' room," are the first words out of my mouth when I realize our very slow moving has ceased and we are fully stopped. I use the term "ladies' room" jokingly throughout the next few weeks. In this case, it's up a hillside about twenty-five yards and around enough corners and trees to be hidden from the road below. Others go off in different directions to find their idea of a "facility," often a larger tree or a particularly attractive hill. Patty and I have known each other for almost twenty years and have had many opportunities to check out "ladies' rooms" together. We were on a master's swim team together for many years, each of us competing in our own events and cheering on the other. We've both climbed all fifty-four of Colorado's fourteen-thousand-foot mountains, about half of them together. This has allowed us multiple camping experiences, from trucks at mountain bases to tents and backpacking together for miles. We have climbed together in heat, cold, rain, snow and sleet. We have been caught in snowstorms in July and electrical storms in August. Running up a hill into an Indonesian jungle while a bus waits on a barely passable dirt road below is just one more adventure. Certainly there is a ladies' room up here somewhere.

The Indonesian driver and crew walk about one-hundred yards ahead and evaluate the road. Some of the American men join them and they all start moving rocks into place, building up the edge of the road so the width will accommodate the width of our bus. Great, this is reassuring! Déjà vu, Honduras. I am thankful the driver stopped. Several of us opt for a walk over the newly constructed portion of the road. I will get back on the bus *after* it passes the narrow section.

Back on the bus. As a child of the '60s, I am reminded of Ken Kesey's saying, "You're either on the bus or off the bus." We are definitely *on* the bus, literally and figuratively. We are exactly halfway around the world; with one finger on Denver on a globe, the other on Nias, draw a line through and connect the two points and you have bisected the globe exactly. One of the surprising things at this point is that even though our trip across Nias appears to be about twenty miles, add another five for winding roads, and an imperfect map, we have now been traveling for an hour and a half and are about half-way there. This is slow travel. We are in a jungle. The sounds are buzzing and high-pitched shrieks and chirps of insects, amphibians and birds. The road is the low point during most of our travel, the hills rising up on each side of us. There are dozens, probably hundreds, of different kinds of trees, bushes, and flowers, and thick, sticky moisture in the air.

Another hour plus of bouncing around and we start to see an increase in the density of houses, people walking along the road, one "house" with five or six small tables on the porch. It's a restaurant! No signs, but there's a glass-covered food case, a counter big enough to hold the cash register and eight or ten people hanging around in front, staring as we go by.

A few minutes later the bus pulls into a parking lot in front of a large old church. There are several tents in the field to the right, the remains of a refugee camp set up two months ago after the tsunami hit. Throngs of people gather in the driveway and parking lot. Someone breaks the padlock holding closed the enormous pair of doors on the front of the church. The crowd parts to let us off the bus as we bravely disembark. With no sense of privacy or personal space, the Indonesians stand back only enough for us to pick our way slowly through the crowd and the short distance from the bus to the church doors seems like a long way as dark, smiling faces watch closely. I sense some internal trepidation. These hopeful people have such expectations. They are so trusting and welcoming. Will I have anything to offer? Is anyone sick or injured with something I can fix? There are so many people here. Will I be able to communicate? Wouldn't it be more useful if I could just rebuild a few thousand houses? But I am not a construction worker – I am a doctor. It's time to trust again. God has me here for a reason. I keep forgetting this part. I'm not alone; there is a God, and it's not me. He is in charge of my life. I just do the footwork, show up, even in a church on a remote side of a remote island in a country of tens of thousands of islands where I don't speak the language, have no laboratory or x-ray facilities, much less surgical capacity. Here I am.

Friendly greetings in a language I have never heard until forty-eight hours ago are coming from everyone. Children are grinning and pointing, women touch our arms as we pass. The inside of the church is dark, layers of dust on windowsills and that closed up, moldy, yet near-the-ocean feel and smell. More evidence of the humid climate is apparent in the deteriorating wood and mold-splotched wall. I do not know how long it has been since this church was used or if this layer of grime is just part of living here and people actually do occupy the pews on Sundays. Or has the church been closed for the two months since the tsunami hit? Even though most will rebuild eventually, many of the locals whose homes were destroyed went to stay with extended family living farther inland.

We accept the conditions and start to set up our consultation and work areas in the front of the church. Two stairs divide a large floor space into two levels. We put our duffel bags and supplies on the upper level and, being American, stake out our personal spaces. The two Philippine dentists on our team need the most light so they put their chairs – red, plastic lawn-type chairs now promoted to "dental chairs" – near the open side door so patients can sit facing the daylight. The other doctor and I each arrange a circle of three plastic or straight-back wooden chairs for our "offices." We each find someone to interpret for us, find our stethoscopes and procure a pen and pad of paper for patient records. The "pharmacy" is set up opposite the dentists, with only a window providing light on that side of the church. Our patients walk down the long aisles from the back of the church, "screened" by mostly non-medical team members. A few words describing why they want to see the doctor or dentist are at the top of a sheet of paper they each carry.

It is quickly apparent that my Indonesian interpreter, Andrew, while well-meaning and volunteering his time for these weeks to work with us, speaks only very basic English. Like many who learn a foreign language in school but never travel to a place where it is spoken, he can understand some of what I say if I speak slowly and clearly, but he misses the context much of the time. He knows some words and phrases but most of them are non-medical and do not apply to our situation. Lack of accuracy in conveying back to me what a patient says can thwart good medical care and even be dangerous.

We muddle through the first few patients: an old man with arthritis who can benefit enormously from ibuprofen and we have plenty to give him; a father and his young son, both with abdominal pain. Better treat both for worms as well as for acid reflux in the father. A young woman is next when Andrew gets up and leaves without explanation. I wait for a minute, trying "sign language" with my patient and wondering if Andrew had to go to the bathroom, had a sudden onset of some illness or is perhaps too shy and finding it politically incorrect to interpret for a young woman. He eventually returns and after this happens several times and the communication goes from bad to useless, I request a change in helpers.

Someone explains to Andrew that for me to work, he has to stay with me. I am useless as a doctor if I do not know why the patient is here and what the symptoms are. Only then does Andrew acknowledge that he doesn't speak Nias, the language spoken on the island by all but the educated men and a very few educated women. It is a separate language, not just a dialect, and Indonesians who don't live here do not speak it. There are more than seventeen-thousand islands that make up Indonesia and many of them have different languages or dialects. The official language of the country is Bahasa Indonesian, which is taught in school, but most girls drop out of school before they learn it and only the older boys and men speak it. Andrew can communicate with the first few patients, men who speak Indonesian, but not with the women. Was he off looking for help? Or maybe just hiding, hoping I would not notice he was gone? One of the lessons of the day is about a somewhat objectionable trait I already see in Indonesian men – they do not like to ask for help. Not unusual for men anywhere, but the difference is that rather than admit that they do not know something, they pretend that they do. They truly want to help, but simply cannot speak enough English or Nias to find what is needed and cannot seem to tell us, so we are left thinking that they are doing what we request and only find later that they are not.

The solution to the interpreting problem is either to find someone who speaks Nias and English, which is rare, or have two interpreters, one who can translate from Nias to Bahasa Indonesian, and another from Indonesian to English. I hit the jackpot and find a young man of twenty-three years old, dressed in military camouflage, who speaks both Nias and English. The rest of the day goes more smoothly.

We treat patients with dermatitis, arthritis, headaches and abdominal pains. Most children are treated for worms. They are assumed to have them unless proven otherwise and we have no lab to check for proof, which requires a stool sample, microscope, staining material, slides and time. Lots of people have respiratory illnesses. Since the December twenty-sixth tsunami, there have been many fires built on the island to burn the debris and the bodies. This is especially aggravating to the lungs of those who have chronic obstructive pulmonary disease or asthma, most of whom are also smokers. Almost all of the men and boys and some of the women smoke cigarettes. Lots of people need to be treated for asthma, emphysema, bronchitis and pneumonia. The strangest things I see are the red mouths. Most men and some women have red tongues, lips and even staining on their teeth from chewing Betel nut.

Betel chewing produces a high, a sense of well-being and euphoria, and like other stimulants, a heightened alertness and increased capacity to work. It sounds similar to cocaine, my former "drug of choice," and we are told it also causes sweating, salivation and a hot sensation in the body. I am so grateful to be free from addiction. I have absolutely no compulsion to use any mind-altering substance, no interest in getting high. I do, however, have a curiosity about the effects of the Betel nut; thankfully, not enough curiosity to consider trying it, taking the risk of liking it and setting up the cycle of drug craving I remember so well.

While in Indonesia, we see many red mouths. Several people proudly tell us they have been able to get off of Betel nut, alcohol and cigarettes; others acknowledge they are struggling to stop. Betel nut is very addictive and part of the difficulty in stopping comes from the ease in acquiring the drug and the almost uniform acceptance. It is obvious from their detached behavior that many of the men and women we see in the clinic and elsewhere are high on this drug. I am thankful to be *present,* not detached and high.

It has been raining on and off and overcast much of the afternoon. The temperature seems to have dropped a few degrees, helping to ease us into this tropical climate. The end of the work day at the church clinic comes with sunset. The dentists can no longer see adequately. Flashlights and headlamps help somewhat but it's really time to stop and pack up. We have seen as many patients as we can effectively see, for most of us probably two or three times what we see in a normal office day in the States. Some people arrive after we stop signing in new patients. The triage crew in front stops taking new people at three o'clock and we work at least three hours longer just to see those who are in line by that time. As the day goes on, word spreads that doctors, dentists and eyeglass techs are in town and people come, most on foot, from every direction. There are clusters of huts down footpaths, up hills and in places well hidden from our sight.

Since the tsunami, there have been aid groups from several places in the world coming for a day or a week. Germany, Holland and the United States have all had a big presence. The locals know that we have medicines and supplies and that there is no cost. Some are tsunami victims but most that were caught in the disaster are either healing or dead. We see a few, especially those with respiratory illness or healing wounds, but most of our business comes in the form of those who need routine medical care. There is no regular doctor on this part of the island. There is bus service to Gunung-Sitoli, about a four-hour trip, for the tiny percent of the island's population who can afford the travel and then afford to pay for a doctor visit and medications. We are told that there are twenty doctors on this island with a population of six-hundred-thousand. I wonder who counts how many people live here and am skeptical of the accuracy.

The island of Nias is seventy-five miles long and twenty-five miles wide with villages consisting of clusters of a few huts each. The island's population is spread into about six-hundred-fifty of these villages, most inaccessible by road. Tiny shacks in the jungle, some barely more than lean-tos, appear old and in disrepair. The constant battering by sea water and salt air takes its toll and it's impossible to know the age of these dwellings. Typically, several generations live in one or two rooms, dirt floor the usual, occasional slabs of cement providing flooring in some. Children play outside each hut, toddlers partially hidden in tall grasses and weeds, no toys visible. Rarely do we see anything but smiles and a little dirt on these small faces. These families love their children just like families everywhere; there is no doubt when we see their happiness, clearly unrelated to lack of material wealth.

A few buildings provide contrast to the majority of the housing. Occasional two-story houses, a remnant from the Dutch Colonial period, still remain. None appear occupied and we never meet anyone who knows more about them, or their possible inhabitants.

It does not matter how many people live on the island. What is in front of us now is a long line of people wanting help for their pain, cough, fever, wounds and skin infections. What happens when no volunteer groups are here the other three hundred-plus days of the year, before the tsunami brought this remote place to the attention of the rest of the world? These dark-skinned, brown-eyed people are uniformly humble, thanking me profusely for the small amount of aspirin, acetaminophen, ibuprofen, antibiotic ointment or antibiotic pills and liquid for their children. It is only in this type of culture, these places in the world where there is no doctor, that I do so little for my patients and get such appreciation.

At the end of this day the "pharmacy" still has antibiotics, antacids, anti-inflammatory medications and medicine to eradicate the ubiquitous worm infections and I am reluctant to leave even though the dentists are packing up because it is getting too dark for them to work. The two Philippine dentists look more like Indonesians than the tall, pale Americans who make up most of our team. With the confidence and purposefulness that distinguishes them easily, plus medical scrubs like the rest of the team, they make eye contact, speak perfect English and go about their business very efficiently. We have gotten to know each other a little by occasionally trading patients during the day. Mix-ups in triage send me some toothaches and some people with headaches to the dentists. Later we find out that these two dentists are committed to helping people in developing countries and do at least two volunteer mission trips every year.

So, with daylight running out, the dentists packing up, the pharmacy in a corner that is now dark, the other doctor and I surrender. We have seen everyone in line. Those who did not get to the line prior to the cutoff time won't be seen. I find out a week later that a group of Muslims arrived too late to be seen. This saddens me, as I want to promote tolerance and harmony between the different religions living in this same community on this island. The group's leader was angry that he didn't know medical help was coming. In fact, I don't believe anyone in the community knew in advance that we would be coming. Only those who see us arrive, and those who live close enough to get word that we are here and either walk or ride bicycles or motorcycles to our location are able to receive treatment. An effective way to find enough patients to fill a day for two doctors and two dentists, this system, or lack of system, is not necessarily fair or efficient. There are undoubtedly people who are much sicker and we don't see them because they don't know we are here or they can't get transportation to reach to us.

After saying goodbye to my last patient, I put my stethoscope away and go out the side door to the outhouse. Another cultural difference: no apparent need for a clean bathroom. I much prefer my hillside with fresh foliage, good smelling trees and plants. This small building houses a typical Asian toilet, the kind found in many European countries as well; simply a hole in the ground around which is a ceramic surface with ridged spots in the shape of footprints for standing on. Stand and squat, aim for the hole, be sure you have your own toilet tissue as there is never any, not even a place for it anywhere near these holes. This is not so bad, easy to get used to for those of us with good knees, but I wonder about the people with arthritis or those who are very overweight and out of shape. There are not many overweight Indonesians, and even fewer who have had knee surgery. Erik on the other hand, who is forty-seven years-old, has had four surgeries on one knee and is grateful for the Western toilets in the hotel. There must be some elderly in this country who do not squat easily. I guess if you do this every day all your life you get so good at it that you don't even notice a problem as you age. I really have no problem with the hole in the ground or with squatting, or carrying my own tissue; it is the filth that makes me cringe.

After waiting in line behind two of the nurses who brave this facility and emerge wincing but surviving the appearance and the stench (what choice do they have really?), I open the door. The smell is overpowering even though I am outdoors. Gagging slightly, I hold my breath and step inside. It is almost dark and I carefully choose spots to place my feet, careful not to let the cuffs of my scrubs fall down around my shoes. It's bad enough that the bottoms of my shoes have to touch this brown-stained, blue ceramic-framed filth. I cannot hold my breath quite long enough. And even though I am hurrying I am reaping the benefits of having kept myself well hydrated throughout the day. I cover my mouth and nose with one hand while holding my pants strategically with the other. One more deep breath and I am okay for the fifteen seconds it takes to finish, pull up my pants and escape. The next person in line points out that my shoes could use a little brushing off on the grass – ugh! I will not miss this part of Indonesia. Most of the toilets I see over this three-week trip look as if they have never been cleaned. It just is not a thought, much less a priority, and is one of the primary cultural differences that stand out.

△◆

Chapter Five

△◆

Back on the bus for the ride home, another two-and-a-half hours of bouncing over twenty-five miles or so of winding dirt road. Does anyone realize that professional marathon runners regularly cover twenty-six-point-two miles in two-and-a-half hours *on foot?* Erik notices one piece of poetic justice when he and several others who are used to getting a little exercise go for a walk one night after dinner. They come across a local knife maker – more accurately, a machete maker – who has a little business just outside his home. His entire family, which includes his wife and a four-year-old son, works the business. His wife pumps bellows to keep a fire going, her arms sporting enormous well-defined muscles, and her smile clearly expressing pride in her job and the products they produce. Placing springs from old buses into the fire, the husband flattens them out to makes the knives. He hammers the molten metal until the shape gradually changes to flattened, sharp-edged pieces he then inserts into a handle. The little boy dances around, keeping his distance from the flame and sparks, pretending to karate-chop Erik and the other large American male visitors. What a happy family and a wonderfully enterprising way to recycle parts of old vehicles. The springs from buses similar to the one that transported us to and from Sirombu are thrown into the fire and transformed into something we can actually use. Several of the men buy knives for about two dollars each. The man makes only about two or three knives a day, seems happy with his day's work and wages, and his family appears happy and well fed. I think there is a lot to be learned from him.

Once again in town, Erik and I move to the hotel where most of the team stayed the night before. It is not until we are almost at the hotel that someone says, "We never saw the actual coastline," the area hit by the tsunami. We did not see where the homes were destroyed or the beaches changed forever because we were two or three kilometers inland. It was too dark to see anything when we finished work, so our drivers did not take us the additional few minutes to the water. Patty really wants to see this area since her work in environmental geology touches on this as much or more than the work of anyone else on the trip. It turns out that we will have the opportunity to go back.

Our trip leader, Jim, needs several of us to stay over one more day in Gunung-Sitoli before heading south because one team member is going to join us late. Communication with the straggler has been cut off and Jim had forgotten about him. Not cool. Yes, he has gazillions of things to attend to but this is an important one. He could ask for help, delegate. We have nearly thirty adults, ages twenty to seventy, many of whom are professionals, all responsible and wanting to help. It is difficult for some people to ask for, or allow help. I had to learn the lesson of how to do this years ago in early recovery, as I wanted to do *all* the jobs in my office from receptionist to nurse to bookkeeper to doctor. I could have made myself very anxious and irritable, seriously reducing my effectiveness as doctor, not to mention driving away excellent employees, had I not used some of the principles of recovery, specifically looking at my own character defects (control, mistrust, fear) that made me want to do everything. I had to surrender some tasks to others and trust them to do it, tempering my problematic "control issues." I am very thankful I was taught, in recovery, to do that, and my staff was thankful, too.

The characters and personalities of people who volunteer for short-term mission trips are interesting. This is the first large trip for me. My other medical missions have been either individual, or with smaller groups. It requires exceptional organizational skills to manage a trip like this; literally, hundreds of details. So, Dan was left without the promised person to meet him at the airport in Medan. He is an experienced traveler and has been on lots of mission trips. He knows our destination, the hotel on the southern part of the island and could undoubtedly find us when he realizes that no one is going to meet him, help him or even communicate with him.

Patty, Erik, Eugene (one of the photographers) and I volunteer to go into town and check email to see if Dan has responded to the one sent yesterday after Jim realizes that he had neglected to send a team member to the airport. Dan is already en route, of course, and may have no way to check email. So, we hire a taxi for the whole day, first to take us back to the Internet café and check email, then to the airport to see if Dan figured out how to get to Nias, then back across the island to see and photograph the area of destruction we did not see yesterday. Seeing and photographing this area of actual tsunami destruction needs to be done for the trip record and especially for those who donated money specifically for tsunami relief. We will see other areas when we head south to Lagundri Bay, but it is important for us to document the destruction on this portion of the northwest coast of Nias.

At the Internet café, we find no email from the lone traveler, so we head to the airport, arriving just before the plane is supposed to arrive. It actually gets in on time; maybe there really is a schedule of sorts. Dan gets off the plane. He has gotten himself this far and is furious at being abandoned in the large Indonesian city of Medan, waiting for over an hour, realizing nobody is coming, and going to a hotel. He is able to get on the first (and possibly only) plane of the day to Nias. Dan declines to join us for the two-hour taxi ride back to Sirombu, wanting to get to the hotel and end his three days of travel. He has successfully used the Indonesian system of random tourist assistance and managed to line up a taxi before leaving the Medan airport. There is always someone in the airport or on the plane who knows someone whose relative or friend drives a taxi or owns a hotel at the next stop.

It is my experience that it's always easy to meet the needs of transportation, food and bed in developing countries because so many locals have jumped into the tourist trade. They find a way to make a better, arguably easier, living than working in the rice pad-dies, and most of them seem to generally enjoy meeting us and speaking a few words of English. It must take great courage to do these two things: leave the familiar for the unknown and learn a new language without formal education. Many local Indonesians cannot read or write their own language but have enough sense of self, cour-age, energy and drive to learn enough English to communicate with us. We never know how much they really understand, probably sometimes more than we think, and to my frustration many times less – and they usually are not honest about not understanding. So many times when I think I am being understood, I find out otherwise.

Dan says goodbye and departs for south Nias to join the rest of the group, ready to "land" after so many days of travel and confu-sion. The remaining five of us – Patty, Erik, Eugene, a second pho-tographer and me – return to Sirombu. The trip is faster by taxi, two hours instead of the almost three by bus. We see the devastation of the beaches, boats and buildings, incongruous with the groups of smiling children vying for our attention. Resilience. The children demonstrate this remarkable quality, as do some of the adults.

Some buildings are gone, just splintered boards scattered around a crumbling foundation. Some are partially gone, perhaps missing two walls, or a second floor. Many are crushed with trees and assorted debris on top. Almost nothing anywhere near the coast is habitable. Yet we see small groups of giggling school children, and adults saying hello and smiling. The spirit of these people is not crushed like their buildings. They have hope and it is contagious.

Rebuilding is already happening in some places. The strang-est sights are the structures that have been gutted, but retain a roof and enough vertical posts or pillars to hold it up. They are empty in the middle leaving only the shell of the building, and some have laundry hanging beside them, evidence their occupants are living their lives in spite of destruction of material belongings. There are lots of these on one dirt street about fifty yards from the water. It's easy to imagine the tsunami waves crashing through, taking the walls of the wooden houses and stores, and the contents, scattering the spoils along its pathway.

People smile, making us feel welcome while they pose for pictures. What goes through their minds, looking at us "touring" their
devastated community? It's time to take some pictures, with cameras
and with our eyes, incorporate the scenes into our hearts, and move on.

I think about rebuilding. In my life, I recall hitting rock bottom with my addiction almost twenty-one years ago. I was lucky to
have lived through the emotional and spiritual wreckage; I almost
didn't. My slide down was gradual at first, then more rapid, a sudden
crash at the end. The visible wreckage from the tsunami that I now
see in front of me is a result of a very sudden crash, with no warning,
no preparation and few having experienced anything like it before. I
am blessed to have had other addicts and alcoholics who had gone
before me and found recovery, to be there when I hit bottom. Many
have hit bottom and died; of those who lived through the disease of
addiction, many have recovered before me. Many wanted to help by
sharing their own experience, their strength, their hope. Here in Indonesia teams from other countries are helping rebuild, but who has
experienced it before? Who can share, like was shared with me, the
experience of survival, of rebuilding better than what was there before?

It is a long way back across the island, then south to Lagundri. The map shows a road down the west coast and taking this route
would cut about three hours from our remaining six- to seven-hour
drive. But there is one minor obstacle; the road does not exist. Two
people we had asked yesterday, and then our taxi driver today, tell
us that even before the tsunami, the road was not really there. So,
why was it on the map? Maybe there was one in the past? Maybe the
map maker thought there should be a road there and simply drew
one in? Or maybe there are dirt trails, put on the map as roads. Fortunately we don't get this information by coming to the end of the
road an hour or two after starting out thinking it will take us all the
way. After the two-hour drive across the island, we go another four
hours south, mostly along the east coast, the side not hit by the tsunami, to Lagundri.

Arriving at the Saroke Beach Hotel, our home for the next
two weeks, feels terrific. I still have not spent two nights in the same
place since beginning our travel from Denver five days and nights
ago. The hotel is made up of more than fifty bungalows, each with a
bedroom and bathroom. Luxury! Things are not always as they appear. The hotel has been closed for four years since the 9/11 terrorist
attack started keeping tourists away from this Muslim country.
Prior to that, surfers from Australia and the U.S. had visited with

enough frequency to keep the hotel busy much of the year. It never occurred to me that the consequences of 9/11 would reach to this tiny island most people have never heard of, and be so devastating that the only hotel in town, actually the only one on the southern half of the island, would close. So many people lost jobs when the fledgling tourist industry closed and the hotel acquired that moldy, closed-up feel that we now get to experience.

Our bungalow is perfectly sufficient but could do without the spotlight outside, presumably a security measure, as many lights surround the hotel. This one is aimed right at the bed and highlights the layer of dust and dirt. These details would be more tolerable if the air conditioner worked well enough to actually cool us off for a few hours at night. The hotel has no Freon, a necessary commodity if one wants to run an air conditioner. Nor do they have money to buy Freon. Each night we weigh whether to close the windows and keep out the mosquitoes, bats and who knows what else, while keeping in the heat; or to open the windows, get whatever slight breeze is present, but risk visits from assorted wildlife. The first night with open windows, a bat does enter. This offers one advantage, as we know he will make a meal of the mosquitoes, but he is scared and flying around frantically. We put a blanket over him and release him back to the outdoors. We will have to rely on the geckos to cull the mosquito population.

We had been looking forward to the promised swimming pool at the hotel. Good that we didn't get too excited as it has been sitting for four years. There is no money to clean it out so it looks like a culture medium set up by a lab to grow bacteria, algae, mold and frogs. No swimming here. The ocean is only a hundred yards away, but what is the story with the flora and fauna there?

Awakening the first morning in our new home, we are awed by the beauty. The dining room is open, has only a floor, roof, railing that is about knee high, pillars and is so close to the ocean that I consider taking my coffee down to the beach. There are no walls, perfect for meals with a view. We only have thirty minutes to eat and get to the bus that will take us to the hospital, so I nix this idea. Do I think I am on vacation or what?

Coming home to the same hotel, our own bungalow, every evening after work is enjoyable. We get used to the routine, getting to know the cooks and other hotel workers and the enterprising sales force from the nearby town that quickly finds us. These are the local men who sell wood carvings, knives and other items made here on Nias.

Most of the crafts are made in one of several tiny nearby villages and all are made completely by hand. Men of all ages carry bags or blankets full of a variety of things to sell and a few have their wares in backpacks. The Indonesian interpreters tell us to bargain and that the salesmen will start out asking at least double the value of the item. I find that if I stop to look at one man's goods, soon three or four other men will come up to me and open their bags, trying to get me to buy their stuff instead. Somehow this just does not seem right. Later, I realize that there is a sense of cooperation between these dozen or more men; they will go to each other to find a certain item if I indicate that I want something specific. They all cooperate with each other when one of them needs change or cannot understand one of us.

As the salesmen become increasingly aggressive as the days go by, I learn the Indonesian word for "no," *tidak.* When they start coming up to the railing around the dining area, we ask the interpreters to tell them that we will not buy until we have had our meal without their incessant pitches and attempts to get our attention. It has started to feel like harassment to have them in front of me, literally becoming enough of an obstacle and risk that I am concerned about tripping over them, every time I am not inside my room. Nevertheless, I have to commend them for persistence, for attempting to make an honest living and for learning enough English and the exchange rate so that they can understand us and accept payment in either dollars or *rupiah.* We do buy lots of souvenirs, most very roughly carved and with an unfinished appearance. The woodworkers are so gifted. Some of the carvings have detachable parts, or moving hinges, all out of wood with no hardware added. A few things are painted black, but most are just rough wood. I am happy with my treasures as I try to buy something from each of the men, spreading around the "wealth."

Some of the local boys bring coconuts or pineapples into the hotel compound to sell. One boy has learned enough English at the age of eleven or twelve to be quite an entrepreneur, undoubtedly picking up the language from the Australian surfers who frequent the island. Like the adult salesmen, the boy comes onto the hotel grounds by either the beach, which is a short walk from the town of Teluk-Delam, or the roadway, easily bypassing the gate. Why is there a gate anyhow? It doesn't keep out anyone who wants to get in; they just go around, through the bushes, or down to the beach. The young fruit salesman strolls from bungalow to bungalow until he sees one of us on the porch or close enough to the open window or door to hear him and not be able to pretend we don't know he's there. He catches me with the door open, putting wet clothes that I had washed in the sink on the porch to dry. He calls, tentatively, "Missus, want pineapple?" He has two, one significantly larger than the other. He asks three-thousand *rupiah* for the large one, twenty-five-hundred for the smaller, equivalent to less than a dollar U.S., but still to much for a pineapple in Indonesia. I would love to give this little salesman five or ten dollars for his trouble and encourage his business, but the consequences would not be positive; every child and adult in the village would be on my steps within twenty-four hours wanting me to buy their goods for five times the value, and this boy would think that everyone should pay many times the fair price for his pineapples. So, we settle on an equitable price for the one I want, the larger of the two. I take it to the dining room and ask the cooks cut it for all of us; they do an artistic display and we enjoy one of the sweetest fruits I have ever tasted.

I eat pineapple and drink coconut milk straight from the coconut almost every day. The other food is good, too, especially the unusual dishes like *chumi-chumi*, squid, served to us almost every day. We eat breakfast and dinner at the hotel, always buffet style, and always with at least three or four dishes from which to choose. The *chumi-chumi* is prepared differently each of the first few times it's served, a repertoire of recipes ranging from bland to spicy, and from few extra ingredients to many. My favorite is mixed with several different vegetables, a spinach-like green, tougher and more flavorful than plain spinach, bits of some tubular stringy affair, and peppers and onions, all in a spicy stew-like concoction. We call the *chumi-chumi*, "chew me, chew me" because the texture is like thin rubber; actually, I doubt if we would know if we were eating bits of rubber cooked in the wonderful sauces. The squid really has no flavor of its own. Its value is in the nutrients it contains, and in providing exercise for our jaws. What we don't finish at dinner, we see for breakfast. That's okay with me, as I am fond of substantial breakfasts and we have no lunch break, only a few minutes for snacks between patients. It's really too hot for lunch anyhow and we are too busy to think about it.

△◆
Chapter Six
△◆

Hilisimaetano. This is the name of the village with the hospital where we will work for the next two weeks. Jim Karl, on his first trip here in January 2005, immediately following the tsunami, managed to get government permission for our team to hold clinic here. On Wednesday, March 2, our team is together again and starting this primary work phase of our three-week trip. The team of more than twenty American adults (all volunteers paying their own way) has grown with the addition of a dozen or more Indonesian assistants who are being paid the tiny amount considered a fair day's pay. We think this pay is equivalent to about ten dollars U.S., but none of us are sure. Other advantages of being associated with us include practicing English, having food for the duration of the time, and the prestige of associating with U.S. travelers. They probably also receive tips from shopkeepers for taking us to specific stores and restaurants. Their pay seems a pittance for the value they add. Without them, we would undoubtedly be taken advantage of when arranging housing, transportation, purchases, and anything else where locals could overcharge the "rich Americans." Together, we board two buses and one car for the forty-minute drive into the interior of the island. We bounce around looking at the countryside, some attempting to take pictures between bounces.

Some knowledgeable person, probably an American Christian missionary who has lived in the country for a dozen years or more, tells us we are passing by rice paddies. The green shoots are in varying stages of growth. Precisely defined areas of fields, each about fifty yards square, are roped off and appear to have been planted at intervals. In one square, pale green, new grass-like straws are just coming up; in the next square are taller, darker green spears; and in the third square, mature stalks bend over with rice weighing heavily on their tips. I have never before seen rice ready to pick. The light brown hulls weigh down their blades, mimicking the bend in the backs of the people picking rice by hand. We see men, women and children all stooped over, hard at work in the paddies. Some are planting rice in a square field of muddy water. This scene is a harbinger of things to come in our medical practices during the next two weeks. It is obvious why so many people have back pain.

The bus makes several turns on the way to the hospital. More and more people are on the road. Whole families ride on one motorcycle; dad driving and mom behind, preschool age child in front of her holding onto dad's back and a toddler in front of him propped in his lap just behind the handlebars. There are lots of walkers in groups of two, three and more, all waving and smiling. After the last turn, only a few hundred yards from the hospital, we slow down, stopping and starting to wait for people in the road to move and make a pathway for the buses to get through.

I hear gasps from the American team members in the front of the bus, just as I look out and see a mass of humanity blocking the road. It takes a moment for me to realize why this crowd is here; they *all* want free medical or dental care *today*. We are three doctors, three dentists, a physician's assistant, five nurses, a fireman EMT, two lay persons, functioning as eyeglass technicians, who have been taught how to measure vision and fit glasses, two other lay persons who have been taught enough about medications to function as pharmacists, several interpreters and other support crew. We later come to believe that our most important support crew are the six large American men who function as security, keeping people from rushing the gate and storming the hospital grounds. How can we take care of these hundreds of people? They are many times the numbers we saw two days ago in Sirombu, but at least we know what to expect. Our motto becomes, "Just Do It," and most of us are, appropriately, wearing running shoes.

Eventually, the bus stops as close to the gate as possible and without creating more patients by running over someone who is not careful to move out of the way. We disembark and for the first time get an unobstructed view of the hospital; a pre-World War II German hospital. What happened to those German doctors anyway? We have been told that cannibalism was still practiced in the interior of some of the Indonesian islands as late as the 1920s and '30s. Maybe there was famine in the community surrounding the hospital, or maybe the German doctors did not "cure" some important tribal chief. Either way, we wonder if maybe they became the main course for a local potluck dinner.

The hospital, apparently abandoned for some time, is now functioning again with one Indonesian doctor (after meeting him, I wonder about his credentials), two nurses (presumably unpaid and doing this work to gain experience), and two security guards. We will not be seeing inpatients (most days there are none) unless asked to do so by the doctor and we will have certain parts of the hospital designated for our use. The hospital actually is a complex of ten one-story buildings, all white with a humidity-induced film of dirt and vegetation that makes them appear to be mottled brown. Connected by outside walkways and stairs, the buildings all are open with windows and doors that have only metal shutters that stay open most of the time. I don't recall seeing any screens anywhere in Indonesia. Cement floors and walls appear as if they were last washed around the time of World War II; maybe just before the German doctors disappeared? Some of the small rooms, each of which has only one window and one doorway, open to the walkway. Each room contains one or two cots, most with a thin mattress that also looks like it is from another century and still holding that century's dirt. Some also have a sheet and blanket; most do not. The iron frames of the cots are rusting; strange for me to see because in dry Colorado most things do not rust. I remember rust and rapid deterioration of materials from my years living in humid, hot North Carolina, another lifetime ago when I was dreaming of doing this kind of work, dreaming of living this kind of life. Now that I *am* living my dream, I remember to be thankful for my life, for being able to pursue my dream, to live my dream. I had forgotten about the dream for decades, becoming sidetracked, and I am now grateful to pick it up again. I hope I can be of some service to this Indonesian population so desperate for any kind of medical care.

Climbing off the bus we walk down the hill, through the crowd and the gate, already guarded by hospital security keeping the crowd out of the compound until some order can be established. Surveying our new workplace, we see that most of the hospital complex is actually outside in the form of walkways and grounds between and around the small buildings. Small square cement rooms off the cement "courtyard" become the pharmacy, optometry office, and the one with the largest windows and best light, the dentistry. Triage is outside between the pharmacy, the administrative office and the storage area. The courtyard is about three times as wide and six or eight times as long as any of the small square rooms where we will work. Going from any one part of the hospital to another requires simply stepping a few feet to the doorway of the building we are in, going outside and hiking up or down a small hill on some type of pathway.

The three doctors will set up in different corners of the large recovery room area outside of the operating room. This is in yet another building connected to the first by a covered walkway; twenty-five yards or so on very slippery tile, down about half-a-dozen stairs and we are there. I choose the far corner and pull together four chairs, having learned that I will need two interpreters for most patients. Four chairs should work, unless the patient has multiple family members. I wonder again how much will be lost in translation.

During my residency training more than thirty years ago, we talked about occasionally having to do "veterinary medicine" when we could not communicate adequately with a patient for any reason; language barrier, mental retardation, comatose patients, and patients with psychological or social problems. Sometimes patients brought from jail refused to talk, as did very young and scared patients. "Veterinary medicine" implies that we must decipher nonverbal communication, grunts and groans, pointing, or withdrawing in discomfort when we poke and prod a painful spot – primitive sign language. I am experienced in this way of determining why a patient is in front of me and maybe I can put it to use here if needed. It was so different in South America when I understood a few Spanish words and Erik spoke fluently, translating easily for me.

So, I am set up in my little "office" where I will spend most of my days for the next few weeks. Soon, the first patients make it through security at the gate, then through triage, down the walkway and begin arriving at the door to our building. There again they are met by a nurse who walks or directs them towards one of the three doctors. The primary patients are the elderly and very young children and infants. One of our first is a very weak, small, thin baby. I am told she is a year old but I doubt it. There is little emphasis on birth dates in this culture, so we are never sure of someone's age. The mother holding her says she has not started crawling yet. She is listless, cries a lot and has "something on her neck." It is hard to determine how long this something on her neck has been there, but at least several weeks. Examining the child, I agree she is weak, pulls away from me and cries, and has purulent drainage from the filthy piercing in her left earlobe. The mother, or whoever pierced the ear, has tied a piece of string through the hole and it is dirty and encrusted with pus. The lobe itself is red, swollen and tender to touch. There are enlarged lymph nodes behind the ear and down the neck. Clearly, this is infected, but it's not the baby's only problem.

I ask the mother, through my two interpreters, speaking in English to interpreter number one who speaks in Indonesian to interpreter number two who then speaks to her in Nias, what the baby eats. I hope that she is still breast fed at least a few feedings a day.

The mother, surrounded by her three other children, the oldest not over six, says "porridge." More questioning reveals that this is what they all eat twice day; porridge, a thin soup of rice and water. The baby is not breast fed, the mother stopped months ago. Was it to work more in the fields? Does the oldest child watch the others during the day? Or is the mother home and just not able to buy anything but rice and thinks it is better for her infant to have something other than breast milk? It is too cumbersome to go through that level of information gathering, so I move on to the infection and the dirty string in the left earlobe, putting the baby on the hospital bed in the corner under the windows so that I can see more clearly the extent of this infection. I ask my wonderful nurse, Shaaron, to begin cleaning off the ear and the neck. The drainage and crusty pus is extensive. Using both sign language and my two interpreters, I tell the mother that I need to remove the string because this is the cause of the infection and it is not likely to clear up with the string still in place. She protests but relents when I am very firm about the need to do that so that the infection does not spread.

I spend too long with this family. So many are waiting for their turns, but I ask again about the baby's age and diet.

"Doesn't she eat anything else?"

"No, that's all we have."

I explain that she needs more, something with protein. "Can she have eggs?"

"Too expensive," says the mother.

"Chicken, fish?"

"No."

"Beans?"

"OK, maybe."

"Also, beans would be good for the other children and her as well. Where is her husband?"

"He is working in the fields."

It occurs to me that I could ask Shaaron to do some "nutrition counseling" and talking about hygiene and cleaning earlobes and skin, but then I realize she cannot; not without an interpreter. Maybe the most important job on this trip is interpreter, not security. So, I do the public health, preventative medicine, hygiene and nutrition counseling. I prescribe antibiotics, oral and topical, to be applied to the earlobe, and vitamins, and send the family off to the pharmacy where Patty and Gail give all the family members vitamins, toothbrushes, toothpaste, soap and the prescribed medications.

All of it is free to our patients. They would not be here if there was any charge, even a very small one. At my special request, they are given some of the high-calorie formula we have brought. It is expired; last year's date is stamped on each can, but it's still good, just not legally usable in the United States. I taste it, knowing it is still good, but check to be sure before giving it to a curious six-year-old boy. A little extra nutrition, this liquid packed with vitamins, minerals, especially calcium and calories can go a long way in this family. But, when these cases of supplements are gone in a few weeks, ongoing nutrition counseling could go further.

What about follow-up? We have none to offer. It's clear that this mother loves her children but doesn't know how to help them grow up healthy. She is only in her early twenties and started her family as a teenager. No chance for birth control; none is available to her. One custom in the community is to pierce the earlobes of infant girls. I wish we could add to the customs to clean the pierced earlobes three times a day, wash dirt from all wounds, breast feed for at least a year or two, and feed themselves and their children a variety of foods, including protein. Peanuts, beans and manioc, a shrub with an edible, starchy root, all are cheap and high in protein.

Two weeks later, toward the end of the trip, I come up with an idea to effect change on this island in a few years instead of a few generations. We could take some of the most interested, energetic, brightest locals to a developed country for education; take those who have a spark and energy and desire to learn. Provide for them as much schooling as needed in a variety of health-related fields, and arrange for their return home to each community to encourage and support public health, basic nursing and health care. I think this could be the most efficient way to change customs and habits; have people from their own community teach and follow-up on patients. I wonder what it would take to actually implement this plan.

I wonder what will become of the baby with the infected earlobe. Most people come to the hospital from too far away to return in the same week or two; too hard to come with three or four young children or to take another day from work. And we have too many people who need to be seen once to ask someone to return. They may never get through security if it is known that they have already been in once. In a developed country, the baby would have lab work, we would know the age accurately and a full assessment would take place. Here, I can only give antibiotics to treat the immediate problem, vitamins and a one-time brief nutrition and hygiene education session. Better than nothing, I guess.

In my early medical school years I was so disappointed that I didn't learn the main thing I thought I wanted to learn when I began those four years: how the brain works. I took neuroanatomy and learned all the nerves, their connections, their vascular supply and their function, but not how the brain works. Those first two years of academics in the classroom went by quickly and then I was a third-year student seeing patients in the clinic and hospital wards. I wanted to fix, to cure everyone. I am sure all medical and nursing students go through this phase. Soon I was disappointed again. Not only could the professors not teach me how the brain works, but there were many patients with many diseases that could not be cured. At first we are overcome with discouragement, but then we learn that it is not a cure we always are after. We can alleviate suffering, or lessen it, and find that diseases improve or go into remission. People heal somewhat, emotionally and physically. We can comfort and show the way toward progress, if not perfect healing.

I am not "cured" from my alcoholism. I am in remission, healing and very healthy. I know that I could reactivate my disease simply by taking a drink. I would not go back to the level of drinking I was doing when I stopped, but would pick up far worse, as if I had never stopped. I would be twenty-one years sicker than I was twenty-one years ago. This is what experience shows: the disease progresses whether or not we are drinking. As long as we are not drinking, we heal, growing emotionally and spiritually, having the opportunity for a healthy life. As soon as we start using anything mind-altering again, we rapidly descend toward the bottom. I have watched so many of the people I know from recovery groups relapse and either die or just get sick with ongoing drug and alcohol use and all of the horrible stuff that accompanies it. Neither am I cured from my hypothyroidism. I am in remission and I stay that way by taking my thyroid medication every day. There are similarities. For each of my diseases, I "take my daily medication." It is just that for alcoholism, the medication is the maintenance of spiritual (not religious) fitness.

So, even though "cure" is often not the goal, offering improvement and a chance to be a little bit healthier at least is progress, if not perfection.

On to other patients. For a few hours we see routine ailments; sore throats, cough, sinus infections, abdominal discomfort and dermatitis. My American Indonesian interpreter laughs as I ask for what seems like the twentieth time in a few hours about diet. Very few eat anything other than rice. Most do not appear malnourished, so they must occasionally have other foods. Why the gastrointestinal distress? Most of the men smoke tobacco, drink alcohol and chew Betel nut. I entertain my interpreter again by requesting elimination of all of the above and explaining that their abdominal pain will most likely disappear with the discontinuation of alcohol, tobacco and Betel nuts. He laughs and says, when interpreting back to me what the patient says, "Oh, he says he'll stop today. No more cigarettes, alcohol or Betel nut."

Both of us know the odds of this are very slim. Just like with drugs in other countries, few actually make the decision to quit, almost none for physical reasons. We know that just showing a smoker a cancerous lung from a cadaver almost never results in his stopping smoking. People who quit drugs usually do so because they hit bottom emotionally and spiritually. They quit for their kids, or because they are so depressed they want to die and somehow figure out the drugs are making things worse; or occasionally because they are in prison or forced to attend treatment or support groups. No, this patient won't stop using his drugs. They are more important to him than the condition of his stomach.

△◆

Chapter Seven

△◆

Just before lunch we see a patient I will never forget. She looks like a man from a distance; taller than most Indonesians, thin, large squared-off jaw and a bandana covering her hair. When she comes into my office I see that she is a woman wearing a bright green dress. A young man, her son, is waiting for her outside the gate. This squared-off jaw is a protruding mouth cancer that has spread in all directions from where it probably started under her tongue, especially apparent downward and into the lower jaw. Her tongue is elevated by the tumor below it. The front of her tongue is attached, more like stuck, to the floor of her mouth about an inch back from its tip. The one remaining lower tooth is protruding out at an awkward angle from the mucous membrane covering the tumor on the floor of her mouth. Her upper teeth appear to be normal. I suspect the tumor goes almost as far back into the deeper structures of the floor of her mouth as it protrudes in the front, but without an

X-ray, MRI or CAT scan, I cannot see the boundaries. What I can see is that even in the United States there is no possibility of recovering from this advanced stage of the disease. I question her, again via my two interpreters. She says that it started as a tiny lump under her tongue. (Most mouth cancers start here and routine physical exams and dental checkups should always include inspection *under* the tongue). She says she saw a doctor three or four years ago when it started and he said there was nothing he could do.

I wonder if it was really a doctor she saw. Whether he was or not, did he know then that it was cancer? Did his training provide him with information to know the course it would take? Did he consider sending her to the Indonesian mainland for appropriate care? Is there appropriate care on the mainland or would she have had to go to Australia or some other developed country for definitive treatment? Or, most likely the cost and logistics of getting her to the mainland, finding care, paying for travel and treatment was all just as impossible as coming to the States would have been. The people on this island have been so disconnected from mainland Sumatra that they have their own language. Most do not even travel to the nearby city of Teluk-Delam, an hour by local bus, much less four more hours to Gunung-Sitoli, where there is an airport. Flying to the mainland for better medical care is an option only for a very few.

My patient's eyes are inquiring and at first she doesn't speak. Has the tumor grown onto her vocal cord or is she just in too much emotional or physical pain? When the interpreter speaks to her in her own language, she responds by saying she is in pain. I never see her complain or whine. She gives no direct outward expression of the pain, other than a statement that yes, she has been in pain for some time. I ask her if I can take pictures and she readily agrees. I reluctantly tell her there is nothing we can do, that even in our country nothing can be done for this, sparing her the information that it could have been treated when it was smaller. In fact, for her that may not be true because of the circumstances of her life. The resources are simply not available to her.

I give her some of the three types of pain medication we have; a large supply of ibuprofen, some Tramadol (a slightly stronger but non-narcotic painkiller) and all of the Percocet we have, which is not much and will last only a few weeks. I carefully go over the progression of strength of these medicines. Use the ibuprofen now once or twice a day, more often if the pain increases. If the pain continues to increase, use the Tramadol. Then, if she develops even more pain (I avoid the word severe in English but I don't know how "even more pain" translates in Indonesian), progress to using the narcotics.

After the patient goes up the hill to the gate to meet the son who will walk her home, my American interpreter shakes his head in disbelief, echoing my own sentiments. How can something like this happen? In 2005, how can a cancer progress untreated? But 2005 in Indonesia is not the same as 2005 in the United States. I tell him I am praying that the tumor grows laterally into the carotid artery and that she quietly and rapidly bleeds out into the internal structures of her neck. Perhaps it could happen so that no blood would be visible to her or her family. Perhaps she could have a painless and rapid way to die. I continue to pray for her. I pray she is at peace and free from pain today, whether or not she is alive.

Doctors lose patients all over the world. Part of good medical care is helping patients and their families ease out of this life with minimal discomfort, physical or emotional. I have seen people die in many ways. Some fight it until the end, struggling, never accepting the inevitable. Others surrender and go peacefully, reassuring their family and saying goodbye, if not in words, then by their attitude. Death truly is part of our existence on this planet; we can help ourselves and others by preparing for it, however we believe we should do that, and welcoming it when the time arrives. I encourage my patients to continue doing the work to heal when it is even remotely possible. Miracles do happen, people can live much longer than anyone expects, even after bleak diagnoses. But acceptance is eventually what is left to those who want peace in their final moments. I am truly impressed with the acceptance of many of my Indonesian patients. They have lived for generations with little or no medical care and with no alternative but to accept that death is part of life.

The afternoon comes with more "routine" patients like those I see in my office in Colorado: headaches, stomachaches, joint pain, chest pain, difficulty breathing, coughing. A few are really sick, but most have minor illnesses that are easily treatable with medicines we have brought. These medicines are routinely available in the United States, many over-the-counter, but they are unheard of by this population. In fact, some are also routinely available in the small towns of Teluk-Delam and Gunung-Sitoli here on Nias, but people this far into the interior rarely get to these cities and if they do they can't afford the medication and wouldn't know what to buy.

I receive profuse thanks for a handful of acetaminophen. A few weeks' supply of antacid is like gold for the middle-aged woman with indigestion. The old man with arthritis has never had an aspirin, much less ibuprofen. Tiny amounts go a long way in a population that never takes any medicines. We prescribe one aspirin a day to treat the mild to moderate discomfort of arthritis, one to two doses of antacid or other stomach medicine for those with stomach complaints.

After several days, we get into a routine of greeting patients and taking the briefest of histories via two interpreters (oh, how my medical school professors would cringe and my students would drop their jaws in disbelief at how little information I am gathering). We do very focused physical exams and rapidly determine what treatment is possible in this culture. My American interpreter and nurse are invaluable. We learn to work together efficiently, my nurse anticipating my needs and fabulously taking care of me and the patients.

On one occasion, as I am about to examine the bare, dirty, infected feet of an elderly patient and reach for her foot to bring it up into my lap to examine closely, as I do with my patients in Colorado, I hear Shaaron exclaim, "No, wait, don't." Glimpsing her out of the corner of my eye, she rushes toward me and thrusts a pair of disposable gloves into my hands, giving me a look only a mother can give. Shaaron is fifty-one going on twenty-five and the mother of two "children" in their twenties, just as I am. We develop a bond from the first day; respect for each other's skills and caring, and have a real fondness and rhythm of working together that makes things flow. I would have spent many hours stumbling through nursing tasks searching for the right supplies and generally being confused without her, and I would have had my ungloved hands on dirty, infected feet. People living on Nias usually walk to the clinic on dusty dirt roads wearing sandals. I have almost no access to hot water and the availability of cold water, soap and paper products, such as lap drapes or paper towels, is variable.

Colin, my American interpreter, is equally easy and fun to work with and is arguably the most valuable member of our trio. Without him, we might have been able to do a "veterinary medicine" assessment by observing and examining patients, but we would never be able to determine exact symptoms and convey treatment; how to take a prescribed medicine, how to care for a wound or pain, what to eat and drink, or not to eat, drink, chew or smoke, to help recover from the particular illness. Colin, having returned from the mission field and currently working as a preacher in Alabama, had previously lived in Indonesia with his wife and children for twelve years as a missionary with the Church of Christ. He had hiked through the jungle on Nias many years earlier, became very ill from contracting malaria and recovered, lived through riots in Jakarta and had come to know, love and respect the Indonesian people. He and his wife, Ellen, are by far the best equipped of all the team members to work in these conditions. I still cannot figure out how they look so cool and freshly pressed each day. Their cotton clothes are perfect for the climate and match their unflappable personalities. They have lived it before. The heat, the food, the people are familiar to them and even though it is sometimes clear they do not approve of everything and everyone, they are calm, accepting, careful to be supportive and not to be overtly critical or judgmental.

For example, Colin and Ellen are realistic when someone reassures the American "security" squad (the six largest non-medically trained men on the team) that while there are hundreds of Indonesians pushing at the gate, clamoring to get in, they will never physically harm any of us. Colin and Ellen roll their eyes and say to us discretely, "Don't you believe it. They have knives and other sharp objects and can be very dangerous, especially in large groups and when we turn our backs." This is not comfortable for us to hear but necessary and our awareness could possibly save us from potential serious problems. We know the men and boys all have knives; we see groups of young boys going off to the jungle with machetes to play. They are quite skilled with knives of all sizes by the time they are adolescents and machetes can be tools *or* weapons.

A certain amount of disorganization with parts of the trip can be expected. Under the best of conditions, in developed countries, it is very difficult to arrange for all parts of transport, living quarters, work place, equipment and permission to work, going through proper channels so as to not break the laws of the country or neglect local authorities. In a Third World or developing country, especially one that has just lost much of its infrastructure, it is impossible. The mentality is just different. Time is not so important; few have watches or clocks. If a busload of thirty Americans has to wait an hour in the heat with no water or facilities, wait until the supplies are purchased and loaded because no one did it before we were boarded, that's just the way it is. Many tasks we take for granted are not possible. There is no way to call ahead, order supplies, or know exactly what is already in place. We are able to hire locals to work loading and unloading, assisting our security contingent, and procuring food and drink, but nothing is absolutely reliable. So, one job of team members is to make suggestions and know that they are only that, suggestions. The leader is in charge and if he chooses to do it his way instead of ours, so be it. Retired career missionaries have much more experience and may have ideas to make things go more smoothly, but are not asked to take on the job of organizing; they simply serve as translators and assist when and where asked.

Colin has never worked in a medical setting before volunteering to interpret for this trip. He rapidly picks up "history taking" and after a day or two is able to anticipate my questions. When I am away from my "office" conferring with one of the other doctors, Colin can get appropriate preliminary information. There are only a few patients he seems to not want to get close to, keeping his distance from our surgeries and from the amputee we see on one of our last days.

Colin and I amuse each other from time to time, a useful thing for people working together day after day for weeks at a time. I find his recap to Ellen about my diagnosis and treatment of one of our patients to be quite interesting, illustrating my attempt to do something honestly.

I always like to have several patients ready and waiting in the immediate area because it's more efficient than waiting several minutes for patients to make their way from the triage area down to me in the back of the hospital. We have a few chairs lined up and usually my four or five waiting patients each have one or more family members with them. Most just sit or squat on the floor, back to the wall, intently watching my interactions with the current patient. Even if I do not want additional people waiting in the immediate area, there are other patients, family and friends, and curious children creeping around the edge of the open doors, or looking through the open windows, bringing back memories of rural Bolivia.

The patients have no qualms about this; there simply is not a sense of privacy. When I want to do a breast exam, I have to stop the woman from just unbuttoning her blouse in front of me and everyone else. I will move the hospital bed to the corner and have my nurse and interpreter hold sheets up around the patient and me. Obviously, this is for my needs, not the patient's. When we need to examine young boys with inguinal hernias or enlarged testicles, we do the same thing. Their parents start undressing them but we stop and provide a screen between them and the ever-present audience. The adolescent boys seemed to appreciate our Western attitudes about privacy even if their parents don't.

In addition to the line-up of waiting patients, there are curious onlookers at the windows. Every morning when we enter our office, we open all the windows, hoping to get some air circulating before the completely still and heavy midday air heated by the tropical sun is upon us. The windows are covered at night by swinging metal doors that latch from the inside and keep people and large animals out. It also keeps heat in and allows free access to insects and small creatures. When these metal window covers are open, there is nothing in the three-by-four-foot window space between us and the great outdoors. Since my office is at the end of the hospital complex, my windows open out into the dense forest; great for throwing the biodegradable scraps from lunch out to the birds and also great for swarms of short, dark, two-legged creatures to peek in. These fast-moving boys are like curious children anywhere else in the world. They move as a unit; a dozen legs attached to dirty, calloused bare feet, sneaking along the outside wall, getting just under the windows and popping up. Either a squeal of delight or a fast movement grabs my attention, and then the grinning brown faces rapidly disappear. Depending on my mood, fatigued, irritable and into my illusion that I have control over something versus being flexible, accepting and tolerant, I decide whether or not to attempt to chase them off, or to simply smile and enjoy their playfulness.

Someone from triage walks a family to our area. A woman who has brought her husband to see me has two infants strapped to her; one on the front and one on the back. I later learn that there had been triplets, but one infant had died. She also has a toddler by the hand. The husband has "seizures" and has not been able to function effectively, specifically to work, since his oldest child was born about three years earlier. He purportedly has these seizures on a somewhat regular basis and none of the doctors he has seen over the years have been able to help him. The local people and hospital workers, including our Indonesian-to-Nias interpreter, know him. While he and his wife and children are waiting, I finish up with a patient. With an inside audience at hand and an outside audience at the window, the possibility of extra attention was not lost on young "Mr. Seizure." Immediately upon arriving at my "office suite," he begins to have an "episode." He starts to shake his head from side to side, carefully guides himself to the floor and lies on his back, moving his head and all four extremities – quite a performance.

I am one-hundred percent sure that this is voluntary. It's not difficult to tell; fluttering eyelids, the occasional glance in my direction, on and off movement of extremities, not at all like a real convul-

sion, and the absence of involuntarily urinating that frequently accompanies real seizures are all absolute signs that he is a fake. His
glances at me and halting his movement when it is clear I am not
looking at him are real tip-offs. I move to the side and tell him, even
though he is pretending not to hear, that I will see him when he
stops shaking. I then invite the next patient to the inner office. "Mr.
Seizure" stops shaking and sits up when he realizes he is getting exactly zero attention from me.

After the next patient, I go over to "Mr. Seizure" and motion
him to the patient chair. He can have his turn now as long as he is
not shaking; all of this told to him through my interpreters. As soon
as I move toward the patient chair, he starts shaking again. I gently
put my hands on his shoulder, turn him around and point him to the
floor, motioning for him to sit. I then start taking care of the next
person in line. This happens three more times. Each time when he
starts up his act, I take the next person in line ahead of him. After
about an hour of waiting, his last attempt at getting me to react is a
single turn of the head from side to side when he is already seated in
the patient chair. He looks at me as if daring me to oust him yet
again. I look back at him, lock eyes and say, in English, "Stop shaking." He speaks no English but gets the message.

Interestingly, the local interpreter, a male nurse employed at
the hospital and living in the village, says, when this patient is ready
to leave, "It's time for another seizure." It seems to me as if "Mr. Seizure" is well known and does these performances on such a regular
basis that all who know him come to expect it at least every few
hours or so. My nurse/interpreter has clearly not yet understood that
these are voluntary movements. When I explain, he laughs, looks a
little skeptical, but seems to understand, if not believe, what I am
saying. "Mr. Seizure" has been successful in convincing every other
healthcare provider he has seen since these episodes started that
they are real seizures. He is clearly getting something out of being
labeled "sick" and "disabled." He doesn't have to be responsible for
feeding his family and can stay home all day. I never find out if his
wife leaves the three-year-old with him when she goes to work in the
fields. She takes the babies with her as she has to breast-feed them
during the day. I wonder if she takes the toddler, too, or can she rely
on her husband to at least care for this child?

With absolutely no resources for counseling or any kind of
psychological support, much less thorough evaluation, I do the only
thing I can. I tell "Mr. Seizure" that I will examine him and I will be

able to tell what is wrong and what to do about it. I do a brief physical exam, emphasizing HEENT (head, eyes, ears, nose and throat), neurological exam, heart, lung and abdominal exam. Everything is completely normal of course. This is a physically healthy, seemingly well-developed, well-nourished man in his twenties.

After examining him, I tell him that his seizure problems are going to stop and that he should immediately return to work. They will not return *if* he goes back to work. I also tell him to ask God to help him (most people from this part of the island are Christian, but I really don't care what religion he is. I just want him to start asking for help from something he believes is more powerful than himself, something outside of himself, while doing his part by returning to work). I tell him that God will keep him healthy and take away the seizure problem while he goes back to work and helps support his family. He seems to hear what I am saying. I say it with his wife and the ever-present audience of waiting patients and those peering through the window all listening. He makes eye contact with me, but says nothing, and has a serious, almost solemn attitude.

He has no further shaking over the next few hours while his family gets their medical and dental care. I wonder what he does mentally, emotionally and spiritually to process what I tell him and wonder if he returns to work. I believe that I do the only thing I can and pray that I might have helped him and his family. I wonder if he believes that God did remove his seizures.

That night, Colin tells Ellen about this patient and laughs as he says that I "told him to pray about it and get up and go to work and he would be healed and stop having seizures." I guess that summarizes it. I do not collude with the patient to pretend he has a genuine seizure disorder, nor do I ignore his distress. I treat him as if he is smart enough to hear what I am saying and to change. This is similar to what I do in the States, except that I cannot offer therapy here on our island of Nias; in the States, I can refer to a counselor or therapist. I do not enable him to continue avoiding responsibility and I give him a way out. As far as I can tell, Colin, and especially Ellen, approve of my patient management.

One patient I am hoping to get a follow-up with is the "Goiter lady." Word spreads rapidly when she comes into the hospital. Her appearance is astounding. Having been in this country and on this island for more than a week already, we have all seen lots of people with large goiters, mostly women. In my medical training in the United States, I had seen an occasional one, all small enlargements

of the thyroid gland in the front of the neck, usually caused by inadequate iodine in the diet. They were common in the United States in
the early 1900s, especially in the Midwest known as the "goiter belt"
to the medical community. Iodine is now added to salt in the U.S.
and goiters are very rare. Today's medical students will not have
much opportunity to see them except in pictures. In Indonesia, the
salt has been iodized for only the past decade or two. Now there is
some iodized salt, but we are told that seventy percent of the salt
that is labeled "iodized" here actually is not. Someone is labeling and
selling salt as iodized, making money on it and doing great harm to
many people. So, the problem with goiters continues. People who eat
fish and other food from the sea get some iodine and other minerals.
Those who live inland and cannot afford seafood do not. Clearly the
soil is missing this mineral, and we see the results: many goiters.

Usually the goiters are small, with the appearance of a lemon
or tennis ball under the skin in the front of the neck. One lady arrives with her shirt collar pulled up over her neck to just under her
chin. Her face is sad, her stare almost blank. Unbuttoning her collar,
she shows us her enormous neck, as if a softball or a large avocado is
pressed into it. She is so embarrassed. We've had to brace ourselves
every day for more of these patients and have very little to offer; no
lab to do blood tests on their thyroid function, no surgeons or operating room equipment for removing the growth. All we can do is start
an estimated dosage of the thyroid supplement to stop the progression of the goiter, and do some basic nutrition counseling. Eat fish!
For those who can't afford it, this is not good news. We take money
from our funds to buy several months' supply of thyroid supplement,
guessing at the dosage and knowing it is not a cure, for several patients. Word spreads and more women with goiters come; so many
goiters! We see more in a day than most U.S. doctors see in a lifetime. Still, no one can prepare us for the patient we refer to as the
"Goiter Lady."

As she walks in, her eyes speak the depth of her sadness and
hopelessness louder and more clearly than words in any language.
She holds her right hand up level with her shoulder, arm bent at the
elbow. Her hand is supporting a tumor, a goiter as large as her head,
attached to the front and right side of her neck. It looks like a skin-
covered basketball and is eerie to touch with its soft brown skin and
visible veins. It is obviously very heavy – what a burden, physically
and emotionally. How long has this been growing and has she ever
tried to get help?

After talking for several hours with other members of the "Colorado Contingency," I begin to shape a plan for her care. We have extra money from the pre-trip fund-raising and I want the team to share in deciding how to spend it. Everyone agrees some of the money will go to help this lady.

Obstacles! Without any, we could just say, "Refer to surgery" and the "Goiter Lady" would receive care, but there are obstacles which include: 1) Getting her to a place where this kind of surgery can happen; 2) Finding the money for her to get there and pay the room and board in the hospital; 3) Being sure that the money goes for her care, not something else. (She could decide to spend it on food or some other necessity for herself or her family, or it might be stolen by a family member, or anyone else, even someone in the hospital); 4) Finding a surgeon who is able to do the surgery and an anesthesiologist able to keep her alive during the surgery; and 5) Finding people able to care for her in and out of the hospital for the recovery period.

Our money can solve numbers one and two. The only medical person we truly trust in this corrupt country is Dr. Derek Allen at the Gunung-Sitoli hospital five hours away from this inland community. We give our patient money for transportation along with instructions on how to get to the hospital and find the New Zealand doctor. We also send a note with her for Dr. Derek saying that we will cover costs for surgery and room and board and that we will pay directly to the doctor and/or the hospital administrator when we are in Gunung-Sitoli in about a week preparing to leave the country.

Concerns about this plan abound, but we see no other solution as we have no phone number for Dr. Derek and no way to reach him. The level of communication and complexity of getting a patient to appropriate care, if available, is so far removed from what we are used to in the U.S. that trying to sort it out further is overwhelming. It's easy to see how disease goes untreated by people living in remote villages on this isolated island when even fresh, high-energy, short-timers like us get frustrated. We can only hope that the doctor can either do the surgery or find someone who can.

△◆

Chapter Eight

△◆

The day finally arrives for half our team, including Erik and two others in our group of six Coloradoans, to leave. Erik and I go to the adjoining bungalow and ask Colin and Ellen to pray with us for his safety and the others as they travel, and also for me and those staying for the duration of the mission. Erik is tearful and I actually do cry. He is concerned for my safety and I later find out that he asks almost every male team member to watch out for me during the coming week. It is common knowledge among mission members that the closer you get to the end of a trip like this the more dangerous it becomes. To avoid last-day problems the trip leader purposely keeps the day and time of our departure quiet, even as the locals guess when we are leaving. In very poor countries, people see the riches we foreigners have and they want to get something, whatever they can as we are leaving; our hats, shoes, clothes, pens, unused supplies and even money. Attitudes can quickly change from cheerfully helping to expecting "gifts." The idea that a gift is something we give is lost on many. There are also those who do not expect or demand, but their quiet presence is overshadowed by the unattractive "grabbing" by less respectful and more aggressive locals.

One fear is that expecting and demanding can turn to stealing. My missionary dentist friend told me about trying to give a gift of some minor value to one of his helpers, a local Papua New Guinea man. The man told him he could not accept it as he would be too indebted. He could, however, steal it. Differences in cultures are fascinating. This behavior is not likely to happen until the end of the trip. Before that, the locals just want to work for pay, get to know us a little and befriend us. I believe most of this is genuine and that most people are sincere and honest. I also know that some have thoughts about how much they can get from us; what we will pay for legitimate work and for items they have to sell and what we might give them at the end of several weeks of depending on them.

Many of the more colorful recovering addicts I know have had the capacity, during the years of their active addiction, to change from honest to dishonest in a split second. I am wary of everyone and am reminded of stories from addicts who would steal your camera, wallet, or iPod and help you look for it! This changes when the addict stops the drug use and gets into recovery. One recovering man told how he used to commit armed robbery and now cannot even accept too much change if a cashier makes a mistake. He is a different man now, honest and clean. The sense of being very close to people who probably have the capacity to steal, or commit other crimes, is unnerving, especially with Erik leaving.

We certainly are dependent on the locals for transportation, communicating the nuances of language that interpreters don't understand, purchasing supplies and getting information about the very few recreational activities we can fit in. We go fishing for half a day and some of the group takes an excursion to a village where there is a native dance performance. We also take a half-day trip to town to purchase some Batik material and a few other souvenirs.

Part of protecting myself requires me to be aware and on guard simply because of being female. Women in Indonesia are thought of as property. They are expected to defer to the men, work hard from morning until night, not complain or ask for help, and to be treated as sex objects to be used by their husband to meet his needs at any time. I did not learn enough about the sexual morals and habits of the people in this community, or in Indonesia as a whole, to get much information about extramarital sex. When I ask one young female patient if she needs birth control, she says no because she is not married, clearly implying there is no way she could be sexually active. All of the women I see with children have husbands, so I get the impression that premarital sex and probably extramarital sex, is not the rule.

Deference to men is not something I was ever taught; in fact, my mother, born in 1910, was one of the original "women's-libbers." I am grateful for her lesson that men and women are different but equal. At the same time, she did teach me self-protection, emotionally and physically. Unfortunately, the message that all women should be equipped to support themselves emotionally and financially came across more like, "Be sure you can do well on your own because you cannot trust men; they are likely to either divorce you or die on you." The negative twist was unnecessary, but I got the point: Don't rely on anyone. Somehow my mother, in spite of her own struggles with her emotional and spiritual health, conveyed the message to me that I *could* rely on God. It just took me a long time, as in over forty years, to internalize that concept and actually put it into practice. Looking back over my life so far, I do see how God has given me what I need, painful and not, to get where He wants me to go.

△◆

Chapter Nine

△◆

On the day that the "two-weekers" leave, the rest of us have the afternoon free. I want to see one of my favorite patients, my

"Asthma Lady." I still have her picture in my house and think about her and pray for her regularly. I meet her on one of the first days at the clinic as she very slowly walks into my "office." She is probably thirty-five, but looks fifty-five and is so thin that I first consider a diagnosis of anorexia nervosa or some other wasting disease. She does in fact have a disease that is keeping her from ingesting adequate nutrition: severe asthma. Extracting her history we find out that she has difficulty breathing and sometimes has episodes of a few days or weeks where it is so bad that she cannot walk, which means she can't go to the fields and work. Listening to her labored breaths, through her thin chest wall, with ribs prominent and breathing a struggle, I immediately understand why. She has severe bronchoconstriction that is partially closing her airway. She breathes with all of the usual respiratory muscles as well as her accessory muscles, chest, neck and abdominal muscles. Even from a distance it's easy to see her retracting, pulling with all of her upper body muscles.

I have very little to offer, only a small amount of bronchodilating medication, aminophylline, the kind that was used in the United States fifty years ago. It is a lifesaving medicine, just not as new and perfected as some of the asthma treatments we now have. Since I too have asthma, I have special empathy with this lady. I have more medications for my personal use and even carry epinephrine injections, the kind used for emergency treatment of the most severe bronchoconstriction (a clamping down and effectively shrinking of size of the airways that prevents normal air movement). I carry this with me at all times, as I have had severe life-threatening episodes of asthma and allergic reactions several times in the past. I start this sad patient on the aminophylline and ask to see her the next day. Since it's much easier for her to come to the hotel than all the way back to the clinic, I give her my room number and ask her to come "after hours" in the early evening.

I am thrilled when she actually shows up and has her husband with her. Having left my stethoscope in the hospital, I ask my nurse Shaaron to once again take care of me and bring her stethoscope so we can both listen to "Asthma Lady's" lungs. There is very little improvement. This time I give her an epinephrine injection from my personal supply, which helps temporarily, start her on prednisone and ask to see her again in two days, or the very next day if she gets worse. Two days later I get a message from an Indonesian team member that she could not come to let me listen to her lungs as she was back to her job of working in the fields. I am concerned and

disappointed that I do not get to see her and also concerned that going back to work in the fields so soon may cause a relapse to severe
wheezing and difficulty breathing. I had been unable to adequately
convey to her, and convince her, that the prednisone, a steroid which
will reduce her wheezing by reducing inflammation and swelling,
causes a false sense of well-being. She will *feel* better, but she needs
to actually *heal* before returning to work and further damaging her
lungs and her already fragile immune system. The reality of life here
is that when people can make it to the fields, they do.

So, as we are standing around the hotel lobby saying goodbye
to the team members who are departing, one of the Indonesian team
members who had been helping get patients from town to the hotel
for after-hours appointments tells me that he will take me into town
by motorcycle to see my asthma patient and several others. This
sounds like an adventure and I really want to see how she is doing
three days after starting prednisone.

Overhearing our conversation, the two Philippine dentists on
the team say they would like to go and see the village as well, so we
collect our cameras, medical supplies and sunscreen and head out.
The Indonesian enlists two other motorcycle drivers, so we each get
to ride with our own driver. What an exhilarating way to make a
house call – a fast, fun, fifteen-minute ride, wind blowing in our hair,
sunlight in our faces, sunscreen our only protection. No helmets in
this country, or at least not on this island. We stop at a tiny roadside
stand to say hello to some of my driver's friends and family, then go
a little farther to a dirt trail that winds off into the jungle, the motorcycles slowing down only enough to negotiate the pathway. A few
twists and turns later, we arrive at the village edge. First stop, the
home of my driver's mother.

Ducking into the mother's dark five-by five-foot square front
room, I see a bench-like bed on one side that takes up the full length
of the room, probably not quite long enough for me to fully stretch
out and a full foot shorter than Erik would need. He would not be
able to be horizontal and would have to curl up. Fortunately, we
don't have to sleep here. A bench outside the front door provides
seating for three; only a few people will fit inside the tiny main room
that is separated by a curtain from the back room, a smaller area
containing a shelf for kitchen items and other supplies. This room
has a doorway to the outside kitchen, a fenced in but open to the sky
"room" with a fire pit for cooking. All three rooms are smoky. The
front is the only area where I can see clearly and the only one into

which I am invited.

My driver brings a patient for me to see, a man perhaps in his mid-forties who also has trouble breathing, especially when walking or working in the fields. I am beginning to be known as the doctor who may be able to help those with asthma. This man, who is also quite thin, wheezes audibly, needs medications now and will probably need them daily for the rest of his life. He says he's had this difficulty breathing for many years and that it's getting worse. I give him some of what I have brought for my Asthma Lady, whom my driver has gone to get. Efren and Roberto, the Philippine dentists, are hanging around outside peeking in at me and filming with a small video cam. When my driver returns empty handed, saying my patient is in the fields and cannot come to see me, I finish up with two other quick medical consults and ask our drivers to take us back to the hotel. Later, Erik admits he had asked the dentists to watch out for me, the reason they came along on my house call. They did at least appreciate seeing the village and the inside of a hut as well as the fun motorcycle ride.

With Erik and a dozen of the other team members gone, I change my focus to moving yet again as we consolidate accommodations. This time I get to move in with Gail, much closer to the beach and ocean. There is no air conditioning in her bungalow, which is not a problem since ours never worked anyhow, sometimes giving us the illusion we were getting cool air when using only the fan. Gail has been happy with the ocean breeze blowing through open windows. The worst time of day is when we return from work, because to save money the hotel turns off the electricity from eight a.m. to six p.m. The windows have been closed by housekeeping for security reasons – as if closed windows could keep anyone out and as if we had anything more valuable than our clothing and toothbrushes. It is stifling and some days the wall thermometer registers over ninety degrees.

After Erik leaves, my antennae perk up and remain that way. I had felt very secure with him here, but once word spreads that we are providing free medical care, free medications and are from the United States, our schedule and comings and goings are publicly known, even to the exact location of our bungalows. Locals who cannot get forty minutes up the hill to the hospital clinic come to the hotel asking for medical care. They also wait for us at the end of the day, sitting in the hotel lobby to meet us when our bus pulls in. Several days after we arrive, two Australian surfers ask if we will see their Indonesian "families." They have spent two to four months a year surfing here for the past several years and plan to move here eventually. They have come to love the families they stay with, have even learned the language and provide enormous help financially and in other ways to this poor community. They are among the first to request "after hours" consultations and take advantage of this service which I am happy to provide. This is why I am here.

Distinctly different, this last week allows me more time with the other women and the joy of getting to know them. The local salesmen become increasingly pushy. And now that I'm closer to the beach, the mosquitoes are biting more and completely ignore my one-hundred percent DEET, biting right through it. After the first night in my new place, I miss the bats. They are several-hundred yards away in their colony near my first bungalow and I'm covered with mosquito bites in the morning. Nobody else on the trip seems to be a mosquito magnet. I can sit beside someone who is not getting bitten and watch the little blood-suckers land on my arms and legs and buzz my ears; I have come to fear and detest that buzzing. One team member takes pity on me and gives me his mosquito netting. His repellent works for him, and he has one of the rare rooms with functioning A.C. I immediately set up the netting over my bed and my life is changed. I can now sleep fearlessly at night and use the occasional daytime free hour to crawl under the net and comfortably read, write, or just visit with my roommate.

Mornings in my new home are spectacular as we get into a routine: Nancy comes over to visit with a thermos of coffee and the three of us watch the sun rise before breakfast. The sky is different each day. Most mornings the picture is peaceful, subtle pinks and oranges moving around each other, calm seas, boats quietly making their way in from a night's work, or heading out for the day. Once we are treated with stormy weather; big black rolling clouds above an ocean louder and rougher than usual, waves higher, small night-fishing boats hurrying home. This quiet time helps us prepare for the chaos that inevitably comes at the clinic.

I see another case of very advanced cancer. A young woman, the wife of the Australian surfer's best friend, is probably about thirty years old and has a toddler by the hand. She has been going blind in her left eye, developing some subtle enlargement in it. I can see from a distance the deformity on the upper aspect of the left side of her face and as I come closer, I see the opacification, the clouding of her eye. I don't have an ophthalmoscope with me but could probably not see any more with it, as the black background in her eye is obvious. I guess that she has a melanoma, a retro-orbital (behind the eye) cancer of the most serious kind. If I'm correct, she will die this year.

She speaks no English, so I talk freely about her to Matt, the tall blond Australian surfer. It's clear that he cares deeply, yet is not surprised by my diagnostic guess. By the time a tumor looks like this, if it is melanoma or another particularly lethal carcinoma, it is undoubtedly in other places in the body and way too far gone to treat effectively. I think out loud to Matt about exactly what and how to tell her and her family. He lets me off the hook by saying he will, of course, tell her and her husband. I am happy they have such a good friend in Matt and yet I'm so sad that they have to deal with this disease. There is no hope of help for her. Again, even if she could magically be whisked to the United States, it is probably far too late to save her life.

The day before our departure from the Saroke Beach Hotel, we hold a free clinic for the hotel and dining room staff and their families. We set up in the lobby and adjacent rooms while the dentists opt for the balcony because it has the best light and they don't need privacy to examine teeth. The eyeglass techs take the large conference room and the pharmacy uses the lobby. I choose a side conference room with an enormous table that can double as a stretcher. I have arranged for three minor surgery patients to see me this last day. I had met them on the Sunday afternoon we held clinic in town, but did not have surgical instruments or an appropriate place, or the time to do the procedures with so many others waiting.

Trying to limit the numbers of patients we see on this last day is like trying to hold water back with a sieve. There is no way to tell who family of hotel staff is and who is not since everyone in town claims to be related. I set up in my familiar way, four chairs, two interpreters, and begin. The usual types of patients come in a never-ending parade.

My most satisfying work of the morning is doing the minor surgeries. The first is a middle-aged lady with a large mole on her upper lip. It is the kind of lesion that draws immediate attention. Everyone who looks at her sees her big black mole first, then works hard to not look at it. The surgery is so simple. After cleansing the lip, I inject some Novocain and cut around the mole with four connecting incisions, making a diamond-shape. I then connect the cuts beneath the mole, kind of like connecting the dots, and remove the whole thing. Since we do not have access to a pathology lab, or even to biohazard waste, I throw this little piece of her face in the trash. It is important to me, not to her or anyone else in the room, that I can tell unquestionably that this is a benign mole. If there was any chance that this was a melanoma, I would have excised a much larger area, still knowing that the chance it will spread is high and the patient could have a recurrence. After I stitch up her lip with suture material that will dissolve in a few weeks, I give her a mirror. She cries with joy, hugging and thanking me profusely. It had taken about fifteen minutes start to finish, and while it doesn't change the length of her life or her physical health, it does add to her feeling of self-worth and self-confidence, and seems to instantly improve her emotional health. For only a few minutes of my life, and such a simple procedure, it is a big thank you. Why am I leaving?

The other surgeries are also on faces of women, one quite elderly who has a large, almost plum-sized, benign lesion hanging from the upper eyelid and covering about half of her left eye. She is about four-and-a-half feet tall, has a wrinkled face and a quiet wisdom about her. She arrives dressed in a long skirt, lacy blouse, sandals and a beautiful patterned shawl covering her head, and already is smiling as if she has won the lottery. It takes only a few minutes to separate her from this piece of tissue, and she is thrilled with the results. The other minor surgery patient is a young girl with a large sebaceous cyst in front of her ear, also an easily remedied problem. Such satisfied customers.

The saddest problem of the day is a pre-school-aged child with a neurological deficit. Unable to walk or communicate; she probably has a degenerative disease and will deteriorate over time until she dies without ever reaching teenage years. We have nothing to offer except sympathy and praise and encouragement for the parents.

Finally, clinic is over. We have seen our last patients in Indonesia. The rest of the day is spent packing, feeling a mix of emotions. Exhilaration accompanies the realization that we have finished with patients – we have seen between three-thousand and four-thousand patients in three weeks. Many days I saw fifty or more myself. Feelings of sadness are mixed in at leaving so much undone – those we had nothing to offer and those we could not see. We could continue to provide care at this rate and not run out of patients for a long time.

The evening finds us at a banquet, served buffet style on the terrace between the hotel and the kitchen, entertained by native dancers. Tomorrow begins the journey home.

△◆
Chapter Ten
△◆

I feel guilty leaving. I can leave this place and this lifestyle; few of the locals here have that luxury. At breakfast I give away the dozen pairs of sandals I bought on our last trip to the city to get medicines. I had noticed so many people going barefoot and was able to buy a twelve-pack of flip-flops, the kind of sandals almost everyone in this hot, island country wears, for about twelve dollars U.S. The kitchen staff and hotel workers are thrilled. On the porch of my bungalow I leave a stack of clothing and my old running shoes, which I brought intending to leave here. These are for the cleaning crew; they will understand. I have a few remaining pens, a pair of Erik's work gloves and a running cap to hand out to some of the locals who are waiting in the lobby to greet us one last time. The fifteen of us bring our baggage up to the lobby and begin our goodbyes. Everyone wants to shake hands and wish us well.

We board the bus, watching carefully to be sure each piece of luggage actually makes it on board, either in the back or on top. Nancy opts to ride on top as it's probably her last chance to do this for a while since it's not usually done in Tabernash, Colorado.

It's hard to leave, both emotionally and physically. The vendors are still trying to get us to buy something. I had looked at a wooden tapioca masher with intricate hand-carved handle several days ago. At that time the salesman quoted one-hundred dollars U.S. for it, saying it was "old." They have learned that we like the old, authentic and preferably actually used items, not the new, carved-for-tourists facsimiles. I declined to purchase it then, but was clearly admiring it. Now he is at the window of the bus asking twenty dollars, then ten. My interpreter nods that it is a good price. I hand the smiling vendor a ten-dollar bill and he gives me the tapioca masher just as the bus pulls away.

By the time we are actually on the road, it is close enough to lunchtime that I'm hungry again. Never without snacks and a bottle of water, I nibble on some Indonesian crackers and wonder if we will get a meal before we drive the four or five hours to Gunung-Sitoli. Less than a half-hour later the bus stops and Nancy crawls down from the top. She describes the danger of being up there with the bus traveling faster than it did on the rough road to the hospital. The three Indonesians who are on top are used to it and remain there.

Nancy also tells us about her near-decapitation when she ducked just in time to miss some low-flying electrical wires! Another moment and she would have had a bad cut on her neck and probably been thrown off the back of the bus onto the ground. I guess the laws in the U.S. about riding on top of vehicles make sense.

Within another hour we are passing through a tiny village. Slowing to almost a stop, I hear music and smell something tantalizing – market day! Shoulder to shoulder people, wall-to-wall booths, and vendors selling everything one could need to eat, wear, or use. With each inch the bus progresses the music is louder and the smells stronger. Now I am really hungry. I see several people cooking and the smells are impossible to ignore. Indonesian burritos? I wonder what is in them. The bus stops. Too many people in the narrow dirt street and many of the tables of goods for sale are just a few feet from the bus, so our driver must be vigilant not to knock over one of the makeshift stores, or a child or dog. People holding their wares up to the bus windows give me the idea to ask Uli, one of our better interpreters, to use her gifts of assertiveness and language to procure lunch on the go. No problem. Everyone in the market is ready to sell anything they have to anyone. If they have nothing to sell, maybe they can get a commission for connecting vendor and buyer. Uli is able to order some of the fried doughy burrito-like pastries for me, and for several others on the bus who can't resist the smells. These tasty pouches are filled with a spicy meat mixture of some kind and make a perfect lunch. They arrive by runner, as the bus is moving slowly again and we pass the stand where they are cooked. I hand some money out the window and wave to the smiling runner. He and the cook are enjoying this interaction as much as I am.

One pit stop and several more hours later we are in Gunung-Sitoli. We recognize our hotel, the one we stayed in our first night on the island. The hotel workers greet us like old friends and it feels like they are. So much has happened since then. Have we really only been here for less than three weeks? Or has it been three years? The familiarity of this hotel is comfortable. We unload the bus and buy cold drinks at the "reception" desk, a small counter in a corner of the lobby with a refrigerator behind it.

A quick trip to put our luggage in our rooms, a few minutes in the air-conditioning, a luxury we have not had in weeks, and we are off to the hospital, another twenty-minute ride, to leave our extra supplies and money to cover the care of patients we have sent here from our clinic in the south. The process of getting someone living on another part of the island to this hospital is complicated and over-whelming, even for us, reinforcing the understanding how disease goes untreated in remote villages. If they are able to get here, they may still get only marginal care. The one doctor, Dr. Derek, is excel-lent, but not a specialist in every field of medicine and limited by lack of equipment and assistants.

We spend most of the afternoon at the hospital settling the bills. As there is no fixed price for care, we negotiate with the admin-istrators. Needing a strong presence to effectively bargain, we gather an impressive group of five. My American interpreter Colin, Uli and two other men chosen for their size and gender go to the hospital with me. Indonesians have very little respect for women, so while Uli understands the nuances of dealing with hospital officials and of the language and can argue and demand with the best of them, she will not command respect like the men, especially Colin, older and fluent in Indonesian. Our little group feels like a "war party" going to do battle with the hospital administrators.

Uli is particularly helpful. She is of Batak heritage from northern Sumatra, descended from a tribe of warriors who were known to be extremely fierce. Their appearance is slightly different than many other Indonesians; short, stocky, somewhat flat-faced and of native Indonesian Indian heritage. Their fierceness has been passed down through the generations so that they are now known to be fierce business people and very tough competitors with a particu-larly abrasive and harsh attitude. This attitude and style of commu-nicating usually covers a very loving, kind human being underneath the cold, hard exterior. Uli is a perfect example of Batak. She can argue fiercely and directly and not hold a grudge or have negative overtones spill over into any relationships, certainly any of those that I see with team members. I learn a beautiful lesson in detach-ment. She does not let anything, especially "what people will think," get in the way of doing what she believes is right, nor will she accept limitations when she knows more is possible

We had sent two adolescent accident victims, the results of a motorcycle-bicycle crash, to the hospital. They both had head injuries and we felt they needed more care than we could provide at our little mountain clinic. We are told that they are improving and while they both had X-rays, only those on the older boy can be found. Great. There is no system of filing; just stacks of X-rays to rummage through, so feeling great concern about the status of the younger boy, we request more X-rays on him. I still question whether they had done any on him to begin with. The X-rays are of very poor quality and are difficult to read. I don't see a skull fracture but am still unconvinced that he does not have one. So much more could be done in this facility if people were appropriately trained, encouraged and somehow learned to be honest as well.

The father of one of the injured boys is here, so we are able to have a conference with him and the hospital administrator. We had told him days earlier that we would pay for half of the care for his son and the younger boy, who had been on the bicycle, when his son on the motorcycle crashed into him. It is traditional for the father or family of the older patient, or the one clearly at fault, to pay the medical expenses for everyone and the fathers of these two boys had previously negotiated without conflict. When we insisted the boys be transported to Gunung-Sitoli to receive better care, the financially responsible father said he couldn't afford it, so we agreed to pay half. Both boys were seriously injured, one of them semi-comatose when we did the preliminary care. I am impressed that they seem to be improving at this time, several days after the accident, with little more than supportive care, fluids, nutrition, and rest. Another lesson here: people heal, sometimes without modern medical care. I thank God for his design, creating us to heal in spite of ourselves! I am also reminded that my own healing has been through many venues, very little of it through "modern medical care for addicts." I have been blessed with ongoing supportive help from others who understand and I have never been a patient in a treatment center. It is possible to heal.

We need to sit down with the financially responsible father and the hospital administrator together to avoid either the father being charged full price and the administrator pocketing the money, or the father declaring that we already paid the administrator for the entire bill and that he owes nothing. How primitive and draining it feels to have to go through this! The five from our team, three American men, one Indonesian woman and me, are crammed into a tiny office, door and windows open, sitting beside each other in a corner in small, straight-backed chairs facing the hospital administrator. He is sitting behind a cluttered desk; an old scratched, wooden affair piled high with papers, none in organized stacks, several topped with empty cups and glasses, some with a layer of dust. Several assistants are walking around the room. One who had earlier searched through the dusty, scattered stacks of X-rays looking unsuccessfully for the one we want, now tells us that the X-ray technician will be in three or four hours later. It seems to us that he will return whenever the spirit moves him to drop in at his job.

The older boy's father is seated in a chair placed behind a table that is between us and the administrator. We are all facing the middle of the room. Uli is up and down, running over to the administrator's desk and pointing, gesturing, rattling off rapid Indonesian, trading exclamations with him. Colin understands them but doesn't have time to translate yet. Later he explains that the father is claiming we said we would pay it all and the hospital administrator is trying to overcharge. Only Uli can note this fact, as she is the one who knows appropriate prices, and negotiates down to a reasonable price for foreigners; of course, quite a lot more than a price reasonable for locals, but still nothing compared to cost in the U.S. Finally, we come to an agreement; about five dollars U.S. per day for lodging. Food is to be brought in by family, but if they cannot get there, which is likely as they are more than twenty miles away, have no transportation and need to work, Uli will need to have extra money and find a way to purchase food for the boys from outside the hospital. We leave more money with her personally; to be sure it is used as we intend. We pay cash, Indonesian *rupiah*, and get a receipt from one of the hospital officials, handwritten on a small piece of unlined paper, ragged edge, torn from a notebook.

We then try to pay for the "Goiter Lady." Unfortunately, Dr. Derek is off island, presumably in Singapore or maybe Vanuatu – he gets around. Unable to communicate directly with him, we have to trust that he will be back and pray he will find a way for "Goiter Lady" to have surgery to remove the enormous mass from her neck. We don't even know Dr. Derek's training. Is he experienced enough as a surgeon to operate on her, or can he get her to the mainland for care? And how can we reliably get him the money to cover her care? We also have a duffel bag of leftover supplies and cash we want to go directly to him, the rest of our Colorado money. All of us from Colorado agree that he is the one doing the most medical care with the least help, is clearly the most honest, and this is where we want our remaining supplies to go. We are leaving the island the next morning and none of us trust the hospital employees to give the money and supplies to Derek. We decide to give the duffel and a note with the cash to Cary, a young Indonesian man who is, in his spare time, a Church of Christ preacher. He speaks some English, actually quite well for someone who has never been to an English-speaking country, and is probably trustworthy. He loves being associated with our

team and I have no reason to doubt his honesty except that he is Indonesian. I am starting to be skeptical, judgmental and prejudiced,
or maybe just realistic.

Ah, honesty. Painful. I have more than a little experience
with this. There have been times in my life when I have wanted to
completely believe in and trust another person, and had to acknowledge that I had not picked the right person to trust. During early
childhood, children and their sense of safety and value in the world
are molded primarily by parents. In an alcoholic home, the parents
are not predictable or consistent, sometimes drunk, sometimes sober,
not reliable. They might show up and be sober, but they might not;
trusting them just results in disappointment and can be crazy-
making for everyone around them, especially their children. The
messages to the children are, "people are not reliable," "don't believe
or trust anyone," and "you are not important enough for me to stay
sober and do what I say I am going to." In medical school, as in early
recovery, the freshman student, like the person newly in recovery,
looks up to those who have gone before. Those in positions of authority or those just inspiring awe from the beginners, such as the recovering person with years of sobriety, the senior medical student or
attending physician, and the parent of the young child, all have similar impact. They are all in positions to mold the junior person looking up to them. Sometimes the admiration they receive is warranted,
sometimes not. There are doctors who are unreliable, unkind and
even unsafe. There are people who have not had a drink or drug for
years who are still dishonest and untrustworthy. And there are parents who are not deserving of the near worship their young children
bestow upon them. Optimists assume they can trust until proven
otherwise. Pessimists do the opposite: demand others prove themselves first, before trusting them. Realists, like me, having grown up
in an unpredictable household but having "re-solved" the old pain to
understand and accept that people are just human – almost all having good and bad, honest and dishonest, kind and unkind traits –
evaluate each situation based on all the information available. I have
learned a balance between trusting and being vulnerable and being
skeptical. Still, it is just uncomfortable to be honest with myself
about being judgmental, to acknowledge that I doubt the trustwor-
thiness of the Indonesian people in general, just because they are
Indonesian. The result of what I have observed while in the country,
my skepticism has developed in the past three weeks.

A few weeks later, after I am safely back in the States, Dr. Derek sends an email saying he has gotten the duffel and the money. Yeah! He is very appreciative and I am thankful that Cary is honest and trustworthy. Derek also says the "Goiter Lady" left the hospital because he could not do the surgery but he will have a goiter surgeon help sometime soon; an additional yeah.

△◆

Chapter Eleven

△◆

The Indonesian government is having an "event" on Nias the weekend of our departure. We have tickets on the only airline that flies to and from the island, and are scheduled to depart Nias for Medan one day before our international flight from Medan back to the States. Apparently tickets on this local airline are only useful if it is convenient for the airline to honor them. More grist for my distrust of people and organizations in Indonesia, more of what feels like dishonesty. We have tickets for a specific day and time, but they are not reliable. On our day of departure, honoring our tickets is not convenient for the airline because of the "event." Government officials have decided to take our seats and leave us to deal with our anger and frustration and to find another way to Medan. After much talking with airline officials, they agree to try to get us off of the island. Sitting, or pacing, in the miniscule Nias airport, we watch several flights come and go, our scheduled nine a.m. flight, one at noon, another a few hours later. We do not dare leave the airport for lunch, or to escape the heat (no air conditioning) for fear of missing a plane if they suddenly decide to board us. We are resigned to spending the day in the airport. It's a small building with one counter that accommodates one agent, a large scale in front of the counter for weighing passengers and baggage, and one waiting room, entered through a door with a metal detector, containing four rows of eight seats each. The bathrooms are typical Indonesian "squatters" and as filthy as anywhere else in this country. To my surprise, there is a food counter in the waiting room. The girl behind the counter serves coffee and packaged pastries, the 1950s versions of flour, sugar and flavoring in a preservative base. I am really glad I have some fruit and crackers with me.

Eventually they "find" an old army plane that can fly only during the daytime (is that because it doesn't have lights?) and bring it in from the mainland. Seven members of our group of eighteen are able to go on this flight and for some unknown reason my name is on the list. We hope that the plane will safely make its one-hour flight, deposit us, and return for our remaining eleven teammates. I consider giving up my seat so that someone else can be on this first flight and I think seriously about it when they weigh all of us, remove some of the baggage, including mine, and tell two passengers with boarding passes that they cannot go on this flight. My concern increases as they put the rear ramp of the plane down for us to board. More adventures in travel. About a dozen of us are crammed into the back of the plane, seven from our team and a few other passengers. We sit on benches facing each other, our backs to the porthole-like windows, knees bent and touching those in front of us. Seatbelts are available, but there are too many people on my bench for the number of available belts. I am beside an Indonesian boy, perhaps twelve years old, traveling with his mother. He is not in his seatbelt yet, so using sign language I suggest we share a belt. He grins, seeming to enjoy the attention we get from the surrounding passengers, mostly my teammates. It's a good thing we are both small.

The plane starts up and someone closes the ramp. Too late to change my mind, I wave goodbye to my suitcase still on the ground, hoping someone in my group brings it. As I pray for safety, I have difficulty "hearing" my thoughts above the loud engine. We get off of the ground safely and enjoy one of the most spectacular sunsets I have seen anywhere in the world. No flight attendants; no one cares whether my seatbelt is on or not; no food or drink service; just shouting to have a conversation above the loud engine noise and sitting on a hard bench a few inches off the floor with no way to protect my personal space. I might just as well enjoy this flight, even if it is the last hour of my life. There is lots of laughter from the Americans and smiles from the Indonesians watching us. I share my bag of raw peanuts, not the roasted salted kind you get on big airlines, and have enough to share with everyone. Even my seatbelt-mate enjoys some.

An hour later we arrive safely in Medan. The teammates who had to stay on Nias wait until dark, and then go back to the hotel. Some arrive in Medan the next morning, and the last few get to Medan just in time to check in for our flight to the States.

When the lucky few of us on the first flight arrive in Medan, we are met by some of our Indonesian team members who left the island the week before. We get the news that Steve, one of our American missionaries who served for two weeks as interpreter, has had a heart attack and undergone bypass surgery, for the third time. He is in Singapore and apparently getting very good medical care. I know that he has heart disease, but I'm surprised that he has had another event. Is it stress? The trip has been very stressful for all of us, physically, emotionally and spiritually, and I start to acknowledge this.

The flight home seems to take twice as long as the flight here just three weeks ago. Each step is exhausting: another layover in Taipei as China Airlines only flies to the U.S. from Taipei three times a week; the added insult of stopping in Seattle to refuel and not being able to take a direct flight to Denver; flying to Houston for the final connection back to Denver; the anxiety when we are late and wonder if we will make the Denver flight or have to spend the night in Houston.

Just to add to the excitement of the trip, and not to be outdone by Steve, our team leader Jim develops chest pain on the last leg of the flight home. His wife asks me to look at him and I find out that he also has heart disease and carries nitroglycerin pills. He has not taken one, even though he has been having pain on and off for hours. We move him up to first class where he can recline and I can monitor his blood pressure, giving him several additional medications and oxygen. We call for an ambulance to be waiting when we arrive in Houston, and pray that this episode does not progress. He makes it safely to the ambulance, and we get to the Denver flight on time.

△◆
Chapter Twelve
△◆

Fatigue. Yes, I do live at high altitude and have been at sea level for more than three weeks, but this is real fatigue. I have done four Ironman races, two fifty-mile ultra-runs and numerous other shorter-distance races and have never been this tired. Some days I just don't want to get out of bed. I am not really sleeping more than my usual six or seven hours, even if I include a nap, but I just cannot seem to get anything done. I work for myself and if I don't do something, it doesn't get done. If I were going to the office to see patients, there would be something in front of me requiring that I do it, but being a consultant and writer, if my reading and writing does not happen, there are no immediate consequences. I am not depressed;

I'm exhausted. After a few days, I return to running and swimming, with an occasional bike ride. Now I am more exhausted. I reduce the physical exercise, but stay tired.

There are talks to give, pictures and small gifts to distribute, supporters to thank. These presentations are somewhat energizing and feel satisfying. Eight days after my return there is an eight-point-seven magnitude earthquake on the north end of Nias. I get email and phone calls from people who want to be sure we are home. The news tells some of the story; the string of email from team members in the U.S. and in Indonesia tells more. The pictures on the news include a helicopter view of the island and we see the hotel that we stayed in on the northern part of the island has become a pile of rubble. We get more pictures and a story from someone still on the island and confirm that both hotels we stayed in, the one in the north, and the southern one with the bungalows, are destroyed. Eight days is a blink in geological time, says geologist Patty. We are blessed to be here, not hurt or killed by a falling hotel, but now we know and care about so many people there, that this is personal, not just a news event.

A distinct emptiness echoes in my core. I don't think too much about it because I am too tired to think, so I just feel. I picture people I know running for their lives, or digging out remains of loved ones. I cannot see myself there. I want to return, but I live here. The emptiness stays with me a long time, along with mental pictures and a minimum of thoughts. I wish I had been kinder to the ever-present salesmen.

Jim Clark, the fireman from California who was with us all three weeks, emails me and says he came home for one week and has returned to Nias. He says that Lagundri Bay where we lived in the Saroke Hotel has been completely changed after a tsunami came through and the place where he had surfed now has an above-water reef. This tsunami was not on the news and I find out that most of the earthquakes and small tsunamis in this part of the world are never reported by our media; there are too many and it is too far away. There are five more small quakes over the next few weeks, information we find only by looking online carefully, specifically for exact locations. Jim says he can help lots of people with minor first aid, finding water and food, and clearing away destruction from falling buildings and will stay as long as he can.

One email from Dr. Derek is entitled "Indonesia still shaking." He says the damage and injury is severe in the city and worse in outlying villages and he is taking medical care to the remote areas of the island.

My children, both in their twenties and fearful for my safety, ask me not to return. I agree with them and will not make plans to go back to Nias at this time. I will continue to communicate with Dr. Derek and with those from my team who do return, and I will continue to send support. After one talk I give at a school, I receive a check for one-thousand dollars to send to Dr. Derek. A group of short-term missionaries from California who are going back to Nias agrees to deliver the money.

A few months later, I give a presentation about the trip in a retirement home in North Carolina, where a favorite cousin lives. After I tell her I am coming to visit, Alma, then eighty-nine and very involved in planning social events at her retirement home, invites me to speak about my trip. She packs the auditorium with her many contacts, both retirees and younger friends from the community, giving us a group of about one-hundred-thirty people, more than for any previous event in this retirement home. The audience is the most attentive and appreciative I have ever had. Several people ask to donate and make out checks for me to send.

The stress of the trip, not being able to fix everyone, unreliable people and emotionally charged days are all familiar to me. I never have to tolerate the intolerable; I am able to let go of outcomes, protect myself emotionally, and do my part in a way that helps others while not doing harm to myself. I am thankful for my history of surviving childhood and addiction, learning coping skills, and becoming able to simply walk through situations without succumbing to the stress.

Many others have also done well on the trip, some saying they would do it again. Others decompensate for moments, hours, or days. Some vow they will never return or do another volunteer medical trip. All of us are changed in some way, learning our own strengths and weaknesses. We all learn that we can help some people a little, but cannot fix everyone.

So it goes on, and lives on in my heart.

You know you are back from Indonesia when

1. You turn on the shower and get hot water
2. You can sit to use the toilet instead of squat
3. You find toilet paper in the bathroom

4. Breakfast does not include fried rice *or* fried noodles
5. The outside temperature is thirty-four degrees Fahrenheit, not Centigrade (in the Colorado mountains)
6. It's nine a.m. and you are not yet sweating profusely
7. Your roommate is your own spouse
8. The only animals in your home are dogs and cats, no bats or geckos
9. You really want to sleep during the daytime and stay up at night
10. The roads are paved and cars are moving faster than twenty mph
11. You can wear a seatbelt
12. Purchase prices for everyday items are in tens or hundreds of dollars instead of thousands or millions of *rupiah*
13. Everyone speaks English

Lessons

△◆

- I need God to direct me in protecting myself, physically, emotionally, and spiritually. I cannot always trust all of his kids.
- Let go of things you cannot control.
- Indonesian men do not like to ask for help; American men do not like to ask for directions.
- Many things are Serenity Prayer issues: accept what you cannot change, change what you can, and have the wisdom to know the difference.
- People in some parts of the world still die of diseases we have long since learned how to treat and sometimes cure in this country
- Tolerance, flexibility, acceptance, and belief that our way is not the only way helps us keep perspective. The jobs eventually get done, except when they don't.
- Simplicity, family (of the knife-maker) working together, promotes joy.
- Delegate
- Detach (Uli)
- People heal, tissue heals, God has designed us to survive.

Crowds wait to see a doctor at the hospital on Nias.

"Goiter Lady"

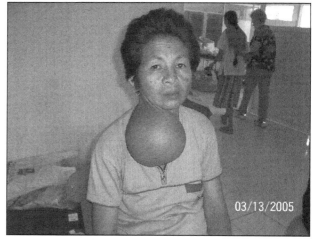

03/13/2005

Two interpreters (Nias to Indonesian and Indonesian to English) work with Dawn to tend to a patient while an audience watches

On the bus.

*Dawn checks her
"Asthma Lady."*

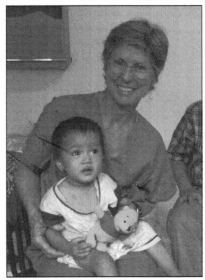

*A young patient gets a
special seat and Pooh.*

*Dawn and Patty at
the Houston airport
traveling "light."*

An Indonesian woman with an inoperable tumor under her tongue.

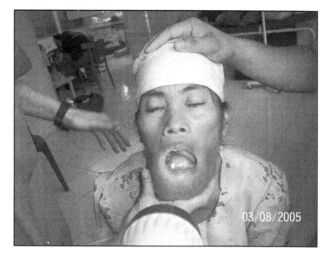

The hotel in Gunung Sitoli before and after the earthquake that hit Nias eight days after our return to the U.S.

School children pose for a picture in the midst of tsunami destruction.

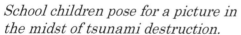

Part Eight

Louisiana
2005

Several months after our return from Indonesia, a major disaster struck in our own country. Hurricane Katrina devastated the city of New Orleans and much of the surrounding area. One of the women from the Colorado contingent of our Indonesia team asked if I wanted to go. I did. We organized. My hospital gave us supplies and we drove to Louisiana and set up a clinic under a canvas tarp. The trip was yet another adventure in providing medical care and, as always, an adventure in personal growth as well.

△◆
Chapter One
△◆

Just say "Yes."

Here we go again.

Hurricane Katrina hits Louisiana, Mississippi and Alabama on Monday, August 29, 2005. A week later, I have spent many hours watching the news, like most people around the country. I am appalled at how things go from bad to worse in New Orleans. Hundreds of thousands of people are without homes, and now have been without food, enough water, medical care, communications and toilet facilities for six days. The media tells unbelievable stories of the deaths from dehydration or lack of medical care among many who survived the initial hurricane. The dead bodies are not being removed from the convention center in New Orleans – there is no one to do it! The infrastructure is gone.

It's getting worse each day. People are in disbelief that this could happen in the United States. We hear things like, "There is no communication." "There is no transportation." "No water." "No toilets." I think of Indonesia. There is often no communication. Many people have no toilets or transportation. This is a way of life. When the tsunami hit just nine months ago, the needs of the people were met rapidly. The long-term repair and rebuilding will take a lifetime, but after the initial event, people did not sit around waiting to die of dehydration – such contrast. Last night on the news I heard that people who tried to walk out of the New Orleans Superdome were not allowed to leave. Some who were walking out of the city were turned back. This is absurd. If those who are healthy help some not so healthy, and travel in the relative cool of night, it is well within the realm of possibility to walk five or even ten miles each day. In two days, one could be ten to twenty miles away from the city to get help from individuals and businesses not in the middle of the destruction. Not everyone can walk, but most can, taking an enormous burden off the scant supplies and facilities.

Another possible solution could be to send buses, hundreds of them, from cities several hours away. Five-hundred buses could make several trips a day transporting thirty-thousand people to communities scattered within a four-hour drive, not overburdening any one place. The response of the local and national government has been as if it is in shock, just looking, wide-eyed, not doing anything useful. The response of many people has been the same, just being, not doing anything to save themselves.

I get calls and email from friends and relatives asking if I am going. As I have said before, my friends know me so well. September 1 is etched in stone as my annual "Lady Doctor Hiking Day." A dozen of us, all specialties, ages and fitness levels, get together each autumn to hike in the Colorado high country for a morning, then have lunch and talk – the day is about talking. This is a permanent engagement on my calendar. Even last year, when I was injured, I went along and walked a little, just enjoying the company of women I respect but rarely see for socializing, except for our annual hiking day and our ski day in February. Almost every specialty is represented and the conversation is unbelievable. One year I had a seriously infected hand, which did not affect my hiking, but required me to have intravenous antibiotics every few hours. I took my medication along and before setting out to hike I had Diane, my urologist friend, run the medication through the line and into my vein. Ah, bonding between doctors!

Some of the hiking chatter this year is about how to help the hurricane victims. I play with the idea of going to the South and seeing if and how I can be useful, but I do not seriously consider it. I have thought, at least for the first days after this devastating event, that the U.S. will deal effectively with it and provide adequate help. With the news reports I am seeing now, it seems to be going from very bad to much worse. Maybe human beings from around the country need to just go there and help, and not wait for the government agencies to get their acts together. People are suffering and dying every hour. So, we women physicians touch on the subject but no one, including me, really considers going.

I think the concept of just showing up someplace and going to work, doing what is in front of us, is foreign to most doctors except those who have worked in a disaster area or in an underdeveloped country. Fire fighters, paramedics, police and many others do it every day, but not us. We are so used to having help from nurses, medical assistants and technicians who arrange things for us. We usually have information about our patients neatly presented to us before, or when, we begin with each one. We are taught to respond to individual patients who present us with a specific problem, or set of problems. In a sense we are spoon-fed. All we have to do is apply the information we have learned in medical training to one patient at a time. One of the best-kept secrets among doctors is that it is often an easy job in many ways. Lots of my colleagues agree that most of us could not do most other professions, especially those that require in-novation, makeshift setups, lack of structure, or uncertainty. Of course there is uncertainty in medicine, but the setting is usually predictable and our role is the same day after day. Think about it. We live and work in a small, protected world of office, hospital, doc-tors, nurses and others with defined roles.

What is difficult is going into a situation that is unfamiliar. We doctors like to control, manage and manipulate our surround-ings. We set up offices, operating rooms and clinics to our liking. Go-ing into a new, different and probably chaotic setting is frightening. We may not know what to do. No one will know our title, our experi-ence, our training. The question I get asked most is, "What is it like" to do medical care in different places? What about lab, X-ray, follow-up? Of course, there usually isn't any follow-up and there is never lab and X-ray. We work with history and physical exam, faith and trust.

I have never worried about licensing on my trips to provide care in other countries. I have never been asked. I simply say I am a doctor and people believe me and ask me to help. Now, as I consider my first medical mission to a disaster area in my own country, a friend asks if I am licensed to practice in states other than Colorado. I am not.

△◆

Chapter Two

△◆

It's clear that there is an overwhelming need for medical care and other help. I'm surprised at the numbers of people who did not get out of the storm's path, the numbers needing medical care and the slow response of agencies in this country.

My friend Nancy, who was with me in Indonesia and lives in the Colorado mountains about an hour from me, calls on Thursday night, September 1, after I return home from my hike and asks, "Do you want to go?" Since I sold my medical practice several years ago and am working from home consulting part-time, I am able to con-sider taking time to do this. I stammer and stutter, trying unsuccess-fully to decline – I have never been good at "No." I don't have this on my schedule. I have work to do, a race I would like to enter if I can stay home long enough to train, and a daughter getting married in two months. Not only that, but my house is on the market and my husband and I are building a home three hours from here, north of Steamboat Springs, Colorado. I am busy enough, thank you very much.

Of course, the thousands of people living along the Gulf Coast did not plan for Hurricane Katrina, either. The news reports continue. Thousands are in the Superdome and thousands more have been moved to the Astrodome in Houston, Texas. There are reports of rape, theft and other assaults in the Superdome. New Orleans is flooded, as the levees have broken. Plans are to evacuate everyone from the city. Patients and staff are stranded in hospitals. Helicopter rescues are happening by the hundreds. This is a nightmare! It is hard to believe it is real and that it is here in the U.S.

I never do get out a "No." But I agree only to *consider* it and make a few calls to see if I can round up some donations of supplies and travel money. After the first three calls, I am in full preparation mode. Erik says, "I guess you're going." He also points out it took me about three seconds to agree to do a little footwork and see if things would fall into place. God stuff again. I just do what I think I am supposed to do and leave the results up to Him. I enjoy thinking that this is what is supposed to happen. It is so easy to get encouragement; it must be meant to be.

Nancy has managed to get two vehicles donated for the trip from a car rental company. She also has procured food and drink donations from a local supermarket. We are unsure about the availability of water and fuel if we drive into the disaster area, so we consider getting a gas can and taking extra gas, ultimately rejecting the idea as too dangerous.

One of my calls is to my chief fundraiser, Patty. She has several contacts that honored her request for support for our Indonesia trip and made personal donations, and she calls some of them again. The support is equally forthcoming, but there is far less time before we travel. I am so grateful for her interest in my adventures. She is a quiet, reserved lady who rarely asks for anything, so when she does, she is taken seriously and the response is usually positive. Before Indonesia we fundraised for more than a month; we leave for Louisiana in about a week. Still, enough is promised for this trip to encourage us to go.

By the Friday morning before Labor Day, less than twenty-four hours after saying to my lady doc friends that I am not going to the disaster site, I have received an overwhelming response to my request for support for this trip and by ten a.m. it's official, I'm going. By noon I have commitments from six doctor friends for donations of medications.

Having just seen my hiking doctor friends, I call several for donations and one in particular is helpful. She is not the kind of woman I would expect to be so responsive to my request and I'm pleasantly surprised at her interest. She is a fast-moving, somewhat harsh, very clinical, East Coast Jewish cardiologist. She is immediately "on it," has lots of hospital contacts and spreads the word rapidly. Her office manager has been looking for a way to help the Katrina victims and is thrilled to be asked to collect cardiac meds and supplies. She even asks around in her professional building and finds a pediatrics office that makes a huge donation of children's medications.

Another hour into my "footwork" and I get a call from a nurse at Lutheran Medical Center who is in charge of central supply. She tells me she has been instructed to give me anything I want. I am stunned. When I go to the hospital to meet with her, she says the CEO says to give us anything we need and he will deal with inventory later. I have been on the staff of this hospital since 1976, almost thirty years, and have never heard of anything like this generous response. I think it is my cardiologist friend who facilitated this. For now I am calling it another "God Thing."

I also go to the offices of several other doctor friends to see if they have extra samples. Lisa's office gives me two enormous trash bags of medication samples. Earlier in the day, they had even asked one of the pharmaceutical representatives to leave additional medications for me. Lisa also presses one-hundred dollars cash in my hand for gas. Carla says to just knock on her office door if I get there after hours and it's locked. I do, and her receptionist opens it. She still has patients even though it's after five. In spite of being so busy, she has a staff member fill yet another huge trash bag with medications. With each stop, I am more convinced that I am doing the right thing. Doors keep opening.

As usual, there is always someone who tries to detract. This time it's a pulmonologist who I have suspected has resented me for some time, as he does not say hello when we pass in the hallway; I am not sure why. We have been in the same medical community for more than two decades, so I may have inadvertently stepped on his toes at some time. I wonder what bothers him, or if he's just fundamentally rude, or maybe shy or preoccupied. Doctors, like everyone else, can be hurt, scared, or angry and they don't always know how to process and resolve issues, or get help. So, when I go to his office asking for extra samples of medications, he has his receptionist tell me to just call the pharmaceutical representative, saying he has only enough for his own patients. The reps are, of course, already unavailable for the long Labor Day weekend. I had put calls in to them hours ago and gotten messages that they will be back next week, after we are already gone.

Clearly, this doctor is not interested in being encouraging or supportive. I am thankful I do not have to live with resentment, thankful I have been given the tools to recover from much of my old pain as well as new issues and difficult people, both old and new, and daily life. Specific patterns of writing, consulting with another person who is using the same tools, looking at my own behavior, and changing are available in recovery programs. Dealing with resentment, hurt and anger in this way has allowed me the freedom from negativity that could, and in the past did cause me a great deal of pain. Anger, hurt, redoing, re-feeling old stuff is so destructive and for an alcoholic is just the kind of thing that causes relapse to drinking. "Resentment" means to re-feel as in the Latin verb *sentir,* "to feel." I pray that Dr. Resentful will someday get similar tools. Meanwhile, everyone else is thrilled about my upcoming trip, and gives me more than I ask, including lots of pulmonary medications. I go to my former office and they give me yet another large bag of medications.

After making my rounds to offices, I meet Erik and my son-in-law, Sven, at the hospital loading dock and pack up as much as three large vehicles can hold. We have a truck and two SUVs full of every medical supply imaginable. Unloading it all into my three-car garage I see it fills about thirty percent of the space. Can we get everything into the two vehicles we will drive to the Gulf Coast?

I send off an email to some of my friends and Erik tells some of his. Word spreads. Soon I am inundated with people who want to give me money for gas, lodging and supplies, and wonder if I can take used clothing, or if they can go with me. I decline the clothing; I have heard that there is already enough being distributed and we are saving room for medical supplies. I accept the offers for cash and checks. The first check in my hand is from Barb, my athletic training partner. Our friendship started in the swimming pool about eight years ago. We have trained in swimming, cycling, and running for years, which translates into *many* hours together. She would prefer if I help Katrina victims by remaining in Denver and providing care for the hundreds who have been evacuated to the old Lowery Air Force Base. Sounds much simpler than my plans, and I could avoid travel and still help, not to mention continue my regular swim, bike, and run routine with her. But I am already committed to traveling south. I will miss her for the weeks we are gone; she is used to me disappearing on short notice and will pray for my safety and welcome me home whenever I get back.

One of my always supportive friends, Holly, says that she and her husband had been considering donating to the Red Cross but decided to "wait and see what Dawn does." She arrives at my house with her own check and several from friends, including some from friends of friends who don't even know me.

An elderly relative calls to ask if I am going. I hear from others, including casual friends like the tellers at my bank, who say they thought I would go. I guess I'm getting a reputation. Maybe when I return, I will start a non-profit organization so my friends can officially deduct their donations.

△◆

Chapter Three

△◆

The team falls into place. Nancy and I are committed to the venture and are making contacts in Houston and Baton Rouge, but don't know exactly where we will go. Our decision is to just start driving and be available. By Sunday, September 4, at least six others express interest in joining us. While most cannot get two weeks off from work or family obligations, our mutual friend and chief fundraiser Patty, who has no medical experience other than being the mother of four children including triplets and a teenager, wants to be part of the trip this time. I encourage her to join us and to arrange for her own return early, since two weeks is too long for her. Her husband had joined us on the Indonesia relief trip and, quite capable of caring for triplets and a teenager singlehandedly, is supportive of her going on this one. Another friend, Dan, the only man who has seriously expressed interest, is between jobs, has been a chef in a treatment center for the past three years and has recently gotten a degree in counseling alcoholics. He spends much of Sunday doing some personal fundraising and calls later in the day to say he is in. He has gotten encouragement all day, and several donations to cover his personal expenses. This will be a first for him, an experience unlike any he has ever considered.

A friend of Nancy's, Paula is a former EMT who decides to join us. Speaking to me on the phone, she assures me she is "stable." We have discouraged other interested people who are well-intentioned but may require more emotional energy than we can give. This kind of event requires the volunteer to be self-sufficient, flexible and able to get along with a variety of people. It is very difficult to have "takers" or needy people instead of "givers" and independent people, as takers detract from the overall energy of the group.

I am grateful to have been given the example of parents who were givers, in spite of their imperfections. As a child, I observed my parents, especially my mother, giving to needy people, strangers and extended family, giving of her time, volunteering at the church, and having an attitude of generosity. Part of an emotionally healthy recovery, just like any emotionally healthy life, allows us to go beyond participating and actually contribute to society, to give back. Some people get here, others don't. One saying that goes around recovery circles is, "Trust God, clean house, help others." This just about sums it up. Positive, healthy recovery requires us to get back to square one of our emotional and spiritual health; grow and "clean up our own messy past" while beginning to feel, or at least behave, as if we are "normal"; and to act like any other human being participating in life, becoming a "giver" instead of a "taker."

By the end of Sunday, it appears as if we have six people, two vehicles, supplies, money, and a vague idea of where we will go. I am reminding myself that God puts these groups together, I just do the footwork and encourage or discourage, leaving the results up to Him. I say out loud, so I can really hear it, "Everything happens for a reason. I just do not get to know the reason most of the time."

Monday, Labor Day, is spent packing. I have procrastinated about packing personal belongings, ambivalent about leaving home again. My life is full, more so than usual now, and I really did not count on being gone, putting everything else on hold for two weeks. How did I ever have time to go to my office and see patients during all the years I worked almost full time? Where is the line between self-care and caring for others? Should I really be doing this? I love spontaneity, but is this just impulsivity? Will I be sorry later that I didn't spend this time getting ready for moving, or for Brie and Dave's wedding? I truly believe I do this mission stuff for me. I get so much out of each trip, each patient, and feel so energized that I am convinced I will return in a few short weeks ready to do double-time at home, picking up the pieces and never missing a beat.

Several friends join us for the ritual of consolidating medicines that come in sample packets of one to four pills, starter doses. As usual, we want them to be packed in full doses to give to patients and we do not want to use the limited and valuable room in our vehicles transporting the extra layers of cardboard and paper. We accumulate two enormous trash bags of paper and plastic packaging, accomplishing a good bit of space-saving. We now have efficient doses of dozens of medications, everything we can think of that does not require refrigeration. One friend has donated a nebulizer that she is thankful her adult son no longer needs. The night before departure our team is five plus a maybe. Dan will arrive at my house at six tomorrow morning to take Paula and Nancy, who have been here packing medicines all day, to pick up the rental vehicles. We will take whatever they give us, but hope for large, safe vehicles that aren't horrible gas-guzzlers. Then we'll pick up Patty at her house and start driving south.

Later that night, I get a call from our "maybe," a nurse practitioner friend of Dan's who helped us pack medicines and who has great energy. She cannot join us, as she does not have as much vacation time accumulated as she thought, and she is still paying off student loans. I am disappointed because I had gotten a good feeling when I met her earlier today about her capacity to work with our team and contribute.

So our final count gives us a team of five: I am the only doctor; there are two former EMTs and two people with no medical experience. Patty plans to return in three days from Houston and is going just to help us drive. There is a chance that one or more of our friends from home will join us after the first week. Erik has said he is available if we need him, and could fly in, work a few days and drive home with us. Remembering to be flexible and to trust God, two of our lessons from previous trips, we remain open to all possibilities.

We're thrilled to find that the two rental vehicles donated for the trip are matching Ford Expeditions. They will hold lots of supplies and are also safe, worth the extra we will spend on fuel. We pack so that one vehicle has only the two front seats empty for driver and passenger and the other has an additional seat in the back for our fifth person. We ask the smokers not to smoke in the car and they promise not to, but after a few days of travel, break that promise. We have radios that allow us to speak from car to car as long as we are only a few miles apart, and we agree to stay close to each other, if not immediately one behind the other. We are off!

Energized to be on the road after marathon preparations, we get all the way to Amarillo the first day and decide to stay in a motel. We get three rooms – Dan deserves his own room, and we deserve him having it. Spending so many hours inside vehicles has its drawbacks, one of which is lack of personal space. None of us want to worry about appropriate bathroom behavior, and some of us might want to lounge around on our beds in scant clothing. At dinner in a chain cafeteria, chosen for efficiency and convenience, not food quality, I get a much appreciated call from Shaaron, a nurse who was in Indonesia with us and who lives an hour north of Houston. She got my email saying we're coming and invites us all to stay at her house. She will be going in to the Astrodome to volunteer for the next few days and will take us with her. This is about the best news we could get now, as finding a place to stay, finding the enormous center, parking, then finding the place to sign up and begin working could be an ordeal.

The next morning after a quick, free breakfast, one of the perks found in the cheap chain motels, we are on the road again. Approaching Dallas-Fort Worth, the traffic picks up and the pace slows down. I am taking my turn driving the lead vehicle, my passengers keeping our second car in sight and in radio communication. Glancing at my rearview window, I see several extremely fast-moving black cars and SUVs behind me, headlights on, gaining rapidly. I move into the slower lane, watching carefully the progress of this line of cars. Using their horns liberally to push slower vehicles out of the fast lane, the first few soon pass me going at least eighty-five miles per hour. I am driving over sixty in the slow lane and they make me look like I am standing still. California license plates and signs in their rear windows reading, "California Cops for Louisiana," "Help for Katrina victims," and other informative phrases announce their destination. They are uniformed police officers from California.

Not one to be left out, I wait until approximately twenty vehicles, each with two to four California cops headed for Louisiana, pass me – then I quickly swerve into the fast lane behind the last one, turn on my headlights, and become part of their convoy. No problem. My vehicle is black, too, and we fit right in. I have driven on the Autobahn in Germany, and am already considering a second or third career as a race car driver. The driver of our second vehicle does not follow, being a bit more timid about speed than me, so we meet up later after negotiating this double city. The big advantage to me is that I easily go through the Dallas-Fort Worth traffic, not having to stop for the usual annoyances of construction, detours and other backups. The Texas police extend courtesy to their California counterparts and wave them, and us, through all kinds of potential jams. And I get to drive *fast!*

Once in Houston, Dan is able to stay with his sister, reconnecting with us the next morning to drive, with Shaaron's direction, to the Astrodome. The doors continue to open; the encouragement and constant thank-yous increase as we get closer to Houston. Picking up Dan from the Starbucks where his sister has dropped him off, we find that they are offering free coffee to all volunteers! I get my favorite, a frappacino topped with whipped cream. By the time we're ready to get back into the cars, I have finished the whipped cream and ask the tattooed, pierced young man preparing the coffee if I can get another "hit" of topping. He says enthusiastically, "Anything you want!" When I thank him and tell him, "You're the best," he responds, "*You're* the best!" for volunteering. Things like this happen on a regular basis during the entire trip, constant acknowledgement and appreciation. It already feels embarrassing, as I don't think of this as a big deal, just an opportunity to practice medicine in a different setting, as a volunteer, and without the hassles of paperwork and complicated insurance company red tape and hoops to jump through.

△◆

Chapter Four

△◆

We are so grateful to have Shaaron directing us. Without her guidance we would probably have taken much longer to find the Astrodome. She knows exactly which exits and side roads to take to get there and doesn't miss a turn. The traffic is bumper-to-bumper starting many miles and many more minutes out of Houston and moving very slowly, even though it's well past traditional morning "rush hour." Shaaron commutes by bus to a "park and ride" lot, a total of about ninety minutes on the days she is either working or taking a class in the city. It's worth it to her to live so far out of the city in a beautiful and peaceful neighborhood – downtown Houston is *busy.*

At the first checkpoint we are told no more volunteers are

needed, but to drive a hundred yards further and check with the next official. Shaaron had already signed us up the previous day, committing us to work this day, so we persist and give additional information that we are a medical team already expected. Now waving us in, this second official tells us to drive to a parking lot for medical volunteers close to the entrance. This complex is *huge.*

We finally make our way to the sign-in area. They are extremely organized, with a bank of computers, photographers and security. They ask for my medical license, which fortunately I have remembered to bring. I usually carry a small wallet-sized copy of it with me now, after providing care to a man having a heart attack on a plane last year and realizing I had no way to prove I am really a doctor. In Houston, they are able to put my Colorado license information into the computer and check me out in about two minutes. Whew. I am who I say I am. I am accepted as a volunteer and in the next three or four minutes they have my picture ID ready. The guards comment that none of the other doctors were smiling so much when their pictures were taken. I guess I am really happy to be here. I would not be here if it didn't make me happy – what's up with the other docs?

Shaaron has signed into the RN area, and the others with me get their pictures taken, the two EMTs and Dan and Patty, not medically trained, now designated as my "assistants." Asked who we're with, we respond, "Just ourselves," and get blank looks from the people making the picture IDs. I guess most volunteers are with some well-known official organization, so we name ourselves CMV, the "Colorado Medical Volunteers." Dan actually has this "official" designation put on his ID behind his name.

Off to the clinical area we go, not knowing what we will face or how we will be useful. We are introduced to the others in the work area by a dentist who is doing administrative work, organizing and communicating with the media. We can now see the setup and the supplies. The whole Astrodome is arranged for patients, pharmacy, free clothing and shoe distribution, and care and feeding of volunteers. Ambulances arrive every few minutes. Partitions made out of yellow curtains strung on poles and rods, some for individual patient "rooms," some for definition of general areas such as intake, records, immunization, pharmacy, etc. fill more than half of the enormous building. The rest of the space is occupied by several trailers, one representing a large pharmacy chain, undoubtedly containing every imaginable product and medication. There is a bank of "Texas Outhouses," several labeled "Medical Staff Only," and a row of a half-dozen sinks, the kind I have seen at large campouts, outdoor concerts and other events. The water is available through a portable system and requires only pumping a foot pedal for delivery – and is clearly labeled, "Not for Drinking." At another location, there is bottled water for volunteers and patients. Antibacterial hand wash is everywhere. Samples for individuals, as well as large bottles, are at every desk and in every patient cubicle. The threat of communicable disease is real, but not so much more than the threat doctors and nurses face every day.

We find lots of work. I evaluate and treat people with respiratory illnesses, abdominal pain, back pain, chest pain, rashes and numerous other ailments. Some of our crew gives hepatitis immunizations to FEMA workers. Dan finds a need for his counseling skills in addiction and alcoholism. I am beginning to take a history on one patient, when an administrative type walks in and asks to speak with me. She takes me out of the room and tells me this lady is a multiple repeat user of the system and asks to speak with the patient. I agree, of course, as the organization of this place is phenomenal with charts generated, patients followed, even insurance information obtained from those who have coverage. All care is free and done by volunteer doctors and nurses, but insurance is billed when appropriate, so some reimbursement for supplies and a few paid administrative staff members can be obtained.

The very kind lady who interrupted me asks the patient to produce her card for a local clinic. This volunteer administrator really knows her stuff and tells the patient that she is to get her medical care at the clinic because the Astrodome setup is for Katrina evacuees, not Houston residents. The patient has been here several times over the last few days, asking for medications and lying about her status as a local. She has been caught each time as she continues to try to milk the system. Without protest, she is escorted by the nurses out of the patient area and just seems resigned to the fact that she has been found out. Maybe she will try again. I wonder what she thinks the Astrodome clinic has that her clinic does not – maybe new faces, different doctors and nurses? She reminds me of the many indigent, mostly mentally ill or alcoholic and drug-addicted street people I have cared for at different times and places in my career. Every city and most small towns have them. I know of no perfect system for caring for this population, but in this country, unlike many others, they do have access to excellent medical care.

Sadness for this woman's level of emotional health reminds me of my own days before recovery. While I did not look or behave like her, I had enormous internal pain. I too received "excellent care" when in the depths of my disease, but not from doctors. The life-saving care I received was from other recovering people who had been caught in the depression and addiction I was in and had recovered. They knew how to help me and provide love, encouragement and guidance through the hard emotional work of recovery. For them to be willing to lead me into and through early recovery, I had to do my part. I had to stop the alcohol and drugs, whatever it took. In spite of how difficult it is to change, the addict is the only one who can change himself, using the tools given freely by other recovering people.

Back to the present. We five Coloradoans meet other volunteers from all over the country; doctors from New Mexico and California, nurses from Texas and surrounding states, and a respiratory therapist from Michigan. These are the few with whom we can take time to speak. There are new patients every few minutes; the system is working and all are seen and treated.

Walking around the Astrodome, it's obvious that there are more supplies than needed; they do not need ours. And while we work all day, they really do not need us either. Convinced there is a place we are supposed to be where there is not such organized and accessible medical care, a place we can provide something needed and not available, we decide to continue on to Baton Rouge, where Nancy has a contact at an Episcopal Church. At the end of our work day, we leave the Astrodome and drive east, going until dark and then trying to find a motel.

None of us realized that evacuees would be filling so many rooms this far from New Orleans. The receptionist at one of the several full motels where we stop to attempt to find lodging calls another motel and talks someone into giving us the last rooms, only because we are volunteers here to help. Most of the motels in town, and everywhere east of here until beyond the hurricane area, are full. That night we actually do some medical care and counseling for an older couple from New Orleans staying in a room near ours. The wife has chest pain and lots of anger, fear and anxiety. After checking to be sure she is stable medically and not having a heart attack, we spend some time letting her vent and tell her story. Expressing enormous gratitude, she says she feels better after talking; we've helped, but wish there was something more we could do. The magic wands are, as usual, on backorder.

The next morning we drive the short distance to Baton Rouge. When we arrive at the church, the people Nancy had contacted are friendly, but do not have either a place for us to work or to stay. Nancy had done the communication with them and they obviously didn't understand that we thought they were arranging connections for us.

I am seeing that in situations like this, many people want to help but few have the skills and initiative to actually do something useful on their own. Most "helpers" are volunteers who follow the lead and direction of the organizer. Only a few are good organizers or instigators. It's not a problem for local charities, shelters, food banks and big, established organizations that can usually put as many helpers to work as they can get. It becomes a big problem during sudden disasters like Katrina, where too few established groups exist to help the many who need help immediately. We need more people with the capacity to set up aid stations of all kinds: food, clothing, shelter, document retrieval and replacement, etc.

Having spent several hours talking with people at the church and coming to understand that we are still on our own in terms of finding a place to help, we are approached by a lady walking into the church foyer who asks if she can help us. I ponder the question for about a millisecond and respond with an assertive "Yes." After she hears of our situation, she swings into action. She is petite, sixty-ish going on thirty, high energy, impeccably dressed and has a more middle-to-north-East Coast accent than a Southern one. I remember that the New Orleans accent is more like New York or New Jersey than typical Louisiana southern drawl. Our new friend asks us to follow her first to a lunch spot where we sample traditional Louisiana "po-boy" sandwiches, then to several places she knows that have set up medical clinics for refugees. All places are well staffed. We get used to being turned away, notwithstanding our expertise, energy and desire to help. The day is coming to an end and it's clear that we do not yet have a place to stay, work, or in a larger sense, a place to be.

This fast-moving, fast-driving lady – it's a challenge to keep her in sight as we follow her through the streets of Baton Rouge – calls her recently divorced son and places us at his home. He is happy to let us occupy his spare rooms and floor space with our sleeping bags. He calls a friend in Slidell, Louisiana, a town just across Lake Ponchatrain from New Orleans, and finds that tomorrow is the day that evacuees are going to be allowed back into Slidell, the perfect day for us to arrive and provide medical care. We are only an hour away, so we make plans to drive there in the morning, using the evening to do laundry, check email, make phone calls home and visit with our host. Three of us also locate and attend a support group meeting receiving, as usual, a boost in the form of a "spiritual radiation treatment."

I share with him my own experience with divorce and, more importantly, the positive aspects of remarriage for me and my children. He is concerned for the emotional health of his daughter and appreciates my reassurance that, while difficult, divorce does not have to severely damage children. I also share with him the part my alcoholism played in my first marriage, my divorce and my current improved emotional health. The next morning he wants to talk about his own drinking problem! Dan and I spend some time with him, noting that God has once again provided a way for us to be useful. We hope it helps this man; we know that sharing our experience, strength and hope helps us.

Recounting the God sightings – some might say miracles or coincidences, depending on personal beliefs – I realize we are at eleven so far: 1) I am able to change all plans, without doing harm to anyone, to take this trip on short notice; 2) We receive enough medical supplies to fill two trucks on a half day's notice; 3) Money for fuel and lodging, as well as extra supplies, just shows up; 4) Two large vehicles are donated for the entire trip; 5) Shaaron has a place for us to stay near Houston, and helps us gain entrance to the heavily guarded Astrodome to volunteer for a day; 6) We receive identification badges at the Astrodome that help us through the rest of the trip; 7) We find lodging just outside of Baton Rouge when almost everything is full; 8) A lady helps us through the maze of looking for a place to help and stay in Baton Rouge; 9) We find free lodging *in* Baton Rouge; 10) We are able to help someone, a recently divorced man struggling with alcohol, in a way we did not expect, even *before* we get to work with refugees from Katrina; and 11) We have a destination for tomorrow – a place we may find we can be useful!

△◆

Chapter Five

△◆

Traffic. We are in bumper-to-bumper, stop-and-start traffic. One lane into the city is open on this first day that residents are al-

lowed back into their hometown of Slidell, after being evacuated almost two weeks earlier. The military has kept everyone who left out
until now, citing multiple safety concerns. Campers and trailers that
have been temporary homes for the past thirteen days number as
many as the cars and trucks in the slow-moving line. People know
that the chances of their houses still standing and being habitable
are slim. The campers will continue to be home for many days to
come.

During the last hours of driving on this third day on the road,
we are seeing increasing evidence of destruction. Billboards and tele-
phone poles are down, buildings are ripped apart, debris is everywhere. Reminiscent of a Salvador Dali painting, the twisted and distorted landscape holds boats, grounded far from water and bent at
grotesque angles, colliding with portions of buildings. Cars are piled
on top of each other, some in ditches, some standing on end, most
partially covered with uprooted trees and shrubs. Faces of other
drivers are uniformly stunned as they seek out familiar landmarks
only to find them missing or far from where they had previously
been.

Our trepidation about just what we will be able to do is
masked by our excitement in being part of this migration back home
for so many thousands of people. Finally, we reach the edge of town
and I see a dirt lot with a temporary food service trailer and a large
canvas tarp covering hundreds of boxes. A sign reads simply,
"MEALS." That's the only cue I need. I make a quick decision to pull
over into the dirt parking, leaving room for our second vehicle just
behind me. I jump out and beckon the others to follow.

"Let's just check this out," I offer, half-walking, half-running
about a hundred yards to where I see people. I am not really thinking, just *doing* and I have no idea why I think we should stop at a
dirt lot where volunteers are serving food. In fact, none of us knows
anything about how we are going to do what we have set out to do.

A tall man, in a red shirt and carrying a radio, walks toward
me and looks like just the person I need, clearly in charge of something. By the time we get to each other, it's apparent that this is a
very large operation, amazingly organized, with an enormous
amount of food in boxes and crates. A small front-end loader, driven
by a friendly man with a Red Sox cap, is stacking some of the boxes.
I am reminded of my Dad's dog food mill and the sacks of feed
stacked so that there were pathways between them. I used to play
hide-and seek with my brother at Dad's mill. It would be easy to hide

in this maze where the boxes of food are stacked so high that I cannot see over them. In subsequent days, I retreat here to make phone calls, or just get a few minutes alone. At this moment, I have no idea that my life will revolve around this dirt lot for the coming two weeks.

Standing as tall as I can in my very flat sandals, I introduce myself to the big guy with the radio and compliment him on his organizational skills. He is cordial, stops talking into the radio, and says they are providing three meals a day to thousands of returning residents. His large Christian group has joined with an Amish group from Pennsylvania to cook and serve, in drive-though style and at no cost, more than six-thousand meals a day! This seems like as good a time as any to ask if he wants to add a medical contingent. He looks at me with a kind of questioning expression, at which point it makes sense to tell him that I'm a doctor and have four assistants and two trucks full of supplies. Never mind my attire, sandals and shorts; all we need is a place to work. Approximately twenty seconds later, he says, "Yes," points to a second enormous canvas tarp and asks if I want to set up under it. We are about to be in business!

There is a flurry of activity as he instructs the driver of the little front-end loader to set up boxes as a barricade at the perimeter of the area covered by the tarp, giving us something resembling a short foundation for nonexistent walls. Several workers materialize to help rake the dirt floor, placing a box over the tree root in the middle of our developing clinic so we don't become casualties with broken toes or sprained ankles before we even see our first patient.

Back to our vehicles to drive around the block, we re-enter the slow-moving line of returning residents and eventually arrive within twenty-five feet of the "front door" of what is starting to feel like our M.A.S.H. unit. Unloading our vehicles and organizing equipment is energizing and convinces us we are about to have a functioning medical clinic. Someone offers army cots to use for patients; another volunteer brings a chair and small table for our team member who will function as receptionist.

As an afterthought, the man with the radio asks me to go to the temporary "city offices" that are set up in trailers nearby to let them know I will be practicing medicine under one of his tents. Again, he gives me that quizzical look. Maybe he does not believe I am really a doctor, understandable when I check out my disheveled appearance, wrinkled shorts, hair and face sticky in the humidity and heat and dirt smudges everywhere. I have never much thought that I look like a doctor either, so it's no problem for me and I take it as a compliment. After the process of getting the official blessings from the city, we're in business. The drive from Colorado, days of wondering how we will help, but trusting God to open doors, is all worth it.

Blessings. It turns out that we are dealing with the 700 Club, an international evangelical organization that produces a Christian television program for its Christian Broadcasting Network; they have the means to do anything they want. I don't actually find this out until a week later; so much for my interest in external factors. I just want to get set up to deal with the medical end of things. I do trust that God will provide a way for us to do whatever it is that He wants us to do, whether or not it is what we have in mind. I am reminded of a favorite saying that one way to make God laugh is to tell him *my* plans.

At the city office, now temporarily housed in a trailer, I introduce myself and my team. We are all wearing the badges we received at the Houston Astrodome and look very official in our shorts and T-shirts – we are the least of the city's worries. But this is the U.S. and they must establish that I am a real doctor, licensed in at least one state, with no "black marks" against me. In disaster conditions, any state license is accepted by any other state. I am normally not able to legally practice medicine in any state other than my home state of Colorado, the only place besides Maryland, where I completed medical school and did one of my years of residency, that I have ever had a license. The exception to this is in government facilities, where any state license is accepted. Here in Louisiana in these disaster conditions, any state license is acceptable and they are glad to have us. I mention to the busy but friendly lady at the main desk that five of us will be here for two weeks (Patty has decided she is so interested and able to be helpful that she cannot make herself break away and go home early as planned) and ask if she has any ideas about a place we could sleep. I make sure she knows we are fine with sleeping outdoors on the cots in our "clinic," but if she just happens to know of anything inside to let us know. I am grateful for cell phones, as she takes my number. Another sixty seconds and she has my entire professional history up on her computer screen, pronouncing me legitimate and welcome to practice medicine in Slidell, Louisiana.

Meanwhile, the cots arrive; fortunately there are six of them, one for each of us to sleep on and one extra to block the makeshift doorway that we set up. We assume we will be sleeping here since there are no intact motels and most homes are completely destroyed. Many of the roads are damaged and no restaurants are open and we find out later that many doctors have already decided not to rebuild their practices and have left the area permanently. Medical records have been destroyed along with the office buildings. Patients are left with what they have, usually a quickly diminishing supply of regular medications and no record of past diagnoses and prescriptions. Even the pharmacies have lost some records, but fortunately many records are computerized and accessible. The pharmacists become my greatest allies in determining what medications patients have used in the past and in trying to reconstruct their medical histories. This first day, I am just beginning to see the magnitude of what needs to be done in the area of health care, so much less obvious than cleanup of hurricane destruction.

Back at our M.A.S.H. unit, we organize supplies and medications. A young man with a cut finger recognizes that we are becoming something resembling a medical clinic and asks if we can help him. One of my team finds a way to clean his wound, digging through our supplies as we unload and finding antibiotic ointment and bandages. He is the first of many injured and ill people we treat over the ensuing weeks.

Dan has disappeared and returns a few hours later with food for all of us. As a former chef, he has found the perfect place to work: food service. Everything is, of course, free for the homeless residents, volunteers and city workers. The food service people are as eager to feed us as we are to take care of any medical problems they incur. We develop an excellent working relationship with the other volunteers working nearby, the construction workers, tree removal guys and others who come to the clinic.

By mid-afternoon that first day, we are treating walk-ins who are actually walking in from all three sides of our space, stepping over the boxes. The area under the tarp is about twenty-five by twenty-five feet, dirt floor complete with tree roots and one wall of boxes that becomes the backdrop for our supply area, and two sides with some boxes marking the easily ignored border. Some astute volunteer notices this and finds a length of red rope to string along the sides above the boxes at waist height. This helps, but eventually we build more of a barrier and make a sign with an arrow pointing to the "door," a space about fifteen feet across one side of the tarp.

We set up our table and chair here and do patient "intakes" to actually get some information about who we are treating. What a concept – just like home. It never occurs to me to keep records of what we are doing, as all of my previous volunteer trips have been to developing countries where I don't even speak the language. I am so grateful for Paula, an EMT and probably the most mature, responsible and organized member of the group, who thinks to do this and arranges for patients to sign in and tell her their needs. She then takes a brief medical history, records their blood pressure and puts them and their new medical record on a cot to wait for me to see them. She is seeing the big picture, unlike me, focused on just the sick and injured person in front of me at the moment.

We really do have a great team: Paula, organized and with a terrific work ethic and enough background in medicine to be comfortable and anticipate many things the rest of us do not; Nancy, also a former EMT, who joined me on the Indonesia trip and is instigator of this trip; Patty, our primary fundraiser who was initially along just to help us drive, but is interested and brave enough to stay longer than planned and also functions as the primary trip photographer; Dan, with no medical background, the most willing worker of all, finding his place helping alcoholics, working in food service and generally doing anything we need, always and consistently with a great attitude and a smile, extremely brave to join four women; and me.

Our first few patients are workers with minor injuries, easy to treat and thankful we can help them to get back to work. Soon we see a preteen girl with asthma who is brought in by her mother. Her medications have been lost and not replaced since she and her family fled their home ten days ago. Her asthma is worse now after spending the day in the remains of her home, inhaling dust and mold. Thanks to someone with more foresight than me, we have a generator. We are able to set up one of the four nebulizers someone in Denver donated, treat her acute, relatively mild asthma attack and send her home with medication and one of the nebulizers. This experience is good and we are feeling useful. Several more patients drift in, including another who has been out of medicine for too long. Blood pressure sky-high and at significant risk for a stroke, this lady has an urgent medical problem which untreated will become an emergency with devastating consequences. She is a moderately overweight, black, middle-aged lady with an endearing smile and that New Orleans accent that has a tinge of New York in it.

While geographically close to Mississippi, the speaking style and accent of these New Orleans and Slidell natives is drastically different. I am used to both as I have several acquaintances from

Mississippi, including a doctor with whom I have been on a committee that requires regular conference calls; his voice is unmistakably sugary Southern! My close high school friend Nancy grew up in New Orleans, "N-Awlins" as she says, and moved back home after college. I hear this lady in front of me speak and immediately think of Nancy and wonder where she is.

I later find out Nancy evacuated to Baton Rouge. Her husband, Jim Amoss, editor of the major New Orleans daily newspaper, the *Times-Picayune*, weathered the hurricane in the paper's New Orleans newsroom and got the paper out every day during this time, a feat that boggles my mind. For the first three days after the hurricane, the newspaper is online only. When they are finally able to get back to a printed version, they pass copies out at shelters around the state at no cost. Jim had called the Dean of the Louisiana State University Journalism School in Baton Rouge, sixty miles from the center of the storm, for help in finding a place where the newspaper staff could work. They function with laptops in a rented space until October, when they were able to get back to their New Orleans newsroom. Having left New Orleans on short notice, Jim was wearing only shorts, T-shirt and running shoes for those first days and after the worst of the storm was over, national television stations wanted to interview him. Nancy, my friend of more than forty years, took her husband to the mall to buy acceptable clothes, apparently more aware than he that he could perhaps dress in something more appropriate than shorts and T-shirt for television.

Back to my patient, I make a guess at what her blood-pressure medication had been and find samples for her to take for the next week. I make her promise to return in a few days to let me check her pressure again, promising in turn to give her a larger supply when we are sure of the right medicine and dose. The next patient needs medication refills and actually has empty prescription bottles. Time to find out if there is a functioning pharmacy in town and let them know who I am. They probably will not have me in their database with my out-of-state license – if they even have access to a database, which means computer, which means electricity, which is variable at best in Slidell at this moment.

No patients waiting, so I walk two blocks to the pharmacy, a Walgreen's which may actually have me in their system because it's a nationwide chain. I introduce myself to the pharmacist and ask if he will have any problem with me writing prescriptions using my Colorado license. He is thrilled to have me available to help sort out and prescribe refills for the hundreds of patients who have lost their medications and who no longer have a doctor. Over the next two weeks, we talk frequently and together are able to re-create countless medical records. The pharmacist is also willing to use a variety of methods to procure medicines for people who cannot pay, have no homes, jobs, or other resources, and who now have no record of their insurance. The Red Cross volunteers have arrived and are in a nearby school building that is minimally damaged. They are dealing with non-medical issues, but have pharmacy vouchers for patients who are not able to pay for medications and very willingly work with us, giving us a supply and offering more when we need them. These are truly disaster conditions and everyone is doing what they can, breaking rules appropriately when doing so can only help.

As I walk back to my medical clinic, I'm overwhelmed with gratitude that we have found a place to help a few people. There are more medical problems than I expected. What did I expect? I had not thought about all the people who would run out of medication for ongoing illnesses, a potentially very serious issue and in some cases potentially fatal. It never occurred to me that so many doctors would lose their records and would permanently leave the community, leaving patients with unanswered questions about their medical histories. Like so many other people, many of these doctors lost their homes and offices and are simply unreachable. There was certainly no special escape for any group of people, even doctors. In subsequent weeks and months the media reports enormous numbers of people reunited with loved ones after many days of wondering if the other is still alive. Our little Colorado contingent cannot save the world or even the city of Slidell, but we definitely can help a few people. I am also aware of the difference between watching reports and actually being here. The media reports cannot capture the tears, smells, feel, humidity and the tiny details we see and hear.

Facial expressions say it all. Surrender is the most prevalent emotion, a sigh both visible and audible, the reaction of many when they see that their material possessions are actually gone. Now they know the truth and can deal with their worst fears. Some show relief, some bewilderment, a few show fear, and the few who are still missing family, or know that someone close has died, appear defeated. Sticky air, sweaty people, body odor on us and our patients seems a fitting atmosphere for dealing with this massive tragedy. Some patients break down in tears when we begin talking with them. The façade of strength that is present during the crisis falls away when someone shows kindness and caring. Just allowing an-other human being to give a hug or even a kind word can break through their tenuous shells. Pretense gone, they are again vulner-able, needing human comfort. Some sob and talk for as long as we can listen, others just briefly and softly weep, soon acknowledging it could be worse, at least their family escaped alive, and most praising God for their own survival. My face is salty with sweat, or is it tears?

After a meal from the Amish food wagon, we begin to think about converting our clinic into our sleeping quarters. The outhouses have been set up by some of the many crew members, and there are even portable sinks with water for washing, again not potable. In fact, none of the water in Slidell is potable now and thousands of bot-tles of drinking water have been arriving every few hours from as far away as New York, California and Wisconsin. Groups of truckers, church groups, service clubs and schools have mobilized to collect food and water and send trucks with cases of supplies. Everywhere I look there are stacks of hundreds of cases of water and food. With so much drinking water, teeth-brushing will not be a problem.

As dark approaches, we get our sleeping bags out and ar-range the cots. Suddenly the prospective bedroom is lit up. A set of bright headlights is aimed right at us. Donna, from the city offices, jumps out of the car and, with amazing energy at the end of the long day she has had, tells us to get in our cars and follow her. She has found us a place to stay! Minutes later we pull up in front of a large, low one-story building with no apparent damage, one of the few in this town. Following her lead and walking to the door, she tells us that the couple who runs the Slidell nursing home, which has been evacuated for more than two weeks, has agreed to let us stay here. There are beds for one-hundred people, mostly in double rooms. The home has been empty, with the exception of the couple who manage it, since the hurricane warnings began several days before Katrina hit. It will remain empty until the town is ready to support the resi-dents again, which is at least several more weeks. The home has wa-ter and electricity, bathrooms down each of the two long hallways, large laundry facilities and an enormous kitchen. Most of all, it has one of the kindest, most paternal men I have ever met, who manages the home along with his wife. They and their staff, who evacuated with the patients, take care of up to one-hundred elderly men and women.

The look of joy on the faces of the couple when we walk through the large, wheelchair-accessible, front door is a wonderful

welcome. The man clearly in charge, says hello, and his wife ex-
claims, "Oh, faces. We have faces!" They have stayed in the home
twenty-four hours a day, since the departure of all other staff, to
care-take the facility and await the return of "their" patients. They
are thrilled to have someone to care for, to again make them useful
and to interrupt their loneliness. And by housing and feeding volunteers, they can do their part to participate in rebuilding their town.
Over the next two weeks we have some wonderful typical Southern
breakfasts of eggs, toast, grits, sausage, coffee, juice and lots of love!
When we allow them to, they also cook an evening meal for us. They
are just a few of the many Southern black men and women we meet
who would do anything they can for us. We treat each other with the
utmost respect and appreciation and develop a strong bond over the
next weeks.

When it's time to find our bedrooms, we are told we can sleep
in any of one- hundred empty beds. We choose separate rooms, each
of us now relishing privacy we have not had for days and had not
expected for more days to come.

△◆

Chapter Six

△◆

Heat, humidity and a film of dirt greet us when we return to
our "clinic" the next morning. Word is not out that we are here and
many people have yet to return to town, so we decide to split up and
take turns staffing the clinic and touring the town. I take my cell
phone with me, back into the routine of being "on call," and assure
the two we leave behind that I will be back in an hour. Later we're
glad we take this opportunity, as on the days that follow we are
working non-stop into the evenings. We are limited by light, as we
have no electricity, so we open at seven a.m. and close our "doors" at
dark, around eight p.m., putting a chair in front of the space we have
kept within the makeshift walls.

Touring the town is overwhelming. When I arrived in Indonesia earlier this year, the tsunami had left its mark seven weeks earlier. Some repair had begun and cleanup teams had preceded us. I
arrive here in Louisiana just days after the hurricane and am among
the first to re-enter the area. There is destruction everywhere and no
cleanup has begun. Posted signs warn against drinking the water,
other signs have street numbers written on them and are posted on

trees in front of flattened houses. Large numbers written with paint on houses indicate the number of living and dead found by military searches. "God Bless" and "We all lived" signs are scrawled on anything standing, partial walls, plywood, small pieces of scrap wood nailed to trees. Three of us drive slowly, just looking. A small group of people is standing in front of a mostly destroyed house. Seeing their home for the first time since the storm, they appear to be somewhat in shock. We stop, tentatively say hello and find them very friendly and seemingly pleased to have someone with whom to process what they are finding. After a few minutes of chatting, they allow us to look inside, to walk into the remains of their small house where they point out the water line along the walls, the height where the water reached during the peak of the hurricane. It is above my head. There is a coating of mud over everything, and all the furniture and appliances are destroyed. The family begins to talk of how they will handle it, of the possibility of moving, or of rebuilding, bringing other family from out of state to help. One young man, a nephew, has driven from California and talks about how long he can stay to help, maybe for the next month or two.

Their resilience amazes me. I have never been a victim of this type of disaster. What I know about is emotional rebuilding and moving on with life after not being so sure it was worth living. I share eye contact that says I care, and hugs. Each of these people demonstrates an inner strength and gratitude for being alive and having their health and their family; the loss of material things, even a house, does not take away their spiritual fitness. We give them hugs and say goodbye, telling them to come to the clinic if they need anything medical. The lady, about my age, does stop by. I will never forget her as her name, Martha Johnson, is the same as a friend of mine who donated to the trip. My new Martha Johnson is Southern and black; my longtime Martha in Colorado is very white and redheaded. I give a small amount from our donations to new Martha, telling her it is from her namesake many miles away, wishing her good luck in rebuilding.

The days that follow blur together and we get into a routine beginning with the town meeting every morning at seven. Most days I attend this meeting in the trailer that houses the city offices, while others get started in the clinic. The meeting is held by the mayor and includes updates on available services from representatives of the fire department, public service, water, police and medical community (which apparently is only me, as to my surprise we are the only clinic in the center of town; other groups arrive, but days later). The mayor is a "no-nonsense, won't-take-no-for-an-answer" man. He demands that city services get back to an acceptable level of functioning. He does it nicely, but leaves no question that it must be done, now.

By the end of the first week, we are seeing more than seventy patients a day. I am so grateful for my crew, as I cannot possibly make more than a dent in this number without them. Dan, Patty, Nancy and Paula are all able to help. Their minimal medical experience is not a hindrance, as the main need is for human kindness, gentleness and listening, cleaning of wounds and simple bandages. Most patients are easily treated and I find that the big difference we make is to empathize with the returning residents about their losses. We treat sprained ankles, abrasions, rashes and respiratory ailments, and only a few are serious medical problems; many would heal on their own, but some would become dangerous if left untreated. What is serious, even potentially life-threatening, is the depression from the trauma they are enduring. My patients talk about their shock at returning to their homes, saying what they need to say while allowing me to connect with them by touching to examine their injury, clean and treat it, whether with a bandage, an Ace wrap, or a few stitches. Poignant stories from everyone illustrate what is truly valuable. One family in which no one was injured, fled with almost no personal belongings and returned to find their youngest child's bedroom almost intact in an otherwise destroyed house. On the wall are the child's drawings from grade school and on the dresser a family photograph. Would these be the only tangible representatives of years past?

In my medical practice at home, I often see patients who have told the receptionist that they need an appointment for a headache, stomach pain, back pain or some other relatively minor physical complaint. They have convinced themselves this is why they need an appointment, or maybe they have waited until developing a physical complaint to make an appointment, thinking those issues are more legitimate than emotional ones. Rarely is this the only reason they want to see me. More often than not, there is some underlying, or maybe additional issue that they feel is not worth an appointment in and of itself. They may be in denial about depression or anxiety. They may not realize the back pain is a reflection of their emotional stress, and that if we treat the stress the pain will resolve.

These Slidell, Louisiana men, women and children are no different; they are just in a more acute emotional crisis. They want a

sympathetic ear. For many, every member of their family has sustained enormous loss. They don't have anyone from the outside to
talk to and they feel as if they cannot complain, or just cry with each
other, afraid of their intense feelings of fear and sadness and the unknown future. Very few want to see a therapist and no therapist is
available anyhow. They don't need hours of looking at their feelings,
figuring things out, and processing childhood losses, just acknowledgement of their *present* ordeal, listening and hugs. We are the
logical solution: go to see the volunteer medics and get care for the
small cut and while there get care for the larger wound in your
heart. The physical touch I am able to provide is as important as my
diagnostic skills. Listening to someone's lungs and heart requires me
to touch them. The comfort from human touch says more than words
when we don't know what the problem or the solution is – we just
want to know we are not alone on earth. This touch is much of what
we provide over the ensuing weeks, and this is what our patients
need and seek to begin to heal the emotional wounds. I don't believe
this is a conscious thought for most, but the many thank-yous and
hugs we get as our patients say goodbye are not just for the Band-
Aids.

Some patients provide a change, even comic relief, among the
dozens with minor illnesses. One middle-aged couple comes in with
rashes around their ankles. We have seen lots of these from people
wading through mud and filthy water to access parts of their homes.
This couple wants treatment for the skin infection, and while we are
caring for them they tell us about going to their boathouse. Their
small boat was overturned and when they righted it, there were a
dozen water moccasins, very poisonous snakes that had taken up
residence in it; they are thankful they were not bitten. This is a reminder to me to offer tetanus boosters to everyone who cannot remember being immunized in the past five years. Snake bites can introduce the tetanus organism, but a more common danger is a punc-
ture wound from some of the debris that is everywhere in town. We
urge people to wear boots when entering their homes and boat-
houses. We run out of tetanus boosters early on and are able to acquire more from a group of black Christian physicians from the East
Coast who have been working out of a church across town and donate what they have left over when they leave. In all, we give about
two-hundred boosters in the two weeks we are here. If anything
changes or saves lives, it could be this. Fifty percent of people who
contract tetanus die from the disease. During my years of training at

the University of Maryland, I watched people die horrible deaths from this preventable disease.

While I am not sure he would have lost his life, there is one patient who might have lost a limb, or effective use of it, without our care. A volunteer from Michigan working with a crew that is removing fallen trees from the tops of houses comes into our clinic with a T-shirt wrapped around his forearm. He sustained a significant laceration when a piece of sheet metal fell on his arm. Since some of my favorite months of post-graduate medical training were spent in the Shock Trauma Unit at the University of Maryland, and other months and years in the Denver General Emergency Room, I am delighted to repair this wound. To me, the injury under the shirt is not a big deal, but requires careful assessment and treatment. When I ask for help preparing the patient, Dan volunteers and stays with us throughout an extensive repair. He comforts the patient and is invaluable to me, helping hold the patient's arm in position, handing me instruments and keeping the wound as exposed as possible so I can see what I'm doing. I anesthetize the area and reassure the patient, who is increasingly relaxed thanks to Dan's support and constant effort to engage him in conversation. I am able to see the damaged tendons, muscle layers and other tissue, and have the right equipment to repair them. Patty joins us and takes pictures, and the team confirms that this patient is the most seriously injured that any of them have ever seen close up. Anxious to return to work, the patient does well and keeps his part of the bargain by showing up for follow-up every day. I am relieved that he heals well, and ask him to check in with the doctors to whom we turn the clinic over when we leave. So many things can go wrong with this type of injury: infection, failure of the underlying structures to heal, or poor return of function, especially under these conditions. Thankfully this one heals without complication.

I have been out of touch with the news and don't know much about what is going on except what is in front of me. During these weeks, my world is a dirt floor, tarp overhead, stacked boxes for walls, and cots with patients on them. At night I return to my room at the nursing home tired, happy, feeling blessed to have been useful all day and thankful to be in a comfortable air-conditioned building. We can't find any information about support meetings for the three of us who are in recovery. No problem, as recovery for us now is about maintaining spiritual health and simply knowing that each other is here is a good reminder to stay in touch with God. Weeks later, after returning home, I hear that doctors from the American Society of Addiction Medicine, my specialty society, are being recruited to staff counseling centers for alcoholics and addicts and their families in several towns along the Gulf Coast. I am tempted to return in this capacity.

△◆

Chapter Seven

△◆

As we approach the end of our trip, we begin to meet other doctors who are arriving to make their contribution. The organization around us and whose tent we are under, the 700 Club becomes more involved with our operation. They invite a TV crew to interview us and bring in a thirty-eight-foot trailer for use as an indoor clinic, with one corner already set up for minor surgery. The ambiance will not be the same without the wind blowing dirt dangerously close to the wounds, passersby stopping to look at us and people stepping over barriers and into the middle of our clinic. Our little unit is going to be upgraded and made semi-permanent with a system for bringing in volunteer doctors who will rotate every few weeks.

As I prepare for the "sale of my business," taking leave of my office and passing on my supplies, watching my baby enter adolescence, I feel as if I am saying goodbye to a child who is ready to grow up. I am thrilled at what God is doing and feel grateful to have been a part of it.

We have seen hundreds of patients, more than seventy on some very busy days, working from daylight until dark seven days a week. We treat people with serious skin infections and mystery rashes from the filthy water they are encountering in their homes, and volunteers from other states who are injured while moving trees and debris. Each injured person who is not up to date on tetanus shots receives an immunization. Elderly and children, many with chronic illness requiring ongoing medication, come for prescription refills, as their former physicians are gone. Due to smoke in the air from burning debris, anyone with respiratory illness is at risk and we make use of all four nebulizers we have. Unlike the smoke in Indonesia, much from burning bodies of those killed by the tsunami, this smoke is from burning downed trees and destroyed houses, a significant consolation.

We have provided free medical care, medications, and supplies to workers, volunteers, and returning residents of Slidell, Louisiana. At home in Colorado several weeks later we feel blessed to have been able to help. This is my drop in the bucket to do a little for a few who have lost so much; my way to help save a few starfish.

△◆

Lessons

△◆

◆ Trust. Just start driving, good attitude and medical supplies in tow, and doors will open.

◆ Flexibility makes life easier; be willing to sleep outdoors on a cot and you might not have to.

◆ People respond differently to tragedy; all need encouragement.

◆ The slightest bit of help is met with gratitude.

◆ Minor medical problems are the ticket through the door for people to talk about their losses and get a hug.

◆ Hugs, ears and empathy are more important than Band-Aids.

◆ Hitting bottom can be treated like landing on a trampoline; if we let it, it will bounce us right back up!

To see a video clip, go to www.cbn.com and in the Search field, type *Slidell, medical.*

The medical clinic in Slidell, Louisiana with tree-stump décor.

△◆

Dan with a helper outside the medical clinic tent.

Dan stands next to a tree uprooted by Hurricane Katrina.

△◆

Doc Dawn with patients in the clinic tent
while volunteers unpack supplies in the background.

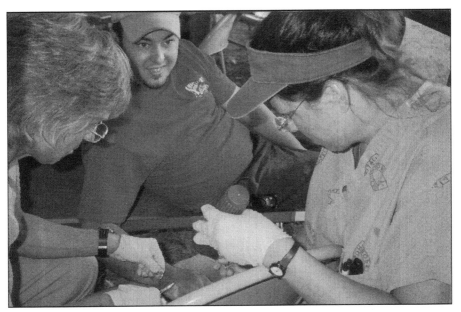

Dawn performs minor surgery.

△◆

Dawn's ID from the Houston Astrodome
and Hurricane Katrina medical bulletins.

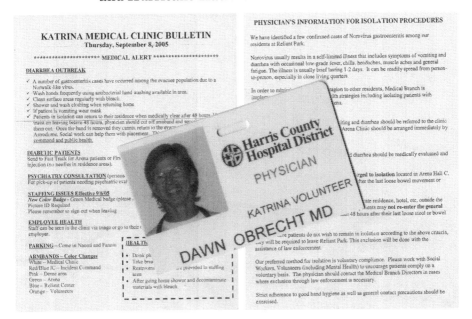

△◆

Generalities

△◆

◆   Always keep a current passport for yourself and everyone in your family, even children. You never know when you might have an opportunity to go somewhere.

◆   Just say "Yes" to opportunities.

◆   Travel stretches our brains.

◆   If you are the kind of person who likes to participate, do so. Spectator sports are not for everyone.

◆   If you realize that it feels good to help, do that too. Find a way to contribute, either supporting by donating, fundraising, or going on a work trip.

Packing

◆   Tips for packing for hot and humid climates, where much of the developing world is located:

◆   Cotton is cool.

◆   Synthetic fibers dry faster; I take a cotton skirt or jumper and microfiber pants.

◆   Pants with zip-off legs are convenient and allow packing one item for two uses.

◆   Some tops are tiny, thin material, no extra length or bulk; easy to pack two or three in the space one large shirt or blouse occupies.

◆   Pack some things you can leave at the end of the trip. Donate them to your favorite or neediest local. This makes space for bringing home something new from your travels.

◆   Assume you can wash out small items, even larger ones if you want, each night; then do so.

◆   Four or five pairs of underclothes are plenty; these are easy to wash out and easy to replace.

◆   Two pairs of pants, or one skirt and one pants, is plenty, and more than most of the people you will be working with own; wear one of them for travel and you only have to pack one.

◆   Tops are smaller and can change the "outfit."

◆   Take small sizes of toiletries and personal medications.

◆   Include insect repellant and sunscreen.

◆   Never go anywhere without a bathing suit (this tip is from my mother); even if you are not going to swim, there is always a chance you will have limited shower facilities and need the suit to actually "bathe" in public.

◆ Camera, journal, pen, books (I recommend soft cover that can be left when finished)

Personal Packing Experiences

We traveled in Europe for five weeks when our daughters were ten and thirteen. The four of us each packed what we thought we would need, and very little of what we would want but not need. Each of us had the responsibility of carrying our own pack, even the girls. We had small packs for them, moderate for me, large for Erik. We each marked our packs with color-coded cord, making them easy to pick out from other luggage, and each pack was small enough to carry on our flights. The girls had to choose which clothing to bring. The heaviest items, shoes, were the limiting factors. Finally, each of us chose a pair to "live in" for five weeks, knowing we were going to civilized places and could buy another pair if needed. We also each took a pair of very lightweight sandals, just flip flops, for beach and shower. One swimsuit, swim goggles, two pairs of shorts, one pair of long pants, one skirt (second pair of pants for Erik), a few small tops, four pairs of underwear and we were set. I encouraged paperback books, as the only place we could purchase reading material in English was in Great Britain, and we would be away from there and on the continent for four weeks. My pack included a tiny medical kit, sunscreen, antibiotic ointment, over-the-counter fever and pain medicines, skin cream, allergy medication, Band Aids, and any personal medicines. Oh, and we each had sunglasses and a cap. I am a runner, so I made sure that the shoes I took could double for running. I hear all you runners out there, saying one should only run in running shoes and not wear them for everyday use. I do not adhere to that philosophy when I am traveling and going 'light'...deal with it. ☺

Kara, who was ten, opted to buy a special pair of shoes somewhere in France. She has always been a collector of shoes, still is at age twenty-eight, and has more shoes than the rest of the family together. At one time during high school, she begged her older sister to *not* tell me how many pairs she had. We did not change our travel rules and would not let her sneak her shoes into our packs, so she decided to leave the old pair in the bed and breakfast in France.

Brie, at thirteen, wanted to bring home about half of the Berlin wall! We were in Berlin on July 4th 1990, shortly after the wall started to come down in 1989. It was exciting to be there and see the remains of the wall, be able to participate in tearing it down, and take pieces of it with us. Brie loaded up a large and heavy bag of rocks and cement from the wall and added them to her pack. They are still in my home in Colorado, and I have moved four times since then, Brie, now thirty-one, lives in St. Louis and knows her piece of the wall is safe in my home. She always carried exceptionally heavy packs in high school, college, and graduate school, drawing on that experience of doubling the weight of her pack in Europe. Now that I think of it, she carries a heavy pack today – her son and my grandson, Alex!

Packing for Indonesia

We had *so* much equipment to take! We also had to pack enough personal belongings in carry-on bags to last the three days it would take to get to our Indonesian island. Once you pack for three days, you really do not need more. I was able to pack for the entire three weeks in one moderate-sized pack, easy to carry onto plane, bus, and into hotels. If the rest of the gear was lost or stolen, at least I had my personal items. Very little is irreplaceable. If anything you own is, don't take it with you. Medications and a journal, at least what is already written, are the only really important things to keep on your person.

Medicine: Even if you take a regular prescription medication and happen to lose it, you can probably replace it without much difficulty. In many countries medicines are easy and cheap to buy. I actually brought home a six-month supply of an asthma inhaler from Thailand in 1995. It cost me about $15 for each inhaler in Thailand, $100 each if I ordered it from Canada, and it was not yet available in the U.S. It is in the U.S. now, and it is still very expensive. Many of the medicines one needs a prescription for here are over-the-counter in Mexico, South and Central America, and Asia, sometimes even in Europe. They may be made in different facilities, by the same company, just in its foreign plant, and thus look a little different. Use caution in reading the label; ask someone to interpret for you if you are unsure of the language. Many labels are in both the language of the country and in English. Do not ever hesitate to talk to the pharmacist and get recommendations for similar medicines if your particular brand is not available. It helps if you have the exact name, generic name and dosage written down.

Jewelry: Don't. I leave my antique diamond ring here when I

travel. It is only worth about $800, but was worn by my paternal grandmother. It has sentimental value and is truly irreplaceable. I wear my wedding band, a pair of cheap earrings and a cheap but reliable watch. That's it. None of these contribute to an outer appearance that says, "Steal my pack, I am wealthy." And this is of course, the point. Do not appear to have things worth stealing! I usually buy several more pairs of cheap earrings, my weakness, and a skirt.

△◆

Thanks to the generosity of our donors, we were able to give $200 to each of several dozen Nias families who had lost everything in the tsunami. With this money, each family was able to buy:

2 pigs
Rice to plant
Rice to eat until the crop comes in
Farming implements
Full kitchen set (pots, pans, utensils, etc)
Bedding
School supplies
School uniforms

△◆

This saying was given to me by a friend from my spiritual support group prior to my mission trip to Indonesia:

"We see that regardless of the presence or absence of material success in our lives, we can be content. We can be happy and fulfilled with or without money, with or without a partner, with or without the approval of others. We've begun to see that God's will for us is the ability to live with dignity, to love ourselves and others, to laugh and to find great joy and beauty in our surroundings. Our most heartfelt longings and dreams for our lives are coming true. These priceless gifts are no longer beyond our reach. They are, in fact, the very essence of God's will for us."

△◆
Epilogue
△◆

Without my own recovery from addiction, I would never have been able to participate in anything I have written about in this book. Truthfully, it is not likely I would be alive. Recovery has given me the emotional and spiritual strength to give, and also to receive. I have truly gotten many times over what I have attempted to give and am so grateful.

Consider what you want to do with your life. What fills your heart? Try giving, try coming out of your comfort zone. What is important? Nothing fills us more than touching another human being and in turn allowing ourselves to be touched.

Reflecting on the energy and focus these medical mission trips have required from me, I am grateful for my strengths. I thank God for having been allowed not only to survive my childhood in an alcoholic household, but to use it to grow. I have been given the gift of enlisting my past to move me forward. The lessons from childhood have been refined in recovery, and are applicable to most areas of my life.

I have learned to be realistic about when to trust people and situations and when not to. I learned to protect myself emotionally, and to take precautions to protect myself physically. If not for this, I might not have made it through early recovery when I was especially vulnerable. At that time, after my shield of alcohol and other drugs had been removed, I was emotionally labile, unstable and vulnerable, overly sensitive to anything anyone said, or that I perceived them to have said. I had to get it that human beings are imperfect, even doctors and people with many years of sobriety. Most of the time, anything anyone says has nothing to do with me, so taking things personally is not appropriate. I am simply not the center of other people's lives. At the same time, I need to be careful about those I allow into my life, realizing that not everyone is safe just because they have stopped drinking and drugging, or have an advanced degree. I have to make decisions about my safety like staying home when the weather in the mountains is too dangerous to drive, or not getting into a car with a driver I don't trust. My emotional safety is also my responsibility. Refusing to engage in a potentially destructive conversation, defending myself when verbally attacked, and choosing healthy people as my friends, are all part of my self care.

I have become resilient. Even when disappointed and frustrated, I learned to move forward, postponing dealing with the feelings until immediate danger is over, or appropriate progress has been made. This is common in households where children are not helped immediately, if ever, to resolve the craziness of unpredictable parents. In my case, sometimes Dad was sober and emotionally available; sometimes he was a vulgar, abusive drunk. I had to tolerate it or it would have killed me. The saying, "What doesn't kill you makes you stronger" really does apply to me.

I could not fix my parents. I nearly killed myself from the pain of childhood. If I could have changed them to be sober, stable, consistent and emotionally present, I would have done it. No one could. And I was a child. A child who thought it was her fault that her parents were drunks who abused each other. I learned I could not fix everything.

In contrast, I learned to not accept the unacceptable or tolerate the intolerable. This one came directly from my mother in every setting except her marriage. She consistently stood up to people who did not behave in a way she thought acceptable, or the way she thought they should, especially if one of her children was involved. One example involves my ballet teacher. My mother gave her an earful when the teacher, an internationally famous Prima Ballerina and instructor, said I should be a dancer, not a doctor!

Much of what I have learned in recovery is to let go. This lesson was taught to me by a marriage counselor I saw with my now exhusband. My first, or trial marriage was over and I was holding on to something that did not exist. I have been grateful I did not succeed in "making it work" as that would have made both of us miserable. Finally, I let him go, first physically, then emotionally. We both became free to be ourselves and grow individually. We now have a very acceptable relationship, attending parties for our children in each other's homes, talking about the children when it's important and generally respecting each other's lives. If I do not attach myself to outcomes of other people's behavior, results, or anything else I have no control over, I waste a lot less energy. I also save energy for doing things I *do* have control over, like providing medical care and teaching my patients what they can do to heal themselves. I still cannot control it if they don't take their prescriptions, or if they get dirt in their wounds, and this I must accept.

I have also learned to rely on God. If I remember that He is

God and I am not, it is easier to let Him be God, not try to coach or instruct Him, and accept the things I cannot change. I also get to pray about which things I can change; to ask for His help in doing so, to take action where I might make a difference, not to accept the unacceptable. This is where "The wisdom to know the difference" comes in. That is the hardest part of living by the Serenity Prayer.

SERENITY PRAYER

God grant me the Serenity to accept the things I cannot change;
Courage to change the things I can;
and the wisdom to know the difference.
Living one day at a time, enjoying one moment at a time;
accepting hardship as the pathway to peace.
Taking, as He did, this sinful world as it is, not as I would have it;
Trusting that He will make all things right if I surrender to His
will; That I may be reasonably happy in this life, and supremely
happy with Him forever in the next.
– Reinhold Niebuhr

To schedule speaking engagements contact
Dr. Dawn Obrecht

303-877-5310
△◆
P.O. Box 775596
Steamboat Springs, CO 80477
△◆
docdawn@hotmail.com
www.docdawn.com

Order copies of
Mission Possible
A Medical Missionary's Journey of Healing
at Amazon or through your local book seller